D1599931

The Slave Economy of the Old South

THE SLAVE ECONOMY OF THE OLD SOUTH

Selected Essays in Economic and Social History

ULRICH BONNELL PHILLIPS

Edited and with an Introduction by
EUGENE D. GENOVESE

LOUISIANA STATE UNIVERSITY PRESS
BATON ROUGE

CONTENTS

PART THREE: Industrial and Urban Problems

PART FOUR: A Glance at the British West Indies

PART FIVE: The Legacy

INTRODUCTION

Ulrich Bonnell Phillips as an Economic Historian

For Ulrich Bonnell Phillips the economy formed only one part of the slave regime of the Old South. It never occurred to him to try to study it apart from ideology, politics, and social structure. He would have had no trouble in understanding Gunnar Myrdal's impatient dismissal of the conventional division of historical factors into economic and noneconomic; for Phillips, as for Myrdal, the only question for an economic historian concerned the extent to which an idea, event, institution, or policy was relevant to the economy. Phillips, accordingly, grappled with the ways of thought of those strata which commanded the economy and tried to assess the extent to which economically rational decision-making was probable in daily life. He wasted little time in applying economic models, for he saw clearly, what many of his critics have missed, that standards of rationality developed to study the capitalist marketplace would break down at too many points. Certainly, he understood the essentially capitalistic nature of that system of commodity production to which the South was committed, and one of his great contributions was the exploration of many of its mechanisms. He also understood—in his own terms—the countertendencies thrown up from within the plantation regime itself, specifically the attitudes, policies, and exigencies rooted in the peculiar labor system. Throughout his work there is an implicit distinction between that which might be considered economically rational in a free-labor economy and that which was socially rational (necessary for the maintenance of a special form of social order and class rule) for the slave system.

The social essays at the beginning and end of this collection stress the race question and offer the concern for white hegemony as the "central theme." Yet, these and the more narrowly economic essays may be read somewhat differently, as revealing the process by which a specific form of class hegemony arose, grew, and collapsed. For Phillips, the persistence of the race question proved that slavery itself was not central to Southern history, but we might take issue sharply with his attempt to separate the Southern ethos of paternalism and patriarchal responsibility from the master-slave relationship. This debate might more appropriately be pressed elsewhere. For our immediate purposes, it is enough that he strove with such determination and with such an impressive degree of success to develop a social framework within which the economy could be studied.

Chapters XVIII and XIX of Phillips' *American Negro Slavery* form an indispensable part of his contribution to Southern economic history as narrowly defined. The first, "Economic Views of Slavery: A Survey of the Literature," constitutes an excellent review of the subject as of 1918 and retains great value. Few new arguments have been added to the debate on such questions as the productivity and costs of slave labor. New techniques of measurement have been advanced, most skillfully by Alfred H. Conrad and John R. Meyer, but even if, as we may hope, they prove to be long strides toward the solution of old problems, they have added few new ideas or arguments. After half a century Phillips' survey remains useful as an introduction to the subject in general as well as to the specifics of the debate down to World War I. The second, "Business Aspects of Slavery," offers a good account of Phillips' views, and supplements, corrects, and occasionally supersedes those earlier articles which are included in Part Two of this volume. The concluding paragraph of the chapter brings out two of his main points—that slavery cannot properly be understood in economic terms alone and that, whatever the limited economic advantages of slave labor to planters, the broader effects on the economy as a whole were largely negative:

The slaveholding regime kept money scarce, population sparse and land values accordingly low; it restricted the opportunities of many men of both races, and it kept many of the natural resources of the

Southern country neglected. But it kept the main body of labor controlled, provisioned and mobile. Above all it maintained order and a notable degree of harmony in a community where confusion worse confounded would not have been far to seek. Plantation slavery had in strictly business aspects at least as many drawbacks as it had attractions. But in the large it was less a business than a life; it made fewer fortunes than it made men.

These and other chapters from *American Negro Slavery* have not been included in this volume because the book is again in print and available in a paperback edition. Those who wish to understand Phillips' thought must consult it and its sequel, *Life and Labor in the Old South*. This collection, however useful it may prove to be, ought to be read together with those books.

In a larger sense *American Negro Slavery, Life and Labor in the Old South*, these essays, and almost everything Phillips wrote form a massive contribution to the political economy of the slave regime. Harold D. Woodman, in his excellent historiographical article, "The Profitability of Slavery: A Perennial," has shown that two questions have become intertwined and sometimes confused in the secular debate on the economics of slavery. The first concerns the returns to individual producers, the second, the impact on regional economic growth and stability. As Woodman has pointed out, Phillips' primary interest lay in the second, and much of his finest work was done on its range of problems. Since Phillips saw plantation slavery as a pervasive social institution, its continued existence never presented itself to him as proof of economic viability. So long as the system could pay its way—in this sense any system is proven economically viable by the fact of its being—its preservation would rest on its usefulness as a means of social control.

He stressed the racial component: the presence of an inferior race, undisciplined to sustained labor, required a stern regime. Early in his career, as "The Plantation as a Civilizing Factor" especially makes clear, he viewed slavery as a special case in a general plantation condition. From this probe to the sophisticated "Central Theme of Southern History" he insisted on the primacy of the race question. While slavery seemed the best, and to some the only, means of controlling Negro labor, the system would continue regardless of its glaring economic faults. But there were limits. Past a certain point, he argued, the economic question could no longer be ignored, and the regime would evolve toward a form of serfdom or specially controlled "free" labor.

This viewpoint, which he linked to the thesis on the natural limits of slavery expansion most commonly associated with Ramsdell, contains serious difficulties. Unless Phillips thought that the system would become absolutely unprofitable—a dubious assumption to say the least—he came close to self-contradiction. He could rescue himself only by arguing that, in time, the specific attractiveness of slavery as a system of racial control would yield to the general attractiveness of the plantation system. To this line of argument several objections may be made. First, Phillips himself pointed out repeatedly, and Conrad and Meyer have underscored, that slavery made possible the degree of labor mobility required for the successful operation of the plantation system. Second, conversion to free labor, even if peaceably effected, would have required enormous capital investments that, as Phillips untiringly maintained, could not have come from within the South. It would therefore have opened the way to Northern penetration and domination. Phillips took great pains to demonstrate that the Southern regime created men of a special type—proud, tough, independent, and jealous of their prerogatives. It is therefore strange to confront his insistence that they ever would have faced such extraordinary threats to their hegemony and sensibilities with equanimity.

From one point of view, which I have developed elsewhere, Phillips' work may be read as an effort to lay bare the history and sociology of the slaveholders as a ruling class. His impressive article, "The Origin and Growth of the Southern Black Belts," is simultaneously a contribution to Southern political economy and an impressive introduction to the formation of social classes, especially the planter class. He analyzed the process by which capital became concentrated in relatively few hands but also considered the various countertendencies that prevented the process from running its full course. In his elegantly constructed "Transportation in the Antebellum South: An Economic Analysis," which first appeared in the *Quarterly Journal of Economics* and then served as the opening chapter of his important monograph, A *History of Transportation in the Eastern Cotton Belt to 1860*, he wove economic geography and politics into a discussion of transportation and thereby added another dimension to the history of the slaveholding class. Ordinary economic interest compelled certain kinds of projects rather than others, but once developed, those projects reinforced the existing social regime and deepened the economic commitments beyond anything originally intended or perhaps thought advisable.

Phillips wrote little about town life and the middle classes but apparently retained considerable interest in them throughout his life. His personal papers, deposited at Yale University, contain a great many notes on these subjects, and one of his earliest articles dealt with urban history. His "Historical Notes of Milledgeville, Ga.," published in the short-lived *Gulf States Historical Magazine*, demonstrated what could be done with existing source materials on local history, but, more important, it drew attention to certain essential features of antebellum Southern town life.

Phillips saw Milledgeville as a typically unprogressive town overshadowed by the plantation-studded countryside. Essentially a cotton-collecting and political center, it accumulated businessmen, lawyers, politicians, and planters, all of whom in one way or another lived off the countryside or its proceeds. His brief but suggestive discussion of the leading classes goes to the heart of the urban dimension of Southern life. The country intruded itself into the town; when those who commanded the rural regime and its economy did not strangle the urban bourgeoisie at birth, they bent it to their lifelong will; and the plantation, its ideals and temper, dominated the consciousness of the townsmen. These few pages offer, in addition to their revealing material on slave life, strong hints for further work, which still needs doing after half a century, and provide, in a burst of youthful insight, a firm grasp of the quality of life under the old regime.

In his accounts of transportation, town life, and the plantation system itself, economic problems and developments are treated as an integral part of the social regime. However much we may quarrel with Phillips' specific formulations or wish to revise his priority of race over class in the interpretation of Southern history, there can be little doubt that he posed the difficult questions, advanced stimulating hypotheses, and kept the consideration of economics where it belongs—in the context of an integrated human history.

II

This book consists of twenty-one essays, grouped into five parts. The essays, as might be expected, are of uneven merit and have different functions. Some remain useful sketches of their respective subjects. These contain little to surprise specialists and perhaps contained little original material when first published. The first two selections—the Introduction to *Plantation and Frontier* and "Racial Problems, Adjustments and Disturbances"—are among the best in this category. They ought to prove immensely useful to graduate as well as undergraduate students for the overview they contain, but I also believe, or at least hope, that specialists will find them suggestive and rewarding even after so many years of excellent work by many others.

Some essays ranked as important monographs when first written and still stand up as among the best accounts of their respective subjects. Among the outstanding examples of this type are "The Origin and Growth of the Southern Black Belts," "The Economic Costs of Slaveholding in the Cotton Belt," and "Slave Labor in the Charleston District." The two studies of slave plantations in the British West Indies continue to be cited by specialists as among the finest in the literature. Almost all studies of slavery in the islands are based on official records, travelers' accounts, journals, and so forth; very little work in plantation manuscripts had been done when Phillips wrote or has been done since. Even such commendable recent works as Elsa Goveia's *Slavery in the British Leeward Islands at the End of the Eighteenth Century* and Orlando Patterson's *The Sociology of Slavery* (Jamaica) are no exception. Phillips' studies therefore serve as models for needed work and as important probing operations into virtually uncharted territory. One or two of the others, most notably "Transportation in the Antebellum South: An Economic Analysis," fit both categories and serve as comprehensive introductions to the data and as essays in interpretation. Finally, some of the articles in Parts One and Five do double duty in providing a social context for the others and, at their best as in "The Central Theme of Southern History," in making seminal contributions to the general history of the South.

Phillips wrote well even as a young man, and his prose became increasingly attractive as he matured. He rarely wasted words or struck poses. Professors could do worse than to recommend his writings to their students as examples of how to be concise yet graceful, forceful yet charming. If these essays necessarily lack some of the easy manner of his major books, *American Negro Slavery* and *Life and Labor in the Old South*, they have compensations in their sharper focus and model economy of style.

The strength of Part One lies in the valuable introduction to Southern economic development that the first two essays offer, but the remaining essays, however dated and even quaint they now appear, deserve more than passing attention. They contain little of value as economic history, although they might serve to remind us of some of the graver weaknesses of the Bourbon regime on the countryside. Their usefulness lies in the way in which they lay bare certain of Phillips' ideas on race and social process. His view of the Negro, his concern with economic reform and modernization, and his deep commitment to conservative ideology all stamp him with the mark of the Progressive Era and help us to understand better what he was driving at in his historical studies. To suggest that Phillips' historical work was conditioned by his political and social commitments hardly is to reduce him to a vulgar ideologue. There is a vast gap between a historical investigation that is ideologically informed and conditioned, as all must be, and a historical investigation that is ideologically dictated and restricted. This gap separates flexibility from dogmatism, competence from incompetence, and, ultimately, honesty from dishonesty. Phillips, like the rest of us, had his moments of dogmatism, incompetence, and even dishonesty, but his life's work could hardly be taxed with such charges. The case for careful study of his early polemics on race relations and economics rests on the light they shed on his historical imagination, although something might be said, too, for their intrinsic merits as a conservative's reasoned defense of humane values in a harsh, competitive world.

Scholars will probably find Parts Two, Three, and Four to contain the analyses and data most useful to their work. Rereading the best of these efforts, one is struck by the abundance of material unavailable elsewhere or at least unavailable in a form so compressed and illuminating. Taken together, they comprise the best introduction to the political economy of Southern slavery that I know of and should prove valuable to specialists and indispensable to students. The almost forgotten essays from *The South in the Building of the Nation* well illustrate Phillips' gift for compressing large quantities of important data into a few pages, and their deceptively straightforward style does not hide their far-ranging evaluations of class relationships.

In Part Five we return to Phillips' more broadly social concerns. The first two essays pick up his early interest in the plantation regime. The ideas he formulated as a young man and published in 1903 and 1904 were reconsidered in 1910 and again in 1925. With "The Plantation Product of Men" (1918) he had already begun to shift from an objective view based on a proposed restoration of a plantation regime to a subjective one based on a desired preservation of an older ethos. These brief remarks, taken together with his famous essay on "The Central Theme," tell us much about his social outlook but they also tell us much about the social context he posited for the economic studies constituting the heart of this collection. Originally, I thought to open with "The Central Theme" but decided to close with it instead. It has been reprinted often and probably will be familiar even to upper-level undergraduates. Hopefully, the selections in Part One will adequately substitute for it as a social introduction to those following. It seemed more useful to present "The Central Theme" for reconsideration at the end of a series of economic and social studies that ought to illuminate it as much as it might illuminate them.

MONTREAL   EUGENE D. GENOVESE
1968

PART ONE

The Historical
and Social Setting

1

Plantation and Frontier

IN THE study of industrial society we are concerned with the people earning their living, and in the present volume it is mainly with the people of the Old South.* The South in politics, the South at war, the South at play have been the subjects of much good historical description; but there is a dearth of first-hand information in regard to the South at work.

The history of industrial society is to be distinguished at the outset from the history of industrial processes. The latter is concerned mainly with machines and technique, the former in the main with men and manners. It is a phase of social history. If made inclusive enough, the study of industrial society may touch all phases of human life; but its concern is, primarily, with the grouping and activity of the people as organized in society for the purpose of producing material goods, and secondarily, with the reflex influence of the work and work-grouping upon life, upon philosophy, and upon the internal and external relations of the society.

This history, like all social history, is in one great aspect the record of the adjustment of men to their environment. The problem in America was that of Europeans, and mostly Englishmen, entering a remote wilderness and making a double adjustment of themselves to their habitat and their habitat to themselves. The Indians had made one use of the country; negroes, Malays, or Tartars, if placed in it and left to their own devices, would have developed characteristic systems of their own; and the Englishmen

---

* This essay appears as the introduction to *Plantation and Frontier*, Vols. I and II of *A Documentary History of American Industrial Society* (10 vols.; Cleveland: A. H. Clark Company, 1910–11).

transplanted hither wrought upon the land, grouped themselves, established relations with the inferior races, experienced reactions from their environment, and developed systems in ways which could hardly have been spontaneous with people of any other origin. From Anglo-American beginnings, distinctively American types of industrial society have evolved, which are conspicuous in the world's history for their efficiency in the functions for which they were intended. Relatively free from the bondage of Old World traditions, the people were able to experiment with methods of work and systems of social organization, to discard the less and retain the more successful ones and remould these to a still greater efficiency. The immediate purpose was the exploitation of a continent—the utilization and enjoyment of its resources. Systems were shaped accordingly. These characteristic systems differed in the several regions of the continent; and they replaced one another in various districts, as the conditions of life and prosperity underwent changes. In some districts and industries, the general problems were similar to those prevailing in England and Europe; and in such cases the systems of life tended to be not unlike those of the Old World. These have grown more prominent and more like those of Europe as the country has grown older. Other systems have been, first and last, peculiarly American.

By evolution in the one case and revolution in the other, two systems in American industrial society of the greatest historical importance have now almost wholly vanished. These, the frontier and the plantation system, form a large part of the American past, from which the present with its resources, its industrial and social constitution, and its problems has resulted. The frontier performed its mission in one area after another, giving place in each to a more complex society which grew out of the frontier regime and supplanted it. By this process the whole vast region of the United States, within the limits where the rainfall is sufficient for tillage, has been reduced to occupation in a phenomenally rapid process. The extension of settlement being now ended, the system has died from want of room.

The plantation system was evolved to answer the specific need of meeting the world's demand for certain staple crops in the absence of a supply of free labor. That system, providing efficient control and direction for labor imported in bondage, met the obvious needs of the case, waxed strong, and shaped not alone the industrial regime to fit its requirements, but also the social and commercial system and the political policy of a vast section; and it incidentally trained a savage race to a certain degree of fitness for life in the Anglo-Saxon community. Through the Civil War and political reconstruction of the South, accompanied by social upheaval, the plantation system was cut short in the midst of its career. It only survives in a few fragments and in forms greatly changed from the characteristic type. Both the frontier and plantation systems can now be studied in the main only in documents.

The most perfect types both of plantation and frontier occurred in the Southern colonies, including the West Indies, and the subsequent Southern states. A few plantations existed north of Mason and Dixon's Line; but the climate and crops were not suited to the full routine which typical plantations required. The wilderness of the Northwest was reduced by a great body of frontiersmen; but some of the features of the full type of frontier were usually lacking there, in that the United States army policed the Indians and the popular government was administered directly under the Federal authority. In the Southwest the settlers in general did their own fighting, their own land-office work, their own legislating, when any was done, and their own administering of the laws.

The South, then, gives type illustration of both plantation and frontier; and furthermore, it gives example of great regions in which one or the other of these systems controlled the lives and destinies of the people. In fact, these two systems dominated the whole South. Small farms of the normal type existed in great numbers; towns, factories and mines were not wholly absent; but in the several areas, as a rule, either the plantation system or the frontier shaped the general order of life without serious rival. Hence the antebellum South is peculiarly the region of plantation and frontier and a study of those systems may largely coincide with a study of Southern industrial organization and society.

To make the theme clearer it will be well to distinguish the types. A plantation was a unit in agricultural industry in which the laboring force was of considerable size, the work was divided among groups of laborers who worked in routine under supervision, and the primary purpose was in each case the production of a special staple commodity for sale. The laborers were generally in a status of bondage. Wage earners might be employed; but for the sake of certainty in maintaining a constant and even supply of labor from season to season, indented servants and negro slaves were the commoner resort.

A farm, then as now, was an agricultural unit in which the laboring force was relatively small. There was no sharp distinction between workman and supervisor. A less regular routine was followed and the primary purpose was divided between producing commodities for market and commodities for consumption within the family. Farmers might hire help and might buy slaves. With unfree labor as such, however, they had little or no vital concern. Their need for assistance was in most cases not constant but intermittent; and wage-earning help, which might be hired for a period and then discharged, was better suited to their needs than long-term bonded laborers. Frontier industrial units were on an average still smaller, comprising in many cases only a single person; agriculture was pursued only to supply necessaries, attention was often given mainly to hunting or Indian trading, and the individual or group was in many emergencies concerned with the protection of life more than with the accumulation of property. On a plantation the workmen were distinctly of a laboring class. On a farm they were of the nature of help in the farmer's own work. In frontier industry there were usually no employers of labor at all and no employees of any sort.

These three types shaded from one to another with no distinct line of differentiation, though the types at the two ends of the series, plantation and frontier, were of course in strong contrast. At any given time, each of these types throve predominantly in certain areas in the South, while in others they existed only in subordination, if at all. Where two or all three coexisted in a single area, the systems usually competed for the supremacy; and in the outcome the most efficient for the main purpose at hand would conquer. The representatives of the other types would mostly have to move on. The location of these types, therefore, was somewhat transitory. The great abundance of land available and the short-lived fertility of the soil, together with the prevailing wasteful methods of tillage, caused a great hunger for land and, to satisfy that hunger, a rapid extension of settlement. Thus arose the westward movement. In it each of the Southern types of industrial society took part; and throughout the whole belt of country suitable for exploitation by these systems a running contest ensued between them.

Space is not available to show the origin and early phases of these systems and their contest by the printing of first-hand materials; and furthermore the record from the fugitive documents would perhaps be too fragmentary for the purpose. The text of many documents in our present collection, however, will suggest the fact that there was a never-ending evolution through the competition of industrial units and systems. A rapid survey of the general development by areas will give a setting to our several categories of documents and will show incidentally how much the economic history of the Old South in its plantation regions was made up of extensions and repetitions of the same general phenomena. The plantation system had independent origins in the Spanish West Indies and in English Virginia. In the latter case, which will concern us first, the system and its name evolved simultaneously.

When Virginia was founded, the word *plantation* had the meaning of the modern word *colony*. The Jamestown settlement was the plantation of the London Company in the sense that the Company had founded it and exercised jurisdiction over it. But there was incidentally a closer relation between the settlement and the Company, which the word *colony* does not connote. The Company owned the land; it owned the equipment; and it had property rights in the labor of the settlers whom it sent over. The Company provided taskmasters; it fed and clothed the laborers from its magazine; and it owned the produce resulting from their work. That is to say, early Virginia was the *plantation* of the London Company in the modern sense of the term—it was an industrial establishment rather than a political community. The next step in the development of Virginia came when a decade's experience had shown the many shortcomings of the system of operating the whole province as one estate and caused the Company's plantation to be replaced by smaller industrial units. This occurred through the distribution of land in severalty. Many of the men who acquired land became farmers on a small scale, tilling their own fields. Others, whether individually or in small stock companies, secured large tracts of land, imported labor (comprising chiefly indentured Europeans), and continued with suitable modifications the system with which the London Company had begun, and which came to be known as the plantation system. By virtue of this transition, Virginia, from being a mere plantation owned by the London Company, became a colony or commonwealth, comprising independent farms and private plantations. The discovery of the great resource for profit in raising tobacco gave the spur to Virginia's large-scale industry and her territorial expansion. Not only this, but it brought about the methods of life which controlled the history of Virginia through the following centuries and of the many colonies and states which borrowed her plantation system.

Settlement quickly spread along the banks of the James River from Chesapeake Bay to the head of navigation, where the city of Richmond now stands. Plantations and farms dotted the river shores in a narrow tongue of settlement thrust into the wilderness. For a period practically all the settlers were tobacco producers, all were in close touch with navigable water and the route to Europe, and all, so to speak, rubbed shoulders with the Indians. Seeking fertile lands, planters began to make clearings on the York River about 1630 and then upon the Rappahannock and Potomac. As decades passed, settlement was spread throughout the Tidewater stretches of these parallel streams; and the commonwealth of Virginia, by this broadening of its area, acquired dimensions conducing to its more easy defence and to the geographical differentiation of conditions and pursuits. The Tidewater peninsulas tended to be monopolized by the planters; the mainland, west and south, chiefly attracted the men of little property. A great fall in tobacco prices at an early period forced the less efficient producers out of that industry, and nothing was left them but self-sufficing economy. The fitness of routine methods for tobacco raising and the advantages of producing and marketing on a large scale gave the control of that industry to the planters. The farmers soon found it of no advantage to live within hail of oceangoing ships; and most of those who owned Tidewater farms sold them to neighboring planters and moved inland where lands were cheaper and fresher, and society might be moulded to the wishes of their class. Emancipated redemptioners, as they emerged from servitude, were attracted by the industrial opportunity and the spirit of democracy prevailing on the outskirts of settlement and tended strongly to join the westward drift. In general, the longer settled and the more accessible areas grew to assume the full plantation type, while the newer areas, with a simpler organization, served as a buffer, sheltering the former from the dangers and inconveniences of the wilderness.

As years passed the numbers of planters increased, partly through the division of estates among heirs, partly through the rise of exceptional yeomen into planting estate, partly by the immigration of gentlemen of means from England. The growth of the farming population was much more rapid; for the planters had to serve constantly as immigration agents in order to maintain their supply of indented labor; and redemptioners were as constantly completing their terms and becoming yeomen, marrying and multiplying. The Virginia plantation districts, therefore, as a by-product provided a pioneering population, detached from the plantation system. These occupied the "back country" of Virginia, and also spread into eastern and then into central North Carolina. An entirely similar process was going on in Maryland and, one not widely different, in Pennsylvania. This group of colonies thus produced the first great supply of people for the process of secondary colonization, which we know as the westward movement. They continued to recruit the pioneering population in large volume, as long as the system of indented servitude remained a chief basis of their industry.

By the end of the seventeenth century, Virginia and Maryland changed to the basis of negro slavery as their chief supply of labor.

This had important effects upon the output of pioneers. The negroes being preferred for the gang labor, the redemptioners of the eighteenth century in Virginia tended to be mostly artisans and responsible persons. When achieving freedom they were accordingly of a more capable and substantial type. After the great resort to slave labor, therefore, the output of pioneers from the plantation districts diminished in volume and improved in quality.

As this emigration of freedmen from the plantations slackened, and as the farming districts grew broader and extended more remotely, the planting and farming districts respectively tended to lose touch, and further, the farming districts began to show a differentiation within themselves. The older and nearer portions tended to acquire a steady-going, peace-loving population, while to the furthest and thinnest edges of settlement there were attracted the more restless and venturesome. By these developments, the frontier in Maryland and Virginia had been extended by 1740 to within perhaps fifty miles of the Blue Ridge, while the plantation districts were still confined to the close neighborhood of tide water.

About this time began the entrance into Virginia, through the then remote and little-known Shenandoah Valley, of the great wave of migration from Pennsylvania, made up mostly of Scotch-Irish and Germans. This in the following decades brought multitudinous recruits to the farming and frontier population and caused a very rapid extension of the occupied area throughout the Shenandoah and Piedmont Virginia, across Piedmont Carolina to middle Georgia, and into the valley of East Tennessee, and even across the Cumberland Mountains to Kentucky and the Nashville district.

Meanwhile a new plantation district was growing into great prominence in the lower South. This was in the coast region lying around the budding city of Charleston. The European settlers and their system of industry arrived in South Carolina by way of the West Indies; and it is well for us to follow the same detour, tracing origins and developments as we go.

In the first place, the Spaniards had begun at once after the discovery by Columbus to exploit such wealth as the West Indies could yield. They enslaved the aborigines in immense numbers, and fed them so little and drove them so hard in their gold mines and their sugar fields that the Indians died off as if by pestilence. To replace the Indians, negroes began about 1520 to be imported in large numbers to serve in the Spanish islands as slaves. The development, however, was not rapid. As soon as the wealth of precious metals in Mexico and Peru had been discovered the most ardent fortune seekers hurried to these new acquisitions; and the islands were left to unaggressive settlers who in the main lived passively upon the labor of their negro slaves in sugar culture. The Spaniards maintained a sort of plantation system; but by reason of the listlessness of its captains, their industry stagnated. The resources of none of the islands were at all fully utilized, and many of the Indies were left by them entirely vacant.

Beginning in 1641, the outlying little island of Barbados was occupied by a sudden in-pouring of Englishmen, mostly royalist refugees from the victorious army of the Roundheads. Barbados, measuring only twenty by ten miles in length and breadth, was quickly crowded with people, and its whole area reduced to tillage in small estates. The sugar industry, however, led to the rapid importation of negro slaves and to the enlargement of estates. This caused much cramping. When war began with Spain, the Barbadians eagerly joined in an English expedition and captured the island of Jamaica in 1655. Here there was abundance of land for a large working population. The settlers in Barbados had already borrowed the Spanish method of using slave labor in sugar production: and, from the needs of their case and from their own large capability as industrial managers, they rendered the plantation system much more efficient in the raising of cane and the making of sugar. In Jamaica this improved system quickly expanded and caused the growth of very large and very productive plantations. The average unit of industry in the Jamaican sugar fields came to be a plantation with a total of nearly two hundred negroes, of whom more than half were workers in the field gangs. The laborers were strictly classified and worked in squads under close and energetic supervision to near the maximum of their muscular ability. The routine was thoroughly systematic, and the system as efficient on the whole as could well be, where the directors were so few and the negroes so many and so little removed from the state of African savagery. The Jamaican units on the average were the largest in all the history of plantation industry. The disproportion of the races was greater than in any other Anglo-American colony or commonwealth, and the association of master and slave was the slightest. The huge demand for negroes in Jamaica prevented the rise of opportunity for any great number of white men. The demand for overseers was limited by the number of plantations; and the opportunity for white mechanics, merchants, and laborers was not large.

The acquisition of Jamaica did not wholly relieve the congestion in Barbados. The Barbadian, John Colleton, soon turned the attention of some of his associates to the continental coast as a further opportunity for expansion. Under a charter of 1663 for Carolina, a band of Barbadians and Englishmen planted the town of Charleston in 1670. Ignorant of the local resources, they found little of a profitable character to do. Trading with the Indians and exporting a small volume of naval stores, the settlement followed a self-sufficing economy on a petty scale and languished until the resource of rice production was discovered in 1694. Following this, there was a rapid importation of negro slaves and a rapid extension of settlement along the fertile strips of land in the neighborhood of the water-broken coast. South Carolina became highly prosperous, and spent most of her earnings in the purchase of more slaves to raise more rice. The addition of indigo as a supplementary staple, about 1745, doubled the resources and intensified the system. The typical estate came to be a plantation with about thirty working hands, cultivating rice in the swampy lands and indigo in the drier fields, in a steady routine which lasted nearly the whole year through. The nature of the climate and the work to be done precluded, as in Jamaica, the use of any but negro labor in the gangs. The prevalence of malaria in the hot months caused most of the planters to abandon their estates for much of the year to the care of overseers and foremen. In contrast with this, the usual type of estate in the Virginia plantation districts had only five or ten working hands, of whom part were likely to be white redemptioners; and the master and his family were usually on the estate the year round. The periodical absenteeism in the rice district, together with the relatively large size of the industrial units, brought about a status of race relations more similar to that of Jamaica than to that of Virginia, where the negro servants had gradually replaced the white ones and were often in close touch with their masters' families.

In Georgia, the rulers of the colony tried hard to keep out slave labor; but about 1750 had to yield to the inevitable. Thereafter the sea-island district of Georgia tended to assume the same complexion as that which the South Carolina lowlands had acquired.

The rice and indigo district, unlike the Virginia-Maryland region, developed town life as well as rural. Charleston and, on a much smaller scale, Savannah were centers of commerce and society. These towns developed some interesting relations between slave, free negro, and white labor, which some of our documents will indicate. The Charleston-Savannah district, employing very few indented servants and attracting very few independent white laborers, furnished only a small number of farmers or frontiersmen. Industrial society was not upon a basis to produce pioneers. Furthermore, no gateway was at hand leading to the continent's interior. The great sandy tract which covers most of the coastal plain from southern Virginia to Texas, pine-grown and barren of resources for the men of the period, was widest in South Carolina and Georgia. To reach the country of rolling hills, hardwood timber, and clay soil, the men from Charleston and Savannah would have to journey across a hundred and fifty miles of the vacant and forbidding pine-barrens. Access to the Carolina-Georgia Piedmont from the northeastward was much easier for pioneers, because the route lay through resourceful country, uniform and familiar in character, and already in part occupied. The tide of migration from Pennsylvania and Virginia had reached the Piedmont of South Carolina before any people from the coast had begun to cross the great belt of pine-barrens which shut them in. Thereafter there was but a thin stream from Charleston to join the tide from the northward. In the South Carolina-Georgia coast district there was little opportunity for small farmers, and much for capable planters with their gangs. Farmers, therefore, had little occasion to enter the district, and planters in the eighteenth century no occasion to leave it. This region, accordingly, grew to be one of those most thoroughly dominated by the plantation system; and it came to be less in touch than any other on the continent with the needs and policy of the farming districts and the frontier.

The result of colonial developments may be pictured in a view of conditions prevailing on the eve of the war for independence:

1. The Chesapeake lowlands and the eastern part of the neighboring hill country were the seat of the tobacco industry, then yielding what was still the most important staple on the continent. By far the most of the output was produced in the plantation system and by far the most of the laborers were negro slaves. The units of plantation industry were relatively small, ranging usually below twenty and often below ten field hands to the plantation. There was a large number, also, of free farmers and an appreciable number of indented servants, especially in Maryland. The lands in the older parts of the districts were by this time largely exhausted and industry somewhat depressed. Eastern Virginia on the whole had begun to pass the zenith of her prosperity. The tobacco staple was a resource of decreasing value, and many people were finding it necessary to resort instead to the production of foodstuffs for market. A readjustment was beginning, which involved the decline of the plantation system in that district. There was a striking dearth of towns and of manufacturing. The trade of most planters with London was inconveniently remote. The towns of Baltimore, Annapolis, Norfolk and Richmond were rising to some little consequence; but the Virginia-Maryland community on the whole was overwhelmingly rural. Across the North Carolina boundary, the district about Albemarle Sound was merely a subprovince of the Chesapeake region. By this time it had received some slaveholding immigrants from Virginia, and thus added to its small-farming population a certain number of tobacco planters.

2. The Shenandoah Valley and most of the Piedmont country from Maryland to eastern Georgia was now occupied by a large but thinly scattered population of backwoods farmers, whose area of occupation touched the plantation district in Virginia, but was

widely separated from it in the Carolinas and Georgia by the intervening pine-barrens. The western portions of these settlements
were much of the frontier complexion. The main advance guard
of the pioneers, however, had now reached the "western waters"
in what we now call East Tennessee, and the most adventurous of
them had recently crossed the barrier of the Cumberland range
and staked out claims in central Kentucky and the Nashville
district.

3. The South Carolina-Georgia lowlands were a segregated area
occupied by plantations of a large average size, and with but few
nonslaveholding farmers. Most of the unattached working men
who by chance entered this district either took employment in the
commercial towns or pushed across the pine-barrens to join the
backwoodsmen of the Piedmont.

4. St. Augustine, Pensacola, Mobile, Biloxi, New Orleans, Natchez, etc., in the provinces of Florida and Louisiana, both at this
time held by Spain, were either feeble garrisons or trifling posts for
the Indian trade. No considerable agriculture had been developed
except in a few clearings upon the banks of the Mississippi; and
even in them industry languished. The industrial future of the
country was clearly in the hands of the Anglo-Americans; and the
Gulf region awaited their coming.

The war for independence brought, of course, a severe economic
depression; and this caused some geographical and industrial readjustment. Eastern Virginia suffered a large emigration of its
planters, many of whom removed only to the adjacent Piedmont;
but some were bold enough to make the long journey to Kentucky
with their slaves to exploit the newly famed tobacco lands there.
Others enquired for openings in Georgia and Florida, and only
awaited favorable reports thence to migrate southward. The planters in the rice district were also depressed for the time, because
the withdrawal of the British bounty on indigo had ended their
profits from that staple. As for the Piedmont, the number of farms
was gradually being increased; and so also in East and Middle
Tennessee.

The depression of the planting industry lasted only until the
resort to the new staple of cotton. Sea-island cotton was made

available in 1786, and upland cotton by the invention of Whitney's gin in 1793. The former revived the prosperity of the rice coast; the latter had tremendous results in revolutionizing the economy and the social constitution of the Carolina and Georgia Piedmont and developing the country westward as far as Texas and north to the southwestern point of Kentucky. Slaveholders from all of the older plantation districts now began to pour into the Carolina and Georgia upland. Very many of the farmers in that region at the same time advanced to the status of planters through the devotion of their earnings from high-priced cotton to the purchase of slaves.

In this newly developing cotton belt a pell-mell regime prevailed. In a scrambling, scattered mass of many sorts of people, planters, slaves, farmers, poor whites, and frontiersmen nearly all were concerned with getting cotton lands. The Creeks and Cherokees resisted the pressure upon their hunting grounds; and there was accordingly a mixture of plantation and frontier regimes in middle Georgia, as also afterward in Alabama and Mississippi. The passage of years witnessed a systematizing process in the cotton belt, and in some measure a segregating process which put the planters in control of most of the fertile and accessible areas.

Meanwhile it had been discovered in Louisiana in 1794 that sugar could be produced there with success; and a development of sugar plantations on a considerable scale had begun in the brief remaining period of the Spanish and French dominations. The arrival of the American regime in the sugar district of Louisiana had much the same stimulating and systematizing effect as that which, as we have noted, followed the English capture of Jamaica. Large and thoroughly organized plantations became the characteristic feature. The sugar district was confined by climatic limitations to the southern part of the present state of Louisiana. Soon after the Louisiana Purchase, it became known that the alluvial lands north of the sugar district could be used for short-staple cotton. The bottoms were relatively slow, however, in acquiring a good reputation except for sugar production. The Georgia and Carolina midlands were for a period in more active demand.

The War of 1812 brought another economic crisis, which again hastened the developments already in progress. Eastern Virginia and Maryland were further depopulated, and the Virginia Piedmont also supplied emigrants. The high cotton prices which came with the return of peace brought a new influx from these districts, and also from the Carolina coast, into the cotton belt. The defeat of the Creeks in war by Andrew Jackson had meanwhile forced a cession of a large part of Alabama; and within the next two decades the Southern Indians were obliged to give up all their remaining lands east of the Mississippi. Thereby a large territory was rapidly opened to receive the spread of settlement. The result was a thin occupation at the outset, in a wildly speculative regime, followed by a sobering process, in which a heavy fall in cotton prices assisted. The lowlands upon the Mississippi River, offering the attraction of inexhaustibly fertile soil, became a district of specially large slaveholdings, whether for cotton or sugar production, and specially subject to spasms of inflation and depression. In the same period the population was being increased in Kentucky and Middle Tennessee in more sedate fashion, as well as in the territory north of the Ohio River. Florida, also, received some immigration after its purchase in 1819; but Florida lay without the cotton belt proper and suffered a relative neglect. The only great extension of the plantation area remaining to be mentioned was that into Texas. The attractions of that region were the prairies for cattle and the river lands for cotton. The process of occupation, from the industrial point of view, was not widely different from that of other new districts in the cotton belt, except that the farms and plantations were more sparsely distributed and industry was somewhat more diversified, and the proportion of negro laborers smaller than in the other cases. The occupation of Arkansas and West Tennessee was merely an extension of the movement into the Mississippi cotton region. Rough conditions prevailed for a period; but industry in sober routine was not slow in replacing the regime of legal and social chaos. The settlement of Missouri was marked by an effort to extend the plantation system into a region not suited to the staples. A considerable number of slaves were carried thither; but they were found relatively unprofitable as laborers;

and as years passed their number tended to diminish through sales to the cotton belt.

A factor which strongly marked off the later period in the Old South's history and exerted great influence upon its industrial constitution was the closing of the foreign slave trade by the congressional act of 1808. Thereafter the tobacco and rice districts had a corner on the supply of slave labor which the cotton belt was demanding; slave prices entered upon a great rise and became subject to wild fluctuations; the industrial units and the several plantation districts competed strenuously for the possession of the available slaves; industry reached very much a speculative basis; crises of great severity became periodical; and the stress of the times quickened migration and hastened the segregation of types. Under these stimuli, the people of the South had gotten fairly acquainted with the qualities and relative advantages of every part of their country, by 1850 or 1860, and in each area had to a large degree developed that distinctive industrial system which, under the general circumstances of their legal system and their labor supply, served best to utilize local opportunities.

A survey on the eve of the War of Secession will show the conditions of industrial society as follows:

Tidewater Virginia and the greater part of Maryland had long been exhausted for plantation purposes and were being reclaimed by farmers working with much the same methods as were followed in the Northern states. The large land- and slaveowners mostly followed an example which George Washington had set and divided up their estates into small units in each of which a few negroes worked in the raising of varied crops under the control of a white man who was more a foreman leading the squad than an overseer driving it. Planters, who adhered to the old methods, were now of decayed estate, supported more by the sale of slaves than by the raising of tobacco. Incidentally, eastern Virginia and Maryland had come to have a very large number of free negroes.

The Piedmont in Virginia and the Carolinas had also reached a stage of some exhaustion and depopulation. The great liability of the hillsides to the washing away of their soil made the preservation of fertility peculiarly difficult in this rolling country, while the plantation system as generally administered was notorious for its carelessness of tillage.

The Charleston-Savannah district was moderately prosperous with its rice and sea-island cotton; and still excluded all small farmers except the poor whites, who were too low in the scale of industry and comfort to feel any effects of competition. The pine-barrens, including most of Florida, were vacant of people except for a thin sprinkling of farmers who tended more or less toward the poor white status.

The South Carolina and Georgia uplands were a fairly prosperous region dominated by planters but with a large portion of each neighborhood owned and cultivated by small farmers. The Alabama black lands, running across the state in a belt just below Montgomery and thence up the Tombigbee Valley, together with the Mississippi and Red river bottoms and a portion of Texas, formed the western cotton belt, which for four decades had been buying all the spare negroes from every other part of the South and smuggling in some from abroad to help in meeting its demand. The cotton estates in the alluvial districts tended to have larger gangs than those elsewhere; but of course the greatest industrial units of all were the sugar estates, where the need of the large economies incident to the operation of a sugar mill on each plantation discouraged all small or medium-sized units from attempting to compete. It must be observed, however, that all the western cotton belt and the sugar district was interspersed more or less with barren or remote tracts where poor whites or other small farmers might live undisturbed by offers of tempting prices for their lands.

Kentucky and Middle Tennessee were a region of diversified industry, producing grain and livestock, tobacco, some cotton, and in one district a large output of hemp. Manufacturing, too, reached appreciable dimensions. Some of the agriculture permitted the plantation system; some did not. Much of the region had a considerable minority of negroes in its population, but very few localities had a majority of them.

In the Shenandoah Valley, northern models of farming were followed, producing large crops of grain, hay, fruit, etc. Attempts by eastern Virginians had been made to establish plantations in the Shenandoah, but only to fail. Slaves were sprinkled in the population but served only as help, not as gang labor. East Tennessee was practically a duplicate of the Shenandoah in its industrial society. It had long been shut out by the mountains from any access to markets for its produce; but the building of railway connection to the cotton belt brought a long delayed wave of prosperity. It of course produced none of the southern staples; it had no slaves to speak of, and no plantations.

As for the people living in the midst of the mountains, in West Virginia, Kentucky, western North Carolina, etc., they were so completely isolated, self-sufficing and unprogressive as to have practically no influence upon the rest of the South and little development of their own.

The succession of stages and systems which we have observed in this outline of the development in the several areas on the continent was largely analogous to that which other students have described among the West India Islands. Merivale,[1] for example, has written in substance as follows on the remarkable repetition of industrial history in the West Indies: The same causes, operating in one island after another, produce the same effects. The opening of a fresh soil, with freedom of trade, gives sudden stimulus to settlement and industry; the land is covered with free proprietors, and a general but rude prosperity prevails. Then follows a period of more careful cultivation, during which estates are consolidated, gangs of slaves succeed to communities of freemen, the rough commonwealth is transformed into a most productive factory. But fertility diminishes; the cost of production augments; slave labor, always dear, becomes dearer through the increased expense of supporting it. At this stage, new islands are occupied, and fresh sources of production opened; the older colonies, meeting thus a ruinous competition, descend after a period of difficulty and suffering into a secondary state, in which capital, economy, and increased skill make up in part only for the advantages which have been lost. Thus, the Windward Islands first supplied almost all

[1] *Lectures on Colonization and Colonies* (London, 1841), 92, 93.

the then limited consumption of sugar and coffee in Europe; Jamaica rose on their decay, and went through precisely the same stages of existence; San Domingo in turn greatly eclipsed Jamaica, but was overwhelmed by the great negro insurrection, and never reached the period of decline. Lastly the Spanish colonies of Cuba and Porto Rico, after centuries of comparative neglect, started all at once into the front rank of exporting islands, while the British planters, with the aid of their accumulated capital, were struggling against encroaching decay. The parallel of the history of the islands with that of the staple areas on the mainland is remarkably close, and is useful in confirming the views we have reached of the nature, influence, and history of the plantation system.

Our outline of the history of Southern industrial society suffices to show the striking repetition of process and to indicate the differentiation of types, area by area. It demonstrates that documents to illustrate either the frontier or the plantation regime can be chosen indifferently from numerous areas, provided that a due regard be had to the periods of time and stages of development within which the writings respectively may fall.

Within the several plantation districts, the systems of labor were determined largely by the requirements of the staples. The size of the units was controlled in large measure by the degree of fitness of the soil and the staple for full routine in simple tasks. Sugar cane offered the best opportunity for plantations of great size, because no delicate work was required and there was employment throughout the year for crude muscular force with a minimum of intelligence and painstaking. The rice crop was next in the order of these qualifications. Indigo was so delicate a plant and needed so much care in preparing the product that negro labor was poorly suited for the work. Cotton had the disadvantage of needing delicate handling at some seasons; but it had the great staple virtue of keeping the laborers busy nearly all the year in a steady routine. No time of fair weather at any season need be lost in that idleness and unremunerative work which it was the planter's chief business to guard against. In tobacco, the routine season was shorter and the need of painstaking greater; and tobacco accordingly was abandoned by many planters who turned in preference to cotton or sugar. The cultivation of corn and wheat as main crops gave such long rest seasons, necessary to fill by job work in by-industries, that no slaveowning planter could well compete in their production for the market. Small farms abounded in the several Southern districts in inverse proportion to the fitness of their soil and their staple for full routine with crude labor. For example, the deep and durable soils of the Mississippi bottoms were more conducive to the use of large gangs in cotton raising than were the rolling lands of the Carolina Piedmont which had only a surface fertility. In the Piedmont there was frequent need of clearing new fields in a process which disturbed the routine; and the uneven character of the land promoted a scattering of fields, which wasted the time of the gangs in going to and coming from work and made effective supervision more difficult. Farmers could there compete in producing the staple with less disadvantage than in the alluvial lands, and small planters could hold their own against the great ones. The Piedmont plantations on the whole were accordingly smaller on the average and less formal in system than those in the several lowland districts. That contrasts existed among the numerous frontier areas and types is obvious. The variations were too many and complex to permit of discussion here. . . .

2

Racial Problems, Adjustments and Disturbances

THE INDIANS

I NDIAN adjustments were shaped almost as much by the character and organization of the Red men as by the purpose of the whites.* The Southern aborigines were less warlike and savage than those of the North, but were less docile than the typical sort in the West Indies, and less advanced in the arts than those of Mexico or Peru. The tribes close upon the Atlantic seaboard in the South were petty in size and could be played off against one another. In the interior the four great confederacies held sway, and there the white men and their governments had to act with caution.

The basis of white and Indian relations varied through all the stages from chronic hostility to firm friendship—from the harrying of De Soto's explorers out of the Creek country to the admiring amity of Tomo-chi-chi and the Yamacraws toward Oglethorpe and his settlers at Savannah. The usual relation was one of alternating war and peace. Formal intercourse was confined mainly to trade and diplomacy. On the part of the English colonies and the American states and their citizens, missionary activity was slight.

By the end of the colonial period the petty seaboard tribes had practically all been destroyed. In the latitude of Virginia the whites were masters of the country as far west as central Kentucky. Farther south the Indians were holding their ground with more

* The South in the Building of the Nation (13 vols.; Richmond, 1909–13), VI, 194–241.

success. The Cherokees maintained their title to nearly all the mountain region in North Carolina, Tennessee and Georgia, and the Creeks held sway from the Oconee River in eastern Georgia westward to beyond the Alabama River. The Choctaws, and, north of them, the Chickasaws, controlled the region of Mississippi and western Tennessee, with few pale-face encroachments. The principal trade routes in the period following American independence were as follows: from Baltimore and Richmond to the Cherokees in and about East Tennessee; from Charleston and Savannah through Augusta to the Creeks and Cherokees, and even the distant Chickasaws; from Pensacola, Mobile, and New Orleans to all the neighboring tribes. The Anglo-Americans wanted land more than they wanted furs, and the farmers were continually narrowing the field of the fur traders. Every possible occasion was used for crowding back the Indian tribes, especially after the cotton industry had begun its huge and swift development.

The Cherokees were the allies of the British in the war of the Revolution and the Creeks, in the war of 1812. In each case the Americans defeated the Indian forces and required land cessions as conditions of peace. In the succeeding period there was constant crowding of white settlers against the Indian borders, and individual American citizens even went to settle in the midst of such tribes as would permit it. Relations of the races along the border were often informal and intimate. White farmers at times hired Indians to pick cotton; white men in many cases married Indian wives, or out of wedlock begot half-breed children; many Indian tribesmen adopted the white men's institution of negro slavery and acquired black laborers to help their women in their drudgery. The Seminoles furthermore tended to fraternize with the runaway negroes escaping from white masters and to interbreed with them.

As solutions for the general Indian problem, many plans were proposed. William H. Crawford, when secretary of war, suggested that the Indians be civilized and that the whites intermarry with them wholesale and absorb the race. The press of the day roundly scolded Crawford for his proposal. The general idea of treating the Indians as wards of the government was discussed in the period only to be rejected. On the one hand the federal government was disposed to regard the tribes as foreign states, and on the other hand the body of the whites on the border were anxious to acquire the lands and did not wish any guardianship established over the tribes which would hinder the speedy driving of them away into the western wilderness. Most of the white missionaries preaching Christianity to the Indians labored incidentally to convert them to civilized industry. But success in this effort would tend to attach the tribesmen to the fields which they might clear and the houses they might build. It might make them more peaceable as neighbors, but they were not wanted as neighbors at all. What was wanted was their lands. As soon as the white farming communities in the states concerned saw the tendencies of the missionary efforts, they increased their own exertions to expel the tribes, so that when roving habits should be given over and the tribes settle down to sober industry their homes would be far away in what was then spoken of as the great American desert of the West.

There was no basis found for neighborly adjustment without chronic friction. The Indians and whites had purposes and activities mutually antagonistic. The Indians were not imitative and not submissive. Talented chiefs of mixed blood increased the trouble. The Cherokee chieftains, about 1827 for example, appealed to the assertion of the inherent equality of men which the Americans had made in their Declaration of Independence, and asserted that the Cherokee people constituted one of the sovereign powers of the earth. The white men who wanted the Cherokee lands were deaf to such appeals and contentions. The Creeks, Cherokees, Choctaws, and Chickasaws dreaded an emigration to a country infested with wild Sioux and Apache tribes which would prey upon the partly civilized emigrants, but this counted little in the policy of the whites. The Indians must go. The four great confederacies were sent beyond the Mississippi in successive bodies between 1817 and 1840. In the West the numerous tribes were gradually concentrated, the problem was localized and was no longer a concern of the South in general. No solution of the problem of Indian adjustments had been found save that of expulsion.

THE NEGROES

The negro population on the whole was willing, first and last, to do farm labor and to submit to control. This fact was largely responsible for the very important part which the negroes played in the life of the South. In all the regions successively made available for staple production there were landholders, actual or prospective, anxious to secure labor. The plantation system was a well-known device already at hand for the profitable employment of crude labor, and negroes, whether African or American born, were constantly available in large numbers and furnished very often the only labor supply to be had. Under these conditions, almost inevitably, negro labor was imported from abroad and transported within the South to all districts where there was prospect of large profits from its employment. These negroes when brought in from Africa were heathen savages accustomed only to precarious tribal existence in the jungles. To be fitted for life in civilized, Christian, industrial society, they had to be drilled, educated in a measure, and controlled. Had they possessed the disposition of the Indians this would have been impossible. Their pliability saved them here, gave them homes, and enabled them to increase and cover great fertile tracts of the earth and share in its plenty.

ORIGIN OF THE AMERICAN SLAVERY SYSTEM

The status of the first cargoes of negroes imported into English America was indefinite, and for years remained so. They were understood to be servants under control of private masters; but a definite and universal relationship was only evolved by gradual process. One item after another was added to the regulations; that the negroes should be servants for life, and not for a term of years; that the basis of their status should be race and not religion; that the legal device for securing control to the master should be a fiction of the ownership of the slave's person instead of a fiction of a contract; that children should inherit the status of their mothers and become the property of their mothers' owners; that the chattel thus created by the fiction of the law should be transferable by sale, bequest or inheritance like other chattels; that slaveowners if they so desired might emancipate their slaves under regulations framed for safeguarding the public welfare; that a special system of police and judicature should be applied to the slave and other negro population; that mulattoes, quadroons or other persons of mixed blood within stated degrees should be deemed negroes in the eyes of the law and held to slavery as if full-blooded Africans, and so on. Many of these provisions originated in the custom of the master class and were later made authoritative by legislation. Regulation of some sort for the negroes was imperative, and according to the general American practice regard was given in many cases to the needs of the immediate present rather than to those of the distant future. A system once developed in a commonwealth and appearing to work well was easily borrowed by neighboring colonies or states. In fact the legislation of Virginia was copied with more or less modification by all the governments from Delaware to Mississippi and Arkansas.

CHARACTER OF LEGISLATIVE REGULATIONS

Life was rough in most parts of the South, except perhaps for the planters' womenfolk and the townspeople. The general task at hand was the conquest of a wilderness, largely by the use of involuntary labor. The population was sparse, and while a rude plenty prevailed and there was little suffering among the negroes, there was need for fairly stringent regulation to secure control by the whites. In addition, where the plantations were closely grouped in dense black belts, there was need of offsetting the smallness of the proportion of whites by keeping the blacks in a more complete subjection. There was steady occasion for guarding against the absconding of slaves into the swamps or to the Indian tribes or to the free states, and there were occasional rumors of plots for insurrection. The consideration of these things led to the enactment of laws for curfew, patrol, and fugitive rendition, and of laws for restricting assemblage, for restricting the travel of slaves except in the company of whites, and for prohibiting the teaching of slaves to read. Abundant laws for most or all of these purposes were enacted by each of the slaveholding colonies and states. And a new restriction upon the negroes, whether slave or free, would be promptly enacted in case a new possible instance were discovered where an added disability upon them would tend to safeguard the established order. It became a fixed custom in most states to legislate in prevention of possible emergencies, with a consciousness that if the law should prove inconvenient to the community it would be allowed to lie unenforced until the occurrence of the contemplated emergency should call it into life. In fact most provisions of the repressive legislation were dead letters at all times. The actual regime was one of government not by laws but by men. In fact each slave was under a paternalistic despotism, a despotism in the majority of cases benevolent but in some cases harsh and oppressive, a despotism resented and resisted by some upon whom it was imposed but borne with light-heartedness, submission, and affection by a huge number of the blacks.

ACTUAL ADJUSTMENTS NOT SHAPED BY THE LAW
BUT BY PRIVATE EXPEDIENCY

There was legislation also safeguarding the slaves against oppression and injury, but this likewise played little part in actual affairs. It was the master's interest, comfort, principles, and desire for good repute which mainly shaped the relations of master and slave. The principal other factor in the matter was the slave's own character and attitude. If extremely submissive he might be oppressed; if rebellious he might be flogged or shackled; if an incorrigible runaway, or a chronic troublemaker, or hopelessly indolent or stupid he might be sold to a trader; if disposed to render reasonable service for reasonable sustenance he was likely to be treated with consideration; if faithful and affectionate, as very many were, he was fairly sure to receive indulgence even to the point where it hurt the master's income; and if sick, crippled or superannuated, he would be given medical treatment and support for the rest of his life. Although the laws provided that slaves must not be taught to read, many of them were so taught by their masters or mistresses. Although the laws required that slaves should be kept directly under the control of the masters or their agents, very many of them were hired to themselves and perhaps did not put in an appearance from week's end to week's end, unless to pay their hire out of their earnings. Although there was no legal sanction for marriages among the slaves, weddings were usually celebrated by religious exercises and the rights of husbands and wives were secured to them at least as effectively as the negroes usually desired. The fundamental law of slavery provided that a slave could not own property; but under any master of average consideration any slave disposed to be thrifty could lay up what he acquired by gift or earnings and enjoy full security in its possession; and some of them even made contracts with their masters to work overtime and buy their freedom on the installment plan. In a word, the laws maintaining slavery in fact simply gave to the master a title to the control of his servants' labor and a claim upon his neighbors to aid in returning the servant to his service in case of an attempted flight. The actual adjustments between master and slave were very largely informal, extra-legal, and varied widely. The master's interest, however, and generally his inclination, lay in cultivating the good will and affection as well as in preserving the good health of his slave; for even a slave could be counted upon to do better work from loyalty and in the hope of rewards than from the fear of punishment. The great mass of plantation records, private correspondence, pamphlets, and newspapers preserved in the South, which the historians have failed to use, tend to show strongly that the average master realized that the range of possible relationships was very wide in the slavery system and that it was generally to the master's interest to be indulgent though firm, benevolent though autocratic. There were some severe, grasping, and harsh masters, however, and many of the slaves had so little of the docility and inertia of the typical Guinea negro for whose adjustment the system of slavery was framed, that they were a misfit in the system and were obviously and unjustly oppressed under it.

A few items written by men involved in the problem who had no thought that their letters, diaries or advertisements would ever be used for a historical purpose, will illustrate the regime more vividly than pages of description. The first is from a letter of Ralph Izard of South Carolina, then sojourning in New York City, to his neighbor, Peter Manigault, in Charleston, April 23, 1769: "Scher-merhorn [a ship captain] will deliver my boy Andrew to you; he has run away, stolen, and given me an infinite deal of trouble. I must beg the favor of you to send him to Mr. Postell [Izard's over-seer], as I find the discipline of a rice plantation is absolutely necessary for his welfare; if he was to stay long in this country he would certainly be hanged." (Ms.)

The next is a series of extracts from letters written in 1860, by William Capers, overseer of a rice plantation on Savannah River, to his employer, Charles Manigault, at Charleston. They show that a capable "driver" (i.e., foreman of a plantation gang) might fall into drunkenness and worthlessness when subjected to bad man-agement, but might well be redeemed again under proper encour-agement and control:

1. From a letter of August 5: "If he [John] is the man that I had as driver when at Mr. Pringle's, buy him by all means. There is but few negroes more competent than he is, and [he] was not a drunkard when under my management. . . . In speaking with John he does not answer like a smart negro, but [he] is quite so. You had better say to him who is to manage him on Savannah."

2. From a letter of August 11: "John arrived safe, and handed me yours of 9th inst. I congratulate you on the purchase of said negro. He says he is quite satisfied to be here and will do as he has always done 'during the time I have managed him.' No drink will be offered him. All on my part will be done to bring John all right."

3. From a letter of October 15: "I have found John as good a driver as when I left him on Santee. Bad management was the cause of his being sold. [I] am glad you have been the fortunate man to get him." (MSS.)

The consideration often shown in the selling of slaves is illus-trated in the following advertisement from the Augusta, Georgia, Chronicle, Sept. 2, 1809: "For sale, a likely Negro Fellow, sober and honest: he is a tolerable carpenter, a good cooper, and can make negro shoes, and in many respects is very useful on a planta-tion; he is used to the upper country, and does not like to live in the lower country, for which reason only he is to be sold."

The following letter of a citizen to the editor, printed in the Washington, Georgia, *News*, May 1, 1824, indicates the slackness of slave regulation. The burden of the letter is a complaint at the disorder prevailing in the village on the Sabbath: "I see crowds of negroes around the tippling houses. . . . They slip in and out, and some of them are seen drunk and rolling about the streets, oaths sounding in our own and our children's ears . . . [Furthermore] I often and almost every Sabbath see load after load of wood, hay, fodder and other articles for market hauled through the streets in waggons, carts, etc., and stop in the square until the owner can go and find a purchaser. . . . Slaves have by these means every encouragement to become rogues."

The indulgence of favorite slaves in the matter of clothing may be gathered from the following advertisement by Mr. J. W. Gibbs of Charleston, offering rewards for two runaways, from the *South Carolina Gazette*, Dec. 10, 1784:

Fifty Dollars Reward. Ran away from the subscriber on Sunday morning, a short yellow wench named Sall, well known in this city; had on a blue woolen jacket and petticoat. Also ran away last night a Negro Fellow named Will, husband of the above wench, who took with him all the remainder of her cloathes, and several suits of his own; among the latter were a pair of black velveret breeches and waistcoat, pair of white dimity corded breeches, and two or three silk waistcoats, two or three pairs of linen overalls, a cinnamon-coloured broadcloth coat with a double row of white plated buttons on the breast, a Saxon green superfine broadcloth coat, almost as good as new, with white plated buttons, a drab coloured great coat with plated buttons, a small, round hat with a black band and plated buckle, with a number of other cloaths which cannot be remembered; also two new and four old blankets. These Negroes were absent once before for three years, a great part of which time they were in the employment of a Mr. Stirk, in Georgia, from whence they were brought back about a twelvemonth ago in rags. During their stay there they acquired a great number of acquaintances with Negroes run away from this State, many of whom are now in this City, and it is supposed are harbourers of them.

An ability to read and write increased the value of a slave, as is indicated by the following advertisement by A. Fleym in the

Charleston *Morning Post* for March 6, 1787: "Negroes for Sale, viz.—A mulatto boy, sober, honest and industrious, can take care of horses, drive a coach, and is a good boatman, fisherman and house servant, 22 years old, and can read and write very well. . . ."

The hardships suffered by those who refused to submit appear from this advertisement in the *Louisiana Gazette* (New Orleans), March 11, 1817: "A Negro man who has been two years in jail will be sold at the courthouse in the town of Baton Rouge, on the 4th day of April next, for jail fees. He is about sixty years of age, 5 feet 5 or 6 inches high, and says his name is Baptiste."

Or from this notice published in the *Virginia Gazette*, April 7, 1774, by Nathaniel Burwell, of King William County: "Run away in July last, Matt, a tall, slim Negro Man, by trade a carpenter, and about forty years old; he walks badly, having been Frost-bit in Prison some years ago, by which he lost one of his great Toes, and the Print of the Irons he then had on may be seen plainly on his legs. Whoever delivers him to me shall receive 3l. reward if taken within twenty miles of my House, and 5l. if at a greater Distance."

Likewise from the following by Henry Randolph, in the *Virginia Gazette*, Dec. 4, 1767: "Run away from the subscriber a Mulatto fellow named Aaron, about 5 feet 10 inches high, about 19 years old, and marked on each cheek I. R. . . ."

The occasional severity of slave punishments is indicated by an extract from the diary of Henry Ravenal, of St. John Parish, South Carolina, April 9, 1818: "Set on a jury of inquest over the body of a negro woman named Sue, the property of Dr. Jordan. Verdict, came to her death by excessive punishment of his sister Rebecca Jordan."

Finally, the following letter from Mrs. S. R. Cobb, near Athens, Georgia, Jan. 9, 1843, to her daughter-in-law, Mrs. Howell Cobb, at Athens, illustrates the consideration often shown by the master class. The Matilda who is mentioned in it was a free negro, and Betty's relatives were of course slaves like herself: "Tell Howell I cannot agree for Betty to be hired to Matilda; her character [*i.e.*, Matilda's] is too bad. I know her of old, she is a drunkard, and is said to be bad in every respect. I should object to her being hired to any colored person no matter what their character was, and if she cannot get into a respectable family I had rather she came home and if she can't work out put her to spinning and weaving. Her relatives here beg she may not be hired to Matilda. She would not be worth a cent at the end of the year." (Ms.)

PROBLEMS OF THE MASTERS

The general tendency, as shown by the mass of plantation records and other material extant in the South, as well as by tradition and by many indications to be gathered even from the laws themselves, was for custom to be very much more kindly than the law. The legislators could deal with the theoretical situation as severely as they pleased, and suffer no personal discomfort; but the slaveholders in private life, day after day, year after year, in good times and in bad, in serenity or in stress had to make shift to get along with their slaves. An unfruitful servant could not be discharged. Reprimands were likely to be useless or worse than useless. Some slaves were beaten, some were cajoled, but with most of course some middle ground of treatment was followed. On the whole a great deal of slack-handed service was put up with. A West Indian planter wrote in his diary (Lewis, M. J., *Journal of a West India Proprietor*, under date of April 22, 1817):

Cubina is now twenty-five, and has all his life been employed about the stable; he goes out with my carriage twice every day; yet he has never been able to succeed in putting on the harness properly. Before we get to one of the plantation gates we are certain of being obliged to stop and put something or other to rights. . . . The girl, whose business it is to open the house each morning, has in vain been desired to unclose all the jalousies; she never fails to leave three or four closed, and when scolded for doing so, she takes care to open those three the next morning, and leaves three shut on the opposite side. Indeed the attempt to make them correct a fault is quite fruitless.

Mr. R. L. Dabney, of Virginia, wrote in familiar correspondence in 1840: "It seems to me there could be no greater curse inflicted on us than to be compelled to manage a parcel of negroes." Another Virginia planter said to F. L. Olmsted "that his negroes never worked so hard as to tire themselves—always were lively and ready to go off on a frolic at night. He did not think they ever did half a fair day's work. They could not be made to work hard; they never would lay out their strength freely, and it was impossible to make them do it." Some masters succeeded better than this in making their slaves work, usually because the masters themselves were high-grade captains of industry.

CHURCH ADJUSTMENTS

Race relations in matters of religion varied as did those in industry, all the way from tutelage and complete paternalism by the whites to complete self-reliance and separate organization among the blacks. In the period of early adjustments there were some missionary efforts among the grown-up negroes and informal teaching of the children by their mistresses. In the vast number of families, too, which held family prayers, the domestic servants were required to attend the daily reading of the Scriptures, and the field hands were usually assembled for a family service each Sabbath. It early became customary to set apart seats in every church for the use of negroes and to invite, in many cases to require, their attendance. They were encouraged also to hold prayer-meetings among themselves, and gradually in the cities there came to be a few separate negro congregations of the Protestant sects. Even in the rural districts the contrast between the whites and negroes in temperament and the manner of religious manifestation promoted separate gatherings, though a large number of the slaves continued throughout the antebellum period to attend services regularly with their masters and white neighbors. A number of negroes or mulattoes who were discovered to have talent for preaching were taught by the white clergy and ordained as ministers. Some of these, Henry Francis, of Savannah, in 1802, and the famous preacher, Jack, of Nottoway County, Virginia, for example, were bought from their masters with purses made up for the purpose and set free for their ministry. In addition to those regularly ordained, there was a great number of plantation exhorters, slaves, many of whom could not even read.

Statistics of the churches in Charleston were gathered in 1819 and published in Shecut's *Medical and Philosophical Essays*. The Roman Catholic chapel had 300 white and 150 colored communicants; the Congregationalist church 300 of each; the Lutheran 265 and 50, respectively; of the Presbyterian churches one only is reported, with 85 whites and 80 colored; of the three Episcopal congregations, St. Michael's had 350 whites and 130 colored members, St. Philip's had 390 white and 180 colored, and St. Paul's 65 whites. Finally, the four Methodist congregations had an aggregate of 382 whites and 1,814 colored, the latter reduced from 5,000 by a recent secession of the blacks to form a separate church of their own. The secession of colored Methodists here alluded to had occurred in 1818, at the instigation of negro preachers sent from the Northern states. The Charleston authorities, with the usual antipathy to Northern suggestions, broke up some of these meetings in 1818, under a statute of 1800, restricting negro assemblage. But apparently soon after the Northern missionaries withdrew the statute was allowed to relapse into its desuetude, and several of the colored congregations continued to maintain their separate existence. In New Orleans, in 1839, there was at least one negro congregation (meeting in the negro church on Gravier Street) which had had a separate existence for a number of years. In Baltimore, in 1847, there were thirteen or more separate colored congregations, and similarly in other cities and towns. Repressive legislation following the insurrection which the preacher, Nat Turner, inspired in Southampton County, Virginia, in 1831, tended to discourage the separate meetings of negro congregations, but the effect of this was only temporary.

The general state of affairs in the churches in the later period is illustrated in a series of reports submitted to a convention in Charleston, May, 1845, to consider the religious instruction of the negroes, and printed in its proceedings. Typical for the dense black belt of the rice district on the coast is the report of the Rev. Alex. Glennie, an Episcopal rector in Georgetown District. Glennie relates that he has ten plantations under his pastoral charge; finding on some of them negroes of good character able to read, he gets them to teach the children in the catechism; he tells the negroes that with their masters' consent they may well hold meetings, using the prayer book of the church; he then on his visits explains to them what they have committed to memory, "and the people learn to worship God in a form of sound words, instead of listening to the senseless if not erroneous effusions of an ignorant negro. I cannot say that I have succeeded in this respect; there is ever a strong disposition in the blind to follow a blind leader." The report of Mr. R. F. W. Allston, also of Georgetown District, shows the grounds for an Episcopal clergyman's discouragement. In the parish of Prince George there were about 13,000 slaves, of whom 3,200 worshipped with the Baptist church, 1,500 with the Baptists, and 300 with the Episcopalians. Concerning his own plantation, Allston continues:

I have a place of worship for my negroes, open to all denominations. The Methodist missionary preaches to my people every alternate Sabbath after catechizing the children, about 50. By the rules of my plantation the Methodists and Baptists have prayer-meetings at given houses, each twice in the week, besides Sundays, when they meet and pray and sing together . . . I have had this custom for 15 years, and it works very well . . . Of my own negroes and those in my immediate neighborhood I may speak with confidence. They are attentive to religious instructions, and greatly improved in intelligence and morals, in domestic relations, etc. Those who have grown up under religious training are more intelligent and more generally, though not always, more improved than those who have received religious instruction as adults. Indeed the degree of intelligence which, as a class they are acquiring, is worthy of deep consideration.

Affairs in the Piedmont region are illustrated in the report of Rev. John Douglas, a Presbyterian minister in Chester District:

The relations and intercourse between the whites and the blacks in the up-country are very different from what they are in the low country. With us they [the negroes] are neither so numerous nor kept so entirely separate, but constitute a part of our households and are daily either with their masters or some member of the white family; from this circumstance they feel themselves more closely identified with their owners than they can [on the great plantations]. I minister steadily to two different congregations. More than one hundred blacks attend—and we have about eighteen members. We have no missionaries for them specially. The gallery or a quarter of the house is appropriated to them in all our churches, and they enjoy the preached gospel in common with the whites.

A report, finally, by Mr. J. D. Wilson of Darlington District is valuable not upon religion but upon the moral progress among the slaves:

The truth is their nature is as susceptible of improvement as our own, and were it not for the deleterious effects of ardent spirits, which is stealthily introduced among them at intervals, we might mark the negro character as having undergone a change as great as the white, in proportion to the amount of intellectual culture. The practice now obtaining so generally among masters of giving them either a proportion of the proceeds of the crop, or which is much more general, allowing them sufficient land to make a crop [i.e., of their own] has infused into them a greater regard for the rights of others.

THE FOREIGN SLAVE TRADE: ITS VOLUME

A factor constantly influencing the problem of racial adjustments was the slave trade, which was an agency for distributing negroes to the localities and employers making the strongest economic demands for slave labor. The foreign division of the slave trade was of chief importance prior to 1808, while the lands of the original thirteen states were being settled. The domestic slave trade in its organized, interstate form began shortly before 1808, and grew rather steadily in importance until about 1850, when the great westward movement of the South began to spend its force and when the problem of the territories began to dwarf the preceding issues in Federal politics.

The operations of the foreign slave trade, while conspicuous, were not so perpetually necessary in the South as in the West Indies and Brazil; for while in the Antilles and South America the stock of slaves failed to replenish itself adequately and tended to die off, in the Southern states a stock once on hand almost invariably increased with rapidity by excess of births over deaths. In the

United States, therefore, it did not appear essential to retain the African slave trade in order to maintain a system and a supply of slave labor. In fact, the traffic to the colonies and states comprising "the South" made up only a small fraction of the trans-Atlantic slave trade. While all estimates in the premises are of necessity conjectural, a reasonable approximation would place the total imports into the South, from first to last, at about four or five hundred thousand, as compared with three to four million into the West Indies and Central and South America. The traffic flourished for nearly a century and a half in the Spanish colonies before it reached any importance in the English settlements; and it continued for a generation in Brazil and Cuba after its prohibition in the United States.

THE TRADE IN AFRICA AND ON THE SEA

The great volume of the traffic from the early seventeenth century onward was carried on by English and Yankee vessels, with some competition by the French and the Dutch. Slave cargoes were obtained on the coasts of West Africa, East Africa, and Madagascar, and as the demand for them grew, the tribes on the coast developed a system of buying or capturing slaves from the tribes in the distant interior of the continent. This promoted tribal wars and treachery in the jungle, and in the long run it greatly disorganized and demoralized the African tribal institutions. This was unknown to the traders, and would have been disregarded if known. Many of the traders were professing Christians, and the Puritans particularly were accustomed to give thanks to God at the conclusion of a successful slave-trading voyage. Some of the Pharisees salved their consciences by reflecting that their traffic was bringing heathen savages (or such of them as survived the "middle passage") into touch with Christianity and was giving them a chance for conversion. But in general the slave trade was considered neither moral nor immoral, but non-moral. The deacons in Massachusetts when sending their ships to Guinea would advise their skippers to water the rum and give short measure when buying slaves with it; and when the skipper after buying a parcel of slaves from a chieftain on the coast kidnapped the chief and his family and added them to the cargo, it was praised as a very smart trick. According to the prevailing code, no faith need be kept with the heathen.

The size of the vessels engaged in the traffic was quite varied, and likewise the cargoes carried to Africa. But a very common type in the New England traffic was a sloop, schooner, or snow of about fifty tons burden, say seventy feet long, over all twenty-four feet beam, ten feet depth of hold, and three and a half feet between decks. Such a vessel would be handled by a captain, a mate, three or four men, and a boy. It would take on a lading in Rhode Island or Massachusetts of about a hundred hogsheads of rum, a food supply, and a lot of shackles. On the coast of Guinea or Madagascar, if luck was good, a hundred slaves would be bought at say a hundred gallons of rum per head, and with food and water supplies replenished, the run to the plantation colonies or states would be begun. The negroes crowded into the between-decks could not stand erect, for the ceiling was but three or four feet from the floor. When they lay down they had such scant room that they must lie spoon-fashion one with another. For the greater part of their month or two on the westward voyage they must sit manacled, often storm-tossed, often ill with the flux, liable to epidemics of smallpox, fevers, and opthalmia, liable also to starvation from the spoiling or exhaustion of the food or water supply, and to shipwreck, and to capture by buccaneers. In the nineteenth century when the traffic had been outlawed by the maritime powers, the peril of capture by war vessels on patrol was added to the risks which the traders ran; and the possibility of being flung overboard was added to the risks of the poor negroes. Upon the average vessel a heavy percentage of the cargo died in the middle passage and when they reached America most of the survivors had endured brutal and terrible sufferings. It was a most unhumane traffic, but hardly inhuman, for to be human is often to be callous. The standard of humaneness nowadays is higher all round than it was a century or two ago; but by the standard of some centuries hence our general conduct of today may be judged either brutal or effeminate. It is impossible to say which, and it is useless to heap epithets upon a traffic of the past in which highly honorable men like Peter Faneuil engaged, which few of the Puritans condemned in the colonial period, and to which no large group but the uncompromising Quakers were irreconcilably opposed. It happened that very few Southerners engaged in the foreign slave trade. That is because their genius was that of landsmen and not of mariners, and because there were plenty of other men to do the repulsive work for them.

THE LANDING AND SALE OF CARGOES

The principal interest of Southerners in the African trade began when the voyage ended. A ship with a cargo for sale in Virginia or Maryland in the colonial time when there were no cities would sail slowly along the coast of the bay and the rivers, stopping to seek buyers and to spread information as to its further itinerary. If the demand should be slack, the ship might peddle its cargo for several months. But in the Lower South, where each colony or state had a single seaport focusing its commerce, skippers would usually avoid delay in case of slack markets by depositing their cargoes with local dealers, for sale on commission. The following advertisements are typical—both taken from the Charleston *Evening Gazette* of July 11, 1785:

Just arrived in the Danish vessel *Gen. Keith*, Captain Kopperbolt, and to be sold on Friday the 15th instant, on board the vessel at Prioleau's wharf, a choice cargo of Windward and Gold Coast Negroes, who have been accustomed to the planting of rice. The appearance of the negroes will sufficiently quiet a report which has been circulated of their being much infected with scurvy. The sale to continue from day to day until the whole is disposed of. The conditions will be as moderate as possible, and will be known on the day of sale by applying on board to A. Pleym.

Just arrived in the ship *James*, Captain Forrest, and to be sold on Wednesday the 13th inst., by W. Macleod & Co., No. 17 Elliott St., a choice picked cargo of two hundred and thirty Gambia Negroes, all of which have been inoculated for the small-pox, and recovered without the loss of one.—The superiority of these negroes to any imported into this state (being accustomed to the planting of rice in their own country) is so well known as to render it unnecessary to enumerate any of their qualifications. A considerable allowance will be made for cash or any kind of produce.

DEMAND FOR AFRICANS EAGER

As long as the African trade was kept open the prices of slaves ranged rather low, and there was constant temptation for the planters to increase their stocks by purchase. For example, Charles Calvert, then governor of Maryland, wrote in 1664 to Lord Baltimore: "I have endeavored to see if I could find as many responsible men that would engage to take 100 or 200 negroes every yeare from the Royall Company at that rate mentioned in [your Lordship's] letter, but I find wee are nott men of estates good enough to undertake such a businesse, but could wish wee were for wee are naturally inclined to love neigros if our purses would endure it."

The lure of African purchases was specially irresistible if the credit system prevailed, as it did in the busy ports of the Lower South. In a debate in the South Carolina House of Representatives, March 22, 1887, it is reported that Dr. David Ramsay "made a jocose remark that every man [who] went to church last Sunday and said his prayers was found by a spiritual obligation to refuse [i. e., to vote against] the importation of slaves. They had devoutly prayed not to be led into temptation, and negroes were a temptation too great to be resisted."

PROBLEMS OF SLAVE TRADE RESTRICTION

In spite of the interest of the individual planters in keeping open a cheap supply of slave labor, there were public considerations in the plantation colonies and states demanding more or less restriction of the traffic. For one thing the importation of great numbers of slaves involved the payment of great sums in their purchase, and drained money out of the importing districts. Furthermore the rapid influx of savage Africans and the congestion of the negroes in dense black belts tended to make police control extremely difficult and the danger of insurrection or other disorder very great.

Every English colony on the continent concerned at all with a race problem legislated or attempted to legislate from time to time in limitation of the foreign slave trade. Some of the bills passed by the assemblies looked to a prohibition, others merely to a taxation of the trade. The British crown, meanwhile, was safeguarding the interests of the slave traders, and was prone to veto restrictive measures. The rate of the duties was usually mild, and some historians have discredited the restrictive purpose of these measures, pointing for example, as Alexander Johnston does, to the preamble of the Virginia Act of 1752, which recites that an existing duty had been found "no ways burdensome to the traders." Such attempt to discredit is not entirely just. The assembly had to secure by indirection and in limited measure what the crown would in nowise consent to if presented in downright form. The colonial assemblymen, however, were neither constant nor unanimous in their desire to restrict the traffic. Representatives from newly settled districts were eager to keep the slave labor supply plentiful and cheap, and thought little of the anxiety in the black belts. On the other hand, the representatives from the long-settled plantation districts would feel an added spur to restrict the African supply because their constituents when selling their surplus negroes to the new settlements were anxious to get high prices for them. As in most other matters of practical politics, the point of view depended very largely upon "whose ox was gored."

STATE PROHIBITION OF THE FOREIGN TRADE

The situation from 1776 to 1808, while the several states had full control of slave-trading policy, brought forth just the developments which might have been expected. The states from Delaware to North Carolina, long settled and at that time industrially stagnant, kept a constant prohibition upon the African trade. Georgia, with a rapidly extending industry, kept her ports open for a time until her constitutional convention closed them permanently in 1798. South Carolina maintained a prohibition upon the trade until the labor demands of the new cotton industry became too importunate. Then she opened her ports in 1803. The keenest industrial demand, however, was in Louisiana, after its purchase and the beginning of its invasion by Americans. At the end of February, 1806, the collector of the port of New Orleans obtained an opinion from the attorney-general of the United States that inhabitants of the territory might lawfully import slaves from any state in the Union. A rapid importation of negroes from Africa began at once in ships which had touched at Charleston en route in order to legitimize their trade. The following advertisement is typical, from the *Louisiana Gazette*, July 4, 1806: "The subscribers offer for sale 74 Prime Slaves of the Fantee Nation, on board the schr. *Reliance*, I Potter, Master, from Charleston, now lying opposite this city. The sales will commence on the 25th inst., at 9 o'clock A.M. and continue from day to day until the whole is sold. Good endorsed notes will be taken in payment, payable the 1st of January, 1807. —Kenner & Henderson."

The congressional prohibition of the African trade in 1808 reduced it thereafter to smuggling dimensions. There was no movement in the South for a reopening of the foreign traffic until after 1855.

THE DOMESTIC SLAVE TRADE

The domestic slave trade had points of sharp contrast with the foreign. It involved no upsetting of African tribal life, it had no horrors to compare remotely with those of the middle passage. In fact it involved no great physical hardships of any sort, and the wrenching from the old homes was but a temporary sentimental distress. New ties were quickly made and the old in large measure forgotten. It is a striking fact of the intellectual history of the American negroes that they have preserved no vestige of tradition regarding the concrete ancestral life in Africa, and likewise the children of the slaves who were carried to Alabama, for example, retained very slight knowledge of their parents in an older Virginia home. Typical negroes are creatures of the moment, with hazy pasts and reckless futures.

The domestic slave trade was merely a readjustment of population within the United States, to supplement the volume of spon-

taneous migration and distribute more effectively a labor supply to the districts where it was most in demand. The earliest important occurrence of this traffic appears to have been the selling of negroes south from the states which had taken or were about to take steps to rid themselves of the institution of slavery. The following document from the Chatham County archives at Savannah, Georgia, illustrates the movement to export slaves from Connecticut, for example, after the act of 1784 in that state which provided for the gradual disestablishment of slavery: "This may certify that I the subscriber have this day sold the bearer hereof being a negro boy named Pad about fifteen years of age middling stature & of a yellow complexion to Mr. Benjamin Richards of New London as a servant for the term of ten years only at the expiration of which time he is to be free from said Richards or any other person claiming under him or myself. In witness whereof I have hereunto set my hand at New London, in the State of Connecticut, July 10, 1787.   Witness present, Titus Hurlbert.   Nicoll Fosdich."
Doubtless full many a negro sold thus from the North for a term of years lost his papers and never found the freedom which his native state nominally secured him.

ORIGIN AND PROGRESS OF THE DOMESTIC SLAVE TRADE

The organized slave trade between the several states of the South began to take form promptly upon the closing of the African traffic. For a decade or more previous, in fact, it had been customary for men intending to settle as planters in the Lower South to go to Virginia to secure a gang of slaves who were already adjusted to and probably native in the American environment. In due course of time professional traders arose to save such planters the need of going in person to buy slaves in Virginia.

The restriction of European trade and the War of 1812 checked the migration and the internal slave-trading activity for the time, but the arrival of peace in 1815 gave a huge impulse to both. The cotton industry was expanding with enormous rapidity in the Southwest, and fevers of speculation in both lands and slaves raged periodically. Except for the panic years of 1819, 1825 and 1837, the period from 1815 to 1839 was the heyday of the domestic slave trade. The chief sources of supply were the states from New York to North Carolina, and among them principally Virginia and Maryland. Some were sold also from Kentucky and from the coast of South Carolina. There were warehouses for the display of the slave merchandise maintained by the dealers in all the principal cities from Washington to New Orleans, and rural agencies, whether fixed or peripatetic, in the buying and selling districts. The following are illustrative newspaper items. The first is an advertisement from a country newspaper in Maryland, the Centerville *Evening Times and Eastern Shore Publick Advertiser,* June 21, 1828: "Cash for Negroes. The subscriber wishes to purchase one hundred likely young slaves, from the age of 12 to 25 years; for which he will pay the highest cash prices. Persons disposed to sell will please call upon him at Mr. Lowe's Tavern, in Easton, where he can be found at all times."   J. B. Woolfolk.

The next is a news item from the *Virginia North-Western Gazette,* August 15, 1818: "Winchester, July 11. Several wretches whose hearts must be as black as the skins of the unfortunate beings who constitute their inhuman traffic, have for several days been imprudently prowling about the streets of this place with labels in their hats, exhibiting in conspicuous characters the words 'Cash for Negroes!' "

TRADE ROUTES AND METHODS

When a trader in this interstate traffic had acquired a squad to his satisfaction he would set off with them for the South or Southwest by one of three general routes; by sea in the vessels of the coasting trade from the Chesapeake to Savannah, Mobile, or New Orleans, by land across the Carolinas and Georgia or via East Tennessee, or by both land and water across western Virginia and thence on boats down the Ohio and Mississippi rivers. In the last mentioned branch of the traffic the negroes en route were usually in manacles and bound together in coffles, for the route lay close along states where slave laws did not prevail and whence the recapture of fugitives from the squads might be found difficult or impossible. On the overland route through the heart of the South the traders used the railroads for the sake of speed and economy wherever available; and elsewhere they usually had the able-bodied negroes travel on foot and the more delicate ones in wagons, while the traders themselves were on horseback, in sulkies, or afoot. The gangs in these cases were also frequently bound in coffles, for many of the negroes went unwillingly, the negroes living along the route would gladly harbor refugees, and many of the planters had such contempt for the "soul-drivers" that they could be counted on for little assistance in giving chase to slave-traders' fugitives.

The journey was by no means always a wretched one. For example, Sir Charles Lyell in his *Second Visit to the United States* remarks that when he reached Columbus, Georgia, "the first sight we saw there was a long line of negroes, men, women and boys, well dressed and very merry, talking and laughing, who stopped to look at our coach. On inquiry we were told that it was a gang of slaves, probably from Virginia, going to the market to be sold."

When arrived in the districts of slave demand, the squads were in many cases rested for a week or two and plumped out with plenty of food to improve their appearance, and then peddled among the plantations. In other cases, particularly when the transit had been made by water and the destination was a city, the traders auctioned off their stocks or deposited them with local dealers for sale on commission. In the latter case better prices could usually be had, because credit machinery was available; and the planters would much more rapidly buy when payments could be delayed until after a crop or two had been harvested. The coastwise trade at New Orleans, supplemented at times by smugglings from Africa, is illustrated by a news item which the Augusta, Georgia, *Chronicle* of Aug. 22, 1818, reprinted with the heading "Abominable Traffic" and the comment, "In reading the following disgusting details one is almost led to regret that he is living in a civilized age." The item, originally printed in the New Orleans *Chronicle* of July 14, 1818, is as follows:

The slave market appears to be very brisk—constant demand and high prices—notwithstanding the arrival lately of thirty-six in the brig *Mary Anne*; thirty-nine in the sloop *Thorn*; ninety-seven in ship *Vir-*

gin; 19 in the schr. *Sea;* 17 in the schr. *Fame;* 34 in the brig *Venus;* 38 in the brig *Franklin;* 37 in the schr. *Humming Bird,* all from the states; 159 in the brig *Josephus II.* from Africa.

We are, however, much indebted to the enterprising and successful exertions of Mr. Charles Morgan, for the copiousness of the present supply which with the aid of three or four hundred that have been seized by General Jackson's officers at Mobile, will probably suffice for the next crop.

Jersey negroes appear to be peculiarly adapted to this market—especially those who bear the marks of Judge Van Winkle, as it is understood that they afford the best opportunity for speculation. We have the right to calculate on large importations in future, from the success which hitherto attended the trade.

STATE RESTRICTIONS

In one of its aspects this domestic trade was a means of dumping undesirable negroes into the newly settled districts. If rebellious, torpid, tubercular, or inclined to insanity or heart disease, a slave could be sold "without a character" to a trader who in turn would unload him in the best way he could in the South or Southwest. These dumpings were dreaded, and attempts were made from time to time to guard against them by laws regulating or prohibiting entirely the interstate traffic. Prohibitive laws were enacted for example in Kentucky, South Carolina, Georgia, and Alabama between 1817 and 1820. But public sanction rarely supported such laws, and they usually fell into disuse if they were not repealed. The only effective check upon the traffic was the falling off in the economic demand for it. The great cotton crisis of 1839 and the hard times continuing to 1845 in the cotton belt made it impossible to sell slaves south at any profit in those years; and the revival of agriculture in Virginia in the fifties heightened the price of labor there and destroyed much of the traders' prospect of profit.

VOLUME OF TRAFFIC

Few statistics of this trade were kept, and estimates of its volume are entirely conjectural. The statistics of increase of slave population in the newer states give little clue in the premises, because they do not indicate what proportion of the negroes were carried by their migrating masters and what by the slave traders. Estimates of the average number of slaves carried out of the state by traders varied from 6,000 a year by Professor Dew in 1832, to 40,000 a year by the Wheeling *Virginia Times* in 1836. Mr. W. H. Collins in his recent monograph reasons that the commercial transit of slaves must have been below the usual estimates, because the census returns of population fail to show any undue proportion of young adult negroes in the importing states. This argument, however, is not convincing. On one hand the traders, particularly in the coasting traffic, took slaves of all ages, although of course they preferred youths. A manifest of the cargo of the ship *Missouri,* bound from Baltimore to New Orleans in 1810, included thirty-nine slaves, with their ages ranging from six months to forty-five years. This is probably not far from typical. On the other hand, the young "fellows and wenches" who without doubt made up the bulk of the traders' stocks, were at or near the breeding age and rapidly supplied the new states with children for the census taker. The conjecture of about 25,000 per year, which has often been made for the interstate slave trade is probably as just an approximation as can be had upon the volume of the traffic in its flourishing period.

THE QUESTION OF CRUELTY

The domestic slave trade was always accompanied by a tradition that conditions were severe in the regions to which the slaves were being carried, and that the traders were men of the greatest roughness and cruelty. This was the result of a bugaboo deliberately held by the masters before the slaves in the exporting districts. Masters found it highly convenient to have a bogeyman with whom to threaten their childlike and credulous laborers. Masters had to get along with their slaves, and to avoid as much as possible any reliance upon force. An excellent and constantly used device was to give some distant locality a horrid reputation and tell the darkies listening in round-eyed alarm that if they were not good and obedient to their kind and loving master and mistress they would be sold as dire punishment to a trader with an outrageous temper, who would carry them to work their lives away, with no holidays or frolics, in those dreadful swamps of Georgia or Louisiana as the case might be. This tradition was similar, on a small scale, to the religious tradition of hell. Negroes sold south did not return to disillusion their fellows, and the tradition lived on undisturbed. As a matter of fact, Virginia or Kentucky was little or no more of a negro elysium than Alabama or Louisiana.

The slave trader as a bogeyman was also overdrawn. For sake of profits if for nothing else he must have his stock-in-trade in prime condition at the end of his journey. Fresh marks of the whip, as well as old scars from it, would cause suspicion of intractability and diminish the price to be had for the slave. To bring the best prices, in fact, the slave must be carefree and eager as well as healthy and strong. A trader often lost a good sale because his negroes were surly, and often made good sales through having provided for the jollity and having won the good will of his stock. The slaves usually took pride in fetching high prices, and many a one praised his own good points on the auction block. And in private sales the bargain was often determined by ingratiating advances by the negro toward his prospective purchaser. Slave trading like liquor-selling was looked upon askance by society, and the social stigma upon the business tended to confine it to men of coarse natures. Yet the traders as a class hardly deserved all the ill repute which tradition has given them.

The interstate traffic was at times attacked in controversy and needed defense. The standard apology for it was that by its means many negroes were transferred from masters who could support them but poorly to more prosperous ones who could and would feed, clothe and shelter them much better. There was some reason in this. Travellers through the Virginia Tidewater district in the twenties and thirties, for example, always noted the industrial depression and the poverty-stricken aspect of things in general; and some of them, among whom was the negro Charles Ball, remarked that many of the negroes had ashy complexions and harsh, dead-looking hair. Ball remarks that this appearance was an invariable result of the negroes having no meats or fats in their diet. In the cotton belt at the same time, and more particularly in the Louisiana sugar district the faces of the darkies shone with all the glint of pork and 'possum, their figures were plump or brawny and their hair as crinkly and glossy as wool ever gets to be.

A charge against the trade was that it broke up families, separating children from parents and husbands from wives. It was replied that such separations, while at times inevitable in the system, were much fewer than was conjectured, and that the partings of parents from children were far more seldom than in the restless migrating free society at the North. And this reply was perhaps fairly just.

A charge was made by the anti-slavery men that the states of the Virginia group were breeding slaves for the cotton belt market. In rejoinder it was contended that market-breeding was an absurdity from the mere fact that hardly any one would produce a commodity which must be kept and fed for fifteen or twenty years before it could well be sold. This reply was not wholly convincing. The fact is that many citizens of the border states enjoyed for many years a considerable income from the occasional sale of slaves from their plantation stocks. On the other hand the matter of breeding was without doubt left almost or quite universally to the inclinations of the negroes themselves. The truth in regard to the so-called slave breeders is that the slaves bred spontaneously and the masters sold off the increase.

On the whole the domestic slave trade was an essential part of the general slavery system. It was one of the things which differentiated American slavery from medieval European serfdom. If it had been prohibited and destroyed the general situation regarding slavery itself would quickly have become profoundly modified. Such men, accordingly, as were anxious to perpetuate slavery were correct in judging the domestic slave trade to be vital to their regime, and in beating off attacks upon it.

MALADJUSTMENTS UNDER THE SLAVERY REGIME

The system of slavery was by no means perfect as a method of racial adjustment, nor was its working constantly smooth. There were always many slaves absconding from their masters, a few others being stolen by white thieves, and an indeterminate number more or less definitely plotting insurrection. At one extreme there were negroes too doggedly barbaric to submit to industrial discipline, and at the other there was a class, increasingly great as decades passed, of high-grade, intelligent, self-reliant negroes, mulattoes, and quadroons who were restless necessarily under the restraints of the system. With all its variety and its considerable elasticity the system of slavery was too rigid to be tolerable to all the extremely diverse people who were grouped in the so-called negro race.

RUNAWAYS AND DESPERADOES

A very conspicuous feature of any average newspaper of the slave-holding districts was the numerous advertisements offering rewards for the return of runaway slaves. Some of these runaways merely took to the woods for a vacation and returned to their work of their own accord at the end of the outing. The return of these was sometimes hastened by the noise of bloodhounds in the neighborhood. Others endeavored to establish themselves as free persons of color, or in the case of octoroons to pass as white persons, and perhaps to work their way in some fashion to the northward of Mason and Dixon's Line. Others became desperadoes and held localities in terror until raiding parties were sent against them. The following newspaper items are illustrative. The first which is taken from the *Louisiana Courier*, June 15, 1830, describes a case where provision in advance was made against the expenses of a long journey:

FIFTY DOLLARS REWARD will be paid for the apprehension of the negress slave named ANNY, aged about fifteen years, having a mark of a scald or burn on each shoulder. Said slave ran away from the residence of the subscriber, in the suburb Marigny on the night of the 11th inst., and took with her $300. in notes of the different Banks of this city.

The above reward will be given for the apprehension of the said slave, and return the money; or $10. for taking up the Slave, should the money not be found. All persons are warned, under the penalties prescribed by law, for harbouring said slave.   ANTONIO ACOSTA.

Sometimes a whole group of negroes on a plantation would stampede for the woods or for the North together. A frequent cause in such cases was the maladroitness or the oppressiveness of the master or overseer. Sometimes a runaway would grow into a desperado and perhaps be declared an outlaw by the government with a price upon his head. One of these was mentioned, for example, in a news item from Raleigh, North Carolina, printed in the *Louisiana Gazette,* Feb. 24, 1819: "The notorious outlying negro Billy James, who has been so long depredating on the property of this vicinity, and for the apprehension of whom the Governor offers a reward of one hundred dollars, was on the plantation of Col. Wm. Hinton a few nights ago. The Col., being informed of it, hoped to surprise him, but hearing no doubt, from some of the negroes of the plantation, what was going on, he escaped."

Sometimes a fugitive when pursued stood at bay, and in a terrific fight sold his life most dearly. The following account is from the New Orleans *Daily Delta,* April 11, 1849:

It is our painful task, says the Houston (Miss.) Republican of the 31st. ult., to record one of the most shocking murders that has ever occurred within the bounds of our country, which happened in the prairie, near the quiet little village of Pikeville. It appears that Mr. J. Heggerson attempted to correct a negro man in his employ, who resisted, drew a knife and stabbed him (Mr. H.) in several places. Mr. J. C. Hobbs (a Tennesseean) ran to his assistance. Mr. Hobbs stooped to pick up a stick to strike the negro, and while in that position the negro rushed upon him, and with a dirk, inflicted a wound in his left breast, which caused his immediate death. The negro then fled to the woods, but was pursued with dogs, and soon overtaken. He had stopped in a swamp to fight the dogs, when the party who were pursuing came up and commanded him to give up, which he refused to do. He then made several efforts to stab them. Mr. Robertson, one of the party, gave him several blows on the head with a rifle gun; but this, instead of subduing, only increased his desperate revenge. Mr. R. then discharged his gun at the negro, and missing him, the ball struck Mr. Boon in the face, and felled him to the ground. The negro seeing Mr. Boon prostrated, attempted to rush up and stab him, but was prevented by the timely interference of some one of the party. He was then shot three times with a revolving pistol and once with a rifle, and after having his throat cut, he still kept the knife firmly grasped in his hand, and tried to cut their legs when they approached to put an end to his life. Mr. Boon is said to be seriously wounded. Mr. Heggerson's wounds are slight.

Sometimes groups of runaways would gather in some natural fastness and live for years in freedom. Thousands in the West Indies, particularly in Jamaica, flocked to the mountain defiles and with rude political and military organization held sway over wide areas. The colonial governments, despairing of any subjugation, would at times negotiate a *modus vivendi* with these maroons. On the continent, the Seminole Indians gave refuge to hundreds of runaway negroes, and swamp fastnesses in the Great Dismal or the Okefenokee or on the Savannah River or the Chattahoochee, the Mobile or the Mississippi gave havens where the fugitives could rally on their own initiative. An item from the Charleston *Observer*, July 21, 1827, relates an incident at such a rendezvous: "A nest of runaway negroes were lately discovered in the fork of the Alabama and Tombeckbee rivers, and broken up, after a smart skirmish by a party from Mobile county. Three of the negroes were killed, several taken and a few escaped. They had two cabins and were about to build a fort. Some of them had been runaway for years, and had committed many depredations on the neighboring plantations."

OUTRAGES AND LYNCH LAW

The doings of negro desperadoes are illustrated from the following account of a lynch law execution published in the Gallatin, Mississippi, *Signal*, Feb. 27, 1843, and reprinted in the *Louisiana Courier*, New Orleans, March 1:

NEGRO OUTRAGES. In the last number of our paper, we gave an imperfect account of the summary punishment of two negro men, belonging to a Mr. Burnly, of this county, who were hung according to a statute of Judge Lynch, in such cases made and provided. We have since learned the particulars of the circumstances which led to their execution; and the more we reflect upon them, the more we are inclined to justify almost any step calculated to punish them severely for such a revolting outrage as they themselves acknowledged was committed by them. It appears that they went to the house of Mr. N. during his absence, and ordered his wife to get them some liquor. On her refusing to do so, they cursed her in a most blasphemous manner and threatened her with death if she did not obey. After having got the liquor, they called for some hot coffee and cold victuals, which she told them they should have if they would not harm her and her children, which they promised to do. But after this, they forcibly took from her arms the infant babe and rudely throwing it upon the floor, they threw her down, and while one of them accomplished the fiendish design of a ravisher, the other pointing the muzzle of a loaded gun to her head, said he would blow out her brains if she resisted or made any noise.

They afterwards took quilts and blankets from the beds, broke open the trunks and drawers, and taking their contents, which consisted of forty dollars in specie and a quantity of clothing all of which they carefully put in the quilts and blankets, they even took the shoes from the feet of Mrs. N. and placing the whole of the plunder on the back of a horse which they had brought with them for the purpose, they made off.

We obtained these particulars from a gentleman of the highest respectability. He questioned the negroes on the subject, a few hours previous to their execution, and also interrogated Mrs. N. in a similar manner, and her answers agreed in every essential particular with the statement made by the negroes. What aggravates this affair is the fact that the unfortunate woman had but six weeks previous recovered from child-bed, and her body is bruised and much hurt from the rough treatment she received while in the hands of the negroes, the prints of whose fingers were visible on her neck. We have ever been, and now are, opposed to any kind of punishment being administered under the statutes of Judge Lynch; but when we reflect upon what must be the feelings of the husband and father, and the deep anguish which must pervade the bosom of the injured wife and outraged mother, a due regard for candor and the preservation of all that is held most sacred and all that is most dear to man, in the domestic circles of life, impells us to acknowledge the fact, that if the perpetrators of this excessively revolting crime had been burned alive, as was first decreed, their fate would have been too good for such diabolical and inhuman wretches.

STOLEN SLAVES

Some of the slaves were not lost or strayed but stolen. The *Athenian*, of Athens, Georgia, Aug. 19, 1828, related that "On July 23, a negro fellow belonging to Henry B. Thompson, of Taliaferro county, was met in the road while on his way to work by two waggoners with their waggon, who promised a treat to him if he would assist in moving a part of their loading; after he got in he was seized by the throat and confined, and one staid in the waggon for the purpose of keeping him quiet while the other drove." But the negro preferred his old master to the new, and while his captors slept in camp that night he cut the thong that bound him and returned home.

When the slave to be stolen connived at the theft, as he frequently did in response to false promises by the thief, the stealing was easily accomplished. The slave could be carried off through the woods or by wagon or river boat or coasting vessel, and sold to some unsuspecting purchaser a hundred miles away, and the master might advertise over the whole countryside for his slave as a runaway and perhaps never gain trace of him; for the negro even if he declared he had been stolen would probably be disbelieved, particularly if he were being offered at a bargain to some not over-scrupulous employer in need of an extra workman. Numerous cases are reported where stolen slaves were packed in boxes or barrels for transportation by common carriers, whether steamboats or railroads. The following news item from Richmond, Virginia, was printed in the *Daily Delta* of New Orleans, May 7, 1849:

Early yesterday morning a negro drayman carried to the office of Adams & Co.'s Express, two large square boxes addressed to "Williamson, No.——, Buttonwood Street, Philadelphia." On being interrogated as to whence they came, the negro showed some confusion. Still the boxes were placed on the Express wagon and transported to the cars. As the driver of the wagon turned one of the boxes over rather roughly, he heard a sort of grunt, which proceeded from it. Suspicion was aroused, the boxes opened, and each one found to contain a stout negro, carefully folded up, with a small quantity of bread and a bladder of water, and one of them with a fan—a useful article in his warm situation. On examining the boxes, a large auger-hole was observed in each box, partially concealed by a stout rope knot, which could be withdrawn while in the cars, and allow the entrance of air. The negroes we hear, belonged, one to Mrs. C. Christian, of New Kent, the other to Mr. Govan's estate, and were employed as waiters, one at the Washington and the other at the Columbian Hotel. Their story is, that they had been prepared for transportation by Mr. S. A. Smith, who keeps a small shoe store on Broad street, in Mr. James Lyons' new buildings, and that they had paid him well (some 60 dollars each) for the job. This Smith formerly kept a shoe store at the sign of the "Red Boot," opposite the Old Market, and has also been a lottery-vendor. We hear that some years ago he was intimate with Blevins, the great negro-kidnapper (now in the penitentiary) and that on the trial of the latter, a letter to, or from, the same "P. Williamson," Philadelphia, was read in evidence.

Negro-stealers were of course no respectors of persons. A free negro could be kidnapped and sold into slavery as easily as a genuine slave—more easily in fact, because in a country controlled by white men's interests he had no master with an interest in him to safeguard. The following is from the New Orleans *Daily Tropic* of Jan. 13, 1846:

A CASE OF KIDNAPPING.—The Raleigh (N.C.) *Star*, notices the taking off of a little son of a poor blind free negro, in that vicinity, under such circumstances as to justify the suspicion that he was stolen to enslave him. A strange young man came to the house of the negro, and under pretence of desiring to find the way to a neighboring shop, took the boy behind him to shew him the road—since then neither of them have been heard of. The boy is a dark mulatto, eight years old, spare made, and is named Nelson Dudley Richardson. The young man who took him off was represented to be tall and slim, and between 21 and 25 years old.

GANGS OF KIDNAPPERS

In a few cases there were organized gangs of slave-stealers operating upon a large scale. A group led by John Washburn spent most of a decade, from 1827 until 1837 when their ringleader was hanged, in robbing river boats and mail coaches, picking pockets, rifling stores, murdering wayfarers, and stealing slaves. In 1820 they stole six negroes in one batch and peddled them out among the Louisiana planters for $4,600. A greater and more notorious gang was that under John A. Murrell, operating also in the Southwest, mainly between Memphis and New Orleans. Murrell had scores of accomplices, some of them apparently industrious farmers, others outright desperadoes, and he kept the whole region more or less terror stricken for some years before his final capture by Virgil A. Stewart, in 1835. The Murrell gang followed all the usual activities of desperadoes, but their favorite work was the seducing of slaves. Their most successful plan, and one which they carried out in a large number of cases, was for the thief to connive with a slave and promise if the negro would run with him and allow himself to be sold and then run away from the purchaser and meet his supposititious friend at a rendezvous agreed upon the thievish friend would then give him papers of freedom or help him to reach the free states. Sometimes the gang would sell a deluded negro three or four times in as many neighborhoods, and finally kill him to prevent his peaching on them. It was often a very inconvenient characteristic of slave property, accordingly, that such property could and did give aid in getting itself stolen.

SLAVE CONSPIRACIES AND REVOLTS

The liability of slaves to run away or to be stolen concerned their several masters only. Their liability to conspire and rise in insurrection, however, was a vital concern of the whole community in which they dwelt. On the continent of North America, it is true, the number of actual slave revolts was small, and each of those which occurred was quickly repressed. In the Spanish, French and British West Indies, on the other hand, there were numerous open attempts at revolt; there were constantly forces of rebel slaves living in the mountain fastnesses of Jamaica and San Domingo; and in the one case of Toussaint L'Ouverture's rising, the negro rebellion shattered the European control, expelled or massacred the whites, and established an independent negro state. News of all these occurrences was widely published and read in the slave-holding communities on the continent, and when added to the rumors of plots at home, was enough to foster from time to time a very serious anxiety.

The series of plots and rumors of plots for servile revolt on the continent extends through the whole period from the bringing of the blacks to America to the final destruction of slavery. There was a plot in Virginia, for example, in 1664, shared in by black and white bondmen, when the total negro population of the colony numbered hardly more than a thousand souls. In New York City there was a frenzy of fright in 1721 and again in 1741 at the report of negro conspiracies for rising and burning the city. Each of these alleged plots in New York was repressed with extreme severity, on the flimsiest of evidence. Severity of punishment was a fixed policy in servile conspiracy cases in all quarters; but the trials at law were usually far more adequate and even-tempered than in these New York instances.

In the colonies and states of denser black populations conspiracies were correspondingly early, and were more numerous and perhaps more disquieting than in Virginia and New York.

The preaching of the "rights of man" in the period of the American Revolution tended to stimulate longings for freedom; but the armies of the master class were mobilized in the period and the prospect poor for success in servile risings. The French revolutionists, fifteen years later, were more ecstatic in praise of liberty, and their preachings spread from the French colonies to the United States along with the slaves whom refugeeing masters carried from Hayti to new homes in and about New Orleans, Charleston, Norfolk, and Richmond. At or near each of these cities, as well as elsewhere, there were serious commotions within the eight years following the Haytien exodus of 1792. At Pointe Coupée, Louisiana, for example, in 1796 a plot was discovered of so alarming a nature that although a dozen negroes were hanged for it at the time, the whole community lived in dread and slept on its arms, so to speak, for years afterward.

The most important conspiracy of this period was that matured by the negro Gabriel, with its focus at Richmond in 1800. A thousand blacks and mulattoes were ready to rise at a signal, and the signal was given on scheduled time. The revolt occurred in terror-striking proportions, and the city would have been doomed had not a great freshet made the rivers impassable and delayed the insurgent march upon Richmond until the militia was organized and ready to oppose Gabriel's pikes with commonwealth bullets and bayonets. Gabriel's army scattered, the leaders were captured and executed, but the fright they had given was long fresh in the Virginian memories. A further source of disturbance was noted by John Randolph as early as 1811, when he said that the impetus given by the French revolution was being sustained and refreshed by emissaries from New England preaching disaffection among the Southern negroes, and that in consequence the whole South was living in a state of insecurity.

The next series of plots was in the period from 1816 to 1822, when the whites had relaxed from the tension of the foreign war. George Boxley, a white man, organized a more or less definite negro plot at Fredericksburg, Virginia, in 1816, which was betrayed before its maturity and repressed by hangings. A similar occurrence in the same year at Camden, South Carolina, was similarly punished, and others at Charleston in 1818 and at Augusta in 1819. Then came the great Denmark Vesey plot in Charleston in 1822, widely spread and well organized, but betrayed before its outbreak. After a large number of trials before a special tribunal Vesey and thirty-four of his fellows were hanged, and a number of others transported from the state. Police regulations were then stiffened in the locality and no further plots were rumored there for many years.

The next series of negro commotions began in 1831, and was attributed to incitement by the Northern abolitionists, whether through pamphlets and newspapers or through word of mouth. The only matured plot at this time was that organized by the negro preacher Nat Turner, which broke out in Southampton County, Virginia, and caused the death of about sixty white persons before it was suppressed. About the same time the discovery of plots, whether real or supposititious, was reported from localities in North Carolina, Georgia, Mississippi, Louisiana, and Kentucky. The wildest rumors flew, and at numerous places the greatest excitement prevailed. In 1832 Professor Dew published his epoch-making essay upon the existing regime as regards negro slavery, and scouted the possibility of any general uprising of the negroes. This promoted the return of confidence and sobriety. There were sporadic reports of plots—three for example in Louisiana in the early forties; in West Feliciana Parish in 1841, at Donaldsonville in 1843, and in Plaquemines Parish in 1845—all of which were considered genuine and serious in the localities, but none of which matured or resulted in disaster to the whites. About 1855 and again more notably in 1860, rumors of plots were rife in the newspapers, and many citizens, it seems, were growing to apprehend a general rising. On the other hand, the complete failure of John Brown's dramatic attempt to incite the slave masses justified a sense of security in the minds of conservative men. A great number of Southerners at all times held the firm belief that the negro population was so docile, so little cohesive, and in the main so friendly toward the whites and so contented that a disastrous insurrection by them would be impossible. But on the whole there was much greater anxiety abroad in the land than the historians have told of, and its influence in shaping Southern policy was much greater than they have appreciated.

FREE NEGROES AND MULATTOES

The Southern attitude toward "free persons of color" was shaped largely by considerations regarding the possibility of negro conspiracies. Negroes and mulattoes who were not slaves could not be restricted effectively in their reading and conversation, and by many they were thought to offer a dangerous medium of communication between the abolitionist agitators and the negro slaves. Many men of the South thought of themselves and their neighbors as living above a loaded mine, in which the negro slaves were the powder, the abolitionists the spark, and the free negroes the fuse. Free mulattoes were still more dreaded than free negroes, because generally they were more intelligent and perhaps had a more acute sense of injustice and grievance under the prevailing regime.

The official policy of the slaveholding states and cities, therefore, tended to restrict and if possible diminish the number of free colored persons, and to restrict the degree of liberty enjoyed by them. Accordingly, the plan of African colonization for that class of people was welcomed in the South when it was proposed in 1816; and branches of the colonization society spread rapidly in most of the Southern states. But that movement never had more than a fleeting success. A few years' debate and experience showed that its task was impossible and that its supporters were in two wings with irreconcilable purposes. The anti-slavery wing wished to use the society for promoting emancipation, while the prevailing Southern policy was to reduce the social danger from free persons of color by the double method of colonizing the existing stock and preventing its replenishment through emancipation. After the rise of the abolition agitation in its radical and aggressive form, say in 1831, the South abandoned its hope of substantial relief through colonization, and grew indifferent to the fate of the Liberian scheme. A sprinkling of idealists, mainly in the border states but including prominently John McDonogh of New Orleans, furnished the only exception to the general Southern loss of confidence in the colonization plan, originally considered so promising as a solution.

The private attitude of a great number of persons toward free negroes differed radically from the official attitude. Men whose main concern was with industry and commerce and not with police were disposed to judge other men more upon their industrial ability and worth than upon their color or their legal status. In the eyes of businessmen, many free persons of color were esteemed as doing good work for reasonable pay and thereby promoting the general prosperity, while others who were sluggards were as such held in disesteem. The personal equation and the questions of industry, sagacity, and integrity were the controlling factors in private relations, and private relations of course reacted upon public policy. In consequence much of the legislation unfriendly to free persons of color was annulled through default of public sanction. Immigrant free negroes, however, were usually dealt with strictly in accordance with the official policy of exclusion and repression. They were dreaded as being probably breeders of plots. In some of the cities, furthermore, the free persons of color in the crafts were repressed by regulations established through the influence of the white artisans who wished to monopolize the local opportunity. On the whole the free persons of color in the South were something less than free. By law they must usually have guardians; generally, though not everywhere, they were deprived of the suffrage franchise; in some instances, their industrial opportunity was restricted; at times special taxes were imposed upon them, and official policy was generally directed toward making their lot uncomfortable. But nearly all these statements are equally true of the Northern states in the antebellum period, and the industrial opportunity for this oppressed class was poorer in the North than in the South. The relative degree of friendliness toward the free persons of color locally may be gathered in part from the census returns; in 1860 Maryland had 83,942 free colored in its population, Virginia 53,042, and North Carolina 36,473, as compared with 56,949 in Pennsylvania, 49,005 in New York, 36,673 in Ohio, 28,318 in New Jersey, 9,602 in Massachusetts, etc. The so-called slave state of Maryland in 1860 contained nearly as many free colored persons as it did slaves, and Delaware had only 1,798 slaves compared with 22,794 free colored. In the Lower South the numbers of free colored were very much smaller, except in Louisiana, where they amounted to 18,647 in 1860, and had reached the number 25,507 in 1840, in a period when regulations affecting them had been lax or unenforced. A great many of the free colored persons were much better off in the matter of property than has generally been supposed; whether by earnings of their own or by bequests from their former masters, many of these persons possessed thousands and even tens of thousands of dollars worth of property, often including therein negro slaves.

A statement previously made regarding the adjustments between slaves and masters applies equally to the relations of free persons of color and their white neighbors: conditions varied widely from place to place and from person to person; local laws were diverse and changeable, and custom, more powerful than the laws, was vastly more varied than the legislation.

CONCLUSION

In the two centuries and more of industrial slave-holding in English America, most of the negroes had improved greatly in civilization, the races had grown mutually much better acquainted, and many changes of detail had been made in race relations. No panacea, however, could be found for some of the great social ills, no solution for some of the pressing problems. In particular, no satisfactory adjustment could be found for the class of specially progressive negroes and mulattoes for whom slave status was obviously a misfit. Racial adjustments in the South, of course, never reached a state of complete equilibrium. The progress of conservative readjustments was interrupted by the clash of war, the victory of the radical North, and the overthrow of the whole established South racial policy. To mention these occurrences is to end our theme of antebellum adjustments.

BIBLIOGRAPHY.—Adams, Nehemiah: A *South-side View of Slavery, or Three Months at the South in 1854* (Boston, 1855); American Colonization Society, *Annual Reports* (1818-1860); Ball, Charles: *Narrative of Life and Adventures* (Philadelphia, 1854; a slave's autobiography); Ballagh, J. C.: *A History of Slavery in Virginia* (Baltimore, 1902); Blake, W. O.: *History of Slavery and the Slave Trade* (Columbus, 1858); Brackett, J. R.: *The Negro in Maryland* (Baltimore, 1889); Burke, Emily P.: *Reminiscences of Georgia* (Oberlin, 1850); Buxton, T. F.: *The African Slave Trade and its Remedy* (London, 1840); Carey, H. C.: *The Slave Trade, Domestic and Foreign* (Philadelphia, 1856); Chambers, William: *American Slavery and Colour* (London, 1857); Clarkson, Thomas: *History of the Abolition of the Slave Trade by the British Parliament* (2 vols., Philadelphia, 1808); Cobb, T. R. R.: *Inquiry into the Law of Negro Slavery in the United*

States (Vol. I., Philadelphia, 1858); Collins, W. H.: *The Domestic Slave-Trade of the Southern States* (New York, 1904); Douglass, Frederick: *Life and Times* (Hartford, 1881); Drewry, W. S.: *Slave Insurrections in Virginia* (Washington, 1900); DuBois, W. E. B.: *The Suppression of the African Slave-Trade to the United States* (New York, 1896; contains bibliography); Goodell, William: *The American Slave Code in Theory and Practice* (New York, 1853); Hart, A. B.: *Slavery and Abolition* (New York, 1906; contains bibliography); Henson, Josiah: *Story of His Own Life* (Boston, 1858; a slave's autobiography); Higginson, T. W.: *Travellers and Outlaws* (Boston, 1889); Horsmanden, Daniel: *The New York Conspiracy of 1741* (2d ed., New York, 1810); Hurd, J. C.: *The Law of Freedom and Bondage in the United States* (Boston, 1858-62); Ingle, Edward: *Southern Sidelights* (New York, 1896); Kemble, Frances A.: *Journal of a Residence on a Georgia Plantation* (London, 1863); Lyell, Charles: *Second Visit to the United States* (2 vols., New York, 1846); Moore, G. B.: *Notes on the History of Slavery in Massachusetts* (New York, 1866); Northup, Solomon: *Twelve Years a Slave* (1853; a slave's autobiography); Olmsted, F. L.: *A Journey in the Seaboard Slave States* (1856), *A Journey through Texas* (1857), *A Journey in the Back Country* (1861), *The Cotton Kingdom* (2 vols., 1861); Phillips, U. B.: "The Slave Labor Problem in the Charleston District" (in the *Political Science Quarterly*, 1907; Russell, W. H.: *My Diary North and South* (New York, 1863); Smedes, Susan D.: *Memorials of a Southern Planter* (Baltimore, 1887); Stearns, Charles: *Narrative of Henry Box Brown* (Boston, n. d;. slave biography); Steward, Austin: *Twenty-two Years a Slave and Forty Years a Freeman* (Rochester, 1857; a negro's autobiography); Tillinghast, J. A.: *The Negro in Africa and America* (New York, 1902); Van Evrie, J. H.: *Negroes and Negro Slavery* (New York, 1861); Walker, David: *Walker's Appeal* (1829, a negro's appeal for slave insurrection); Williams, G. W.: *History of the Negro Race in America* (2 vols., New York, 1883); Weston, G. M.: *The Progress of Slavery in the United States* (1857).

3

The Economics of the Plantation

S INCE the end of the Civil War there has been in the South a tendency toward the multiplication of small holdings of land, which has been thought to promise the disappearance of all the plantations.* But a more careful study of the general problem will show that the tendencies in the unsettled periods of reconstruction and later were probably of temporary character, and that something like the old plantation will be established as the predominant type of agricultural organization in the South for the future.

The plantation was evolved in early colonial Virginia as the most efficient system for growing tobacco. That was before African slaves were imported in any appreciable numbers. The negroes were soon found to fit in admirably with the plantation arrangements. A similar system was established in the Carolina districts producing rice and indigo, and in the sugar cane fields of Louisiana. Finally the invention of the cotton gin and the extension of cotton culture into the uplands carried the plantation into the whole of the staple-producing South. Wherever the land was adapted to tobacco, rice, indigo, sugar, or cotton, the plantation won the victory over the small farm. It was the survival of the fittest. The involuntary servitude of the laborers was merely an incident. There is no essential reason why the freedom of the slaves should destroy the plantations.

The conditions of the problem in Southern agriculture were and remain as follows: (1) abundance of land; (2) money crops,

* *South Atlantic Quarterly*, II (July, 1903), 231–36.

with uncertain money returns; (3) ignorant and unenterprising labor; and (4) a large number of efficient managers of agricultural labor, who are usually also the owners of the soil and of such capital as exists. The problem is how to organize this labor under the existing conditions to secure the best returns. In former times the plantation system was developed as the most efficient for the purpose, and today it is not at all clear that the usefulness of that system has departed.

The plantation system was the application of manufacturing or capitalistic methods to agricultural production. The planter was a captain of industry. He owned the land, he planned the work of the year, and he saw to it that the work was done. His problem was to lay out the fields for the best return, to keep his laborers profitably at work in all seasons, to guard against the overworking of his laborers or his mules, and to watch receipts and expenditures with an eye for economy. If the planter failed in any of these requirements, he lost his wages of superintendence. If he allowed expenditures to exceed receipts, he lost first his profits, then his rent, and finally his capital. By overworking his land, his mules, or his laborers, to their injury, he might secure a greater return for one year, but was sure to be the loser in the long run.

In a normal period the small farm could not compete with a well-managed plantation in the production of the staples. A man who is able to manage a small farm to advantage is usually able also to superintend the labor of others in his line of work. Wages of efficient superintendence are always much higher than the wages of mere labor. The tendency, then, in the staple regions where additional labor was to be had, was for the successful farmer to establish himself as a planter. When an independent artisan becomes a foreman in a factory, or advances further to the ownership and superintendence of a mill, he does no wrong to the other artisans or to the factory operatives. By his efficient work on the larger scale he serves the whole world better than before. The advance of a ploughman into efficient plantation management and ownership causes a net increase in production, with a lowering of cost, and usually also means a betterment for the laborers under him.

The plantation system in the South can be no hardship for the negro. If his wages are low and the wages of superintendence high, it is because the laborer is careless and slovenly, and the risk of loss is great. The capable mulatto, and even the exceptional negro under present conditions, may hope to advance by thrift from the status of a hired ploughman or an independent farmer to become an overseer or the owner and manager of a plantation.

In the reconstruction period, there was a complete upheaval in the system of Southern industry. With the manager dead in battle, with labor disorganized, and with capital vanished from the land, some new arrangement had to be devised. As a rule the negroes became tenants, either on the basis of giving a share of the crop for the use of the land and stock, or on the basis of a rental in money or in cotton. By industry and economy, a number of the negroes have been able to buy land and mules of their own, but the great majority remain renters, or croppers, today. A large number even of those who own their farms are in a chronic state of debt to the merchants who furnish their supplies. These merchants require this class of debtors to plant a given amount of land in a money crop, and they often employ inspectors to see to it that the crops are kept in adequate cultivation. Thus they make sure that the debtor will be able to settle his account in full or in part when the crop is sold. In good years the farmer is able to pay off his current debts and perhaps has a surplus left on hand. But when crops are bad or prices are low, a mortgage must usually be made in order to secure the advance of supplies for another year. A second year of failure may establish the merchant as an unwilling landholder, and the debtor as his tenant.

The present system of renting, or cropping, can be but temporary. Under it the negro is superintended in but a half-hearted way. Whenever he fails to raise a good crop and to sell it at a good price, he involves his landlord and his creditor with himself in a common embarrassment. Furthermore, the average negro cannot maintain himself as an independent farmer, because his ignorance, indolence, and instability prevent him from managing his own labor in an efficient way.

The most promising solution for the problem is the re-establishment of the old plantation system, with some form of hired labor instead of slave labor. The whole tendency of American industry is toward organization for more efficient management. It is a dead loss for a good manager to have no managing to do. It is also a dead loss for a laborer who needs management to have no management. The most successful grain farms in the West are really plantations, where great gangs of men and machines work under a single direction. A system of small farms in the South would be an unprofitable reaction from a better system in the past. It would be a lessening of the net output in the staples and in grain, meat, and dairy products. It is necessary to bring Southern industry in agriculture as well as in manufacturing to a modern progressive basis; and the plantation system seems to be the most efficient for the purpose.

For the last thirty-five years the most progressive men in the country districts of the South have been moving to nearby towns or to the Northern cities. This is disastrous to agriculture, and a reverse tendency should be set at work. Under the present regime, a hundred schools of agriculture and dairying would do little good, for the farmer boy now goes to college only in order to leave the farm for good. Efficient managers can be attracted back to the soil only by some arrangement which will offer promising opportunities for management. A new plantation system must offer profitable and attractive careers to well-equipped men, or the pine thicket and the sedge field will continue to be conspicuous features of the landscape in the cotton belt, wasteful methods will continue in use, and the Southern farmers and Southern merchants will ever lag behind those of the North and the West. The colleges of agriculture in Wisconsin, Nebraska, and California have demands always pouring in for twice or thrice as many men as they can equip to fill the attractive positions which are offered upon the large farms in need of managers. In Georgia the college of agriculture has for decades been without students, because the system of renters and croppers and small farmers has prevented the rise of any demand for agricultural managers.

Yet there already exists a tendency for betterment in the South. There are several colleges of agriculture, like that of Tennessee, which are drawing a fair number of students; and the prosperity of these schools indicates that the soil is efficiently demanding a number of trained managers. Model plantations are to be found here and there, which are most attractive as patterns. There are planters in the Georgia cotton belt, for instance, who have withstood the disintegrating tendencies, and who at this day conduct large plantations upon the old system of management, but with hired labor. The Georgia Convict Farm serves as an example in its community. The managers are the most capable men to be had. They adopt the most approved methods, and they conduct experiments in draining, terracing, ploughing, fertilizing and rotating crops, which lead to surprisingly good returns. It is easy to see that the same managers with hired labor instead of convicts might win equal success. This has been done in fact in numerous recent instances by men who have had no special training, but who possess natural or inherited fitness for plantation management.

I am acquainted with a gentleman, born and reared upon a cotton plantation in Troup County, Georgia, who moved to Atlanta, upon reaching manhood, and established himself in business. He achieved moderate success, but always felt that yearning for the soil which is felt by so many Southerners away from the plantation. At length he resolved to return to the country and apply, with hired labor, the methods of cotton raising which his father had applied in antebellum days. He bought a tract of land in the Alabama cotton belt, built comfortable cabins, hired several negro families, selected the best of modern implements and fertilizers, and by good management made such a success that capitalists have offered to buy an unlimited amount of land for him if he will undertake to organize upon it a modern plantation system. A number of other men have received instruction from his example, and his whole community is tending to change from the renting and cropping system to the system of the plantation. This is not an isolated case; but seems to be an earnest of a general movement. The great, new peach orchards of middle Georgia further illustrate the recent tendency toward the plantation system and its adaptation to a variety of crops.

When the plantation comes to be re-established predominantly in the fertile parts of the South, it will bring order out of the existing chaos. By introducing system in place of haphazard work, it will lower the cost of production, increase the output, and enable the South to produce a greater amount of its food and other needed supplies. It will infuse a spirit of thrift into the Southern community, for the competition of plantation managers for the market will not permit of indolence.

The plantation system offers to the South the best means of offsetting the ignorance and laziness of the negro laborers. It offers profitable work for blacksmiths, engineers, millers, carpenters, and other artisans. As in a factory or a great business concern, the system, when thoroughly developed, will put a premium upon ability and enterprise. Capable men will be promoted to responsible positions. And yet it need not involve any hardship upon the ordinary laborer, further than the requirement of regular hours of work. Under present conditions the average negro cropper, or renter, lives from hand to mouth with an extremely low standard of living. Money wages would be much better. Savings facilities could well be established, and perhaps also a profit-sharing system. The unenterprising whites would be drawn off to the factories, or they would continue as small farmers, learning improved methods from the neighboring plantations.

The great fault of the antebellum system of plantations lay in its exclusive devotion to the staple crops, and in its discouragement of manufacturing and other forms of industry. But the experience of latter years has destroyed the belief in the omnipotence of raw cotton. The planter of today and tomorrow must accept his place as only one of many captains of industry, without expecting to become the autocratic master of production or of politics in the country.

Any modern system must take a tone from the active, pushing, world of today; but in essentials the plantations of old could again look with hope to the system which produced the fine type of the

Southern gentlemen of the old regime. The present heterogeneous conditions can only be transitional. The prevalence of small farms would be the prevalence of mediocrity and stagnation. The hope of the South is in the application of the principle of the division of labor to agricultural production.

4

Conservatism and Progress in the Cotton Belt

B Y TAKING thought, a man cannot add a cubit to his stature; and yet he may add materially to his equipment and value as a member of society; he may increase his own and his neighbor's resources.* By taking thought, a people may adopt broad policies which will better its own internal condition and at the same time increase its beneficial influence upon the world at large. The men of the South have been men of action and seldom philosophers. They have done what their hands have found to do, and have usually done it well; yet it appears that their work has too often been each day for that day alone, too regardless of the yesterday and the morrow. They have had respect for the history of the South, but a too distant respect, which has dealt in traditions and oratory and not with the prosaic study of economic and social evolutions. Their study of history was more of the antiquarian than of the practical sort. The leaders of the Old South were fond of ancient and mediaeval history, and of the biblical justification of slavery, but they sometimes failed to comprehend the under-lying causes of the movements in which they themselves were par-ticipants. In spite of their general conservatism, their lack of this knowledge caused them sometimes to be erratic in policy. The South has sometimes followed policies because they were tradi-tional or because there was a widespread superficial feeling that they were right and best, and naturally the South has at times gone wrong. A safeguard against error, weakened of course by our hu-

* South Atlantic Quarterly, III (January, 1904), 1–10.

man limitations, lies in the study of present and future problems in the light of the past, and in the comparison of the views reached by truth-seeking investigators. The present article claims attention merely as one of the efforts in interpretation which may aid future thinkers in gaining a fuller knowledge and a more perfect understanding of the general problem.

Within the last half century the South has gone through a series of political, social, and industrial upheavals and readjustments; and yet the South of today is the historical product of the South of old, with much the same conditions and problems. Progress for the future is conditioned upon the developments of the past and the circumstances of the present; and future advance can be made steady and successful only through correct understanding of the past and sound reasoning upon it.

Conservatism and progress are not essentially antagonistic. Conservatism need not be of the Bourbon type, never learning and never forgetting; the spirit of progress need not be exaggerated into radicalism. The conservatism of the South has in many things been of a distinctly liberal sort. In promoting sentiment leading to the Declaration of Independence, the formation of the union, and the declaration of war in 1812, men of the South were among the most progressive and powerful leaders. The statesmen of the South, of both the critical and constructive types, have been as a rule far from retrogressive, except in certain instances where slavery was concerned; and the South practically controlled the United States government throughout the first half of the nineteenth century. The frontiersmen of the South accomplished the conquest of the trans-Alleghany wilderness, opened the Southwest for cotton production, and by offering a market for food products, called the Northwest into being. The state of Georgia set a mighty precedent in educational lines when in 1785 it chartered the University of Georgia as the crown of its school system and the first state university in America; and the Carolinas, Virginia, Tennessee, and the states of the Southwest rapidly followed the example. The South for years led New England and the Middle States in railway development (a forgotten fact but true); and its strenuous efforts for the development of manufactures were defeated only by the institution of slavery and the superior attractiveness of cotton production. In economic lines, the mightiest work accomplished by the Old South was the establishment of the great plantation system throughout the staple-producing region as a highly organized institution for the most efficient use of ignorant and slothful labor. The Old South developed no very great institutions of learning as such; but the whole system of life was organized for educating the negroes out of barbarism into civilization and for training the youth of the dominant race to attain the highest type of true manhood and womanhood yet developed in America.

In all of these matters the governing class in the South showed strong progressive spirit. But that spirit was hampered and its work partly vitiated by two great adverse influences—the institution of slavery and over-dependence upon the agricultural staples.

Slavery from its very nature put something of a check upon freedom of speech. Washington, Jefferson, and Patrick Henry were great enough to see and bold enough to speak of its actual bad features, but they were men of exceptional greatness and boldness. Other men from mere prudence avoided any public declaration of views which might percolate to the negroes and possibly encourage them to servile insurrection. In the session of the Virginia legislature, 1832, many slaveholding members showed wonderful frankness in condemning the institution; but that was the last great occasion where Southerners gave free expression to ideas which might possibly prove a spark in the powder magazine, the dangers from which had at that time just been shown by Nat Turner's massacre in Southampton County. The rise of the abolition agitation in the North during the thirties brought death to Southern liberalism. The abolitionists made certain false charges against the Southern system. In repelling these calumnies the Southern leaders thought it advisable to ignore all the bad features of slavery and deny their existence, to praise the institution as beneficial to all parties concerned, and to advocate its permanent maintenance instead of its gradual disestablishment. This change in the Southern attitude was to a large degree involuntary. A man of temper who receives a blow or a stab does not calmly look for its justification, but takes the strongest defensive position he can find at the moment and strikes back as hard as he can. A people is more prone to retaliate than a single person. In the absence of effective laws to which it may appeal for protection, it often refuses to parley, and proceeds at once to self-defence. Whether wisely or not for the long run, the men of the South leagued themselves to defeat the instigators of insurrection and maintain the institutions of their country. With the motive of preserving the lives and the welfare of both white and black, they avoided and frowned upon criticisms of slavery. From the exigencies of the case as developed by the historical forces internal and external, conservative men became Bourbons, no longer open to argument upon that subject.

Over-dependence upon the staples led to the over-production of tobacco and cotton; it at times ruined the market and brought distress, and it prevented the economic independence of the South. When the Bourbons arrived at the idea that slavery was right and should be perpetuated, the correlative idea was reached that cotton was king and could never be dethroned. The severe depression of the forties should have shaken faith in the omnipotence of cotton, but the mental bondage of the people and the revived prosperity of the fifties prevented the learning of the lesson. The cataclysm of the sixties should have brought liberalism in race relations. Many planters of the old school felt a positive relief when the economic burden of slavery was lifted from their shoulders, and were disposed to give the most friendly guidance to the freedmen. But the radicalism of the republican majority at Washington and the carpet-baggers in the field in the South excluded the Southern moderates from control and led to the domination of the extremists of the Tillman type when the reconstruction governments were overthrown. Out of the ashes of war and reconstruction there arose the "Solid South." Its people had been the plaything of the fates, and the play was not done. The Democratic party in national politics had shown itself the only friend of Southern interests. The South now swore fealty and service to that party in return for its protection. The domination of the blacks was rightly thought to be among the worst of possible evils; and to avoid that prospect the South pledged itself absolutely to the Democratic Party. But whether chosen by the South or forced upon her, that fidelity has proved a misfortune in the long run. It has prevented her having due influence upon national legislation and administration, and what is worse it has proved perhaps a greater check to freedom of thought than slavery was.

Again, in the Lower South the extremely high prices of cotton in the reconstruction period caused a new and greater dependence upon the fleecy staple. The main object of life was apparently to raise cotton. Neglect corn and meat, manufacture no ploughs or furniture—but buy them—buy every essential thing, so as to have more hands for cotton production; this was the practice of the South. Let the agricultural organization degenerate and small farms replace the remarkably efficient plantation system, let the soil be worn out, let the people move to Texas for fresh lands, let disorder reign and the planters be driven to town, leaving the negroes to lapse back toward barbarism—let almost anything happen provided all possible cotton is produced each year.

For example, observe the census figures for South Carolina:

	Cotton.	Corn.	Wheat.
1860.	353,000 bales,	15,000,000 bushels,	1,285,000 bushels,
1880.	522,000 bales.	11,700,000 bushels.	962,000 bushels.

	Hay.	Sweet Potatoes.
1860.	87,000 tons,	4,000,000 bushels,
1880.	2,700 tons.	2,000,000 bushels.

The population of the cotton belt had increased considerably by 1880; but far less corn, wheat, potatoes, meat, and manufactures were produced than in 1860. Most of their food the people obtained from the Northwest, and all manufactures they bought from the North or from Europe, with the prices doubled or trebled in either case by the exorbitant protective duties and the disorganization of commerce. Such a system of living would be ruinous to almost any people in any age; but the South had practically no choice. She was to all intents compelled to pay an enormous war indemnity, and cotton production was the only way of paying it. The South was at the mercy of the North, and *Vae Victis*, the North had no mercy. The Southern farmers, with capital and system swept away, were living on credit and from hand to mouth. It was a struggle for existence, and cotton offered the only certain livelihood from year to year. The interest upon debts ate up the profits before the crop was gathered, and each year brought a repetition of almost the same battle with debt and disadvantage. Where existence is the immediate problem, rapid progress is out of the question. It was only by tremendous efforts in the cotton field that any surplus was gained upon which to base plans for future advance. For twenty years the South was forced to dispense with all prospect of substantial improvement. She was almost absolutely obliged to depend upon cotton and upon the Democratic party. Her fidelity in politics meant retrogression, while her bondage to the staple meant no more than stagnation.

Dependence upon cotton, in fact, meant a little less than stagnation; for step by step the South advanced out of the painful distress of the later sixties and early seventies. The outer world stood in such great need of the staple that the total productive power of the cotton belt through two decades could no more than meet the demand. But thereafter the increased population and the extensive use of commercial fertilizers rapidly increased the output; and in consequence the price rapidly declined, until in the nineties it reached the level of the cost of production and caused all profits in the industry to vanish.

We have seen that the high prices just after the war were the cause of the exclusive attention to cotton. The declining prices in the eighties should have directed energy into other lines: but the arrival of that result was delayed. Bourbonism had too firm a control in industry as well as in politics. At length, however, the overproduction in the nineties brought widespread distress and forced the people to face the prospect of an absolute loss each year from cotton raising. Diversification of industry was the only possible remedy. Thus in the nineties a partial industrial revolution was forced upon the South. Thousands of white farmers moved from farms to factories. Thousands of negroes were reduced to debt and destitution, but in their lack of initiative they have had no recourse but to raise more cotton, always more cotton. Their creditors demanded cotton of them and advanced them rations only in proportion to their acreage. As the price continued to fall, their only means of keeping body and soul together was to produce their own supplies or to increase the output of cotton, and they found it the easier to neglect everything else and raise more cotton. But in recent years the abandonment of the cotton field by the whites who have gone to the factories, and a succession of bad seasons have worked together to check the output of the staple and to raise the price to the point at which the industry is highly profitable again.

And now arrives the greater need and the greater opportunity for concerted action, under capable leaders, for conservative progress. There is pressing need of better system and greater diversification in the agricultural industry of the South; but unless a strong preventive effort is made, the high price of cotton will cause a return of the people to their hurtful dependence upon the staple. The lesson of the past should be applied for the betterment of the future. The adversity in the early nineties showed the inefficiency of the small farms and of the system of non-resident supervision of negro tenants. The prosperity of today is bringing money into the cotton belt to facilitate the re-establishment of capitalized production, to enable capable managers to organize plantations in an efficient system which will work to the common benefit of the negro ploughmen and the white planters. The inflow of capital and the prospect of heavy returns upon its investment will encourage men of organizing capacity to leave the towns for the country again and to study the best ways and means in agriculture. Such study must result in the investment of more capital than formerly in drainage, terracing, and machinery, and in the greater diversification of crops. Capable managers will produce cotton at a lessened cost and at a greater profit for they will avoid spoiling the market by over-production.

Bourbonism demands the maintenance of the renting and cropping system, for in sooth that system has existed for a generation and the people have meanwhile preserved life and a modicum of self-respect. Radicalism demands the expulsion of the negroes, to rid the country of that whole race and to attempt to make the South just like the rest of America. But the policy of conservative progress, basing its contentions upon the best features of the Old

South, urges the preservation of everything which will tend toward restoring and maintaining the graciousness and charm of the ante-bellum civilization; of everything which will increase the efficiency and add to the resources of the New South; and of everything also which will work toward the actual uplifting and the general better-ment of the negro race. It accepts or rejects nothing because it is old or new, but because it is good or bad, wise or unwise as a means to the great end in view. The policy of conservative progress demands that the present generation stand upon the shoulders of the ones that have gone before; that it take from the past the ut-most advantage that it can, and give to the future what it has re-ceived from the past, with something valuable added as its own contribution to progress.

Slavery was but one element in the system of the Old South. After the negroes had once become fitted into a place in civilized society, the plantation system could have been maintained without the feature of involuntary servitude. If the abolition agitation had never arisen in its violent form to blind the Southerners to their own best interests, it is fairly probable that within the nineteenth century slavery would have been disestablished in some peaceable way in response to the demand of public opinion in the South. Laying the question of slavery aside, the presence of negroes in very large numbers in the population made some system like that of the old plantations essential for the peace and prosperity of the two races. And in view of the still greater proportion of negroes in the black belts of the South of today it appears that a modified form of the old plantation system is the best recourse for agricul-tural progress and racial sympathy in the present and the near future. It will draw the best element of the Southern whites back into the country, where they will afford the negroes a much-needed guidance; it will give the negroes a renewed association with the best of the Southern people (always the negroes' very best friends) and enable them to use their imitative faculties and make further progress in acquiring the white man's civilization.

The extensive revival of the system is of course conditioned up-on the capability of the planters. If they follow slipshod methods of cultivation, or if they fail to use their resources for the production of grain, hay, meat and dairy products, and spoil their market by raising too much cotton, the project will prove a failure and the South will have profited little from the attempt. But if capable men in large numbers establish themselves as captains of plantation industry, the present wave of prosperity can be made a lasting thing, and the South will quickly take rank well forward in the industrial world.

The political outlook is still overcast, but rifts are breaking through the clouds. Dominated by the Bourbons, the South has long esteemed its political solidity not a hindrance but a positive advantage. But men of the South of late have begun to think on these things, and regrets are heard that the present generation in politics proves unworthy of the generation of the fathers. Embarrassing questions are being asked of the Bourbons as to the causes of the decadence of statesmen. A divine discontent is working, and results must come in time. The path of progress out of the slough of political solidity and mental bondage and intolerance is visible only a step at a time, but the steps are being taken. The movement to disfranchise legally all the negroes but the exceptional ones is surely in the right direction, for it tends to lessen irritation and to enable the white people to follow their own judgments in questions of current politics and restore the South to its former national influence. And it is an earnest of greater harmony and greater improvement that the moderates are now in such control in the country at large that no important outcry has been raised against this invasion of the negro's so-called right and equality. When the zealots of the school of Charles Sumner and Thad Stevens shall have subsided in the North, the Bourbons must needs lose their control of the South and give way to the moderate-liberals of the school of Henry Grady and J. L. M. Curry.

The whole scheme of things entire in the South hangs together. Every detail of policy should be regulated upon sound principles of conservative progress. Problems of politics, industry, education, and religion are closely interwoven, and should be treated with a view to their complex bearings and not as unrelated questions. The fundamental principles underlying progress in general apply with special force to the South because of its backward condition. The states and the people should maintain and spread education and encourage freedom and vigor of thought. A well-trained citizenry with sturdy morals and powerful intellects is the greatest treasure which any country can have. The South cannot afford to neglect any possible means of further developing the strength of her people. She certainly cannot afford to be niggardly or even economical in the support of her schools and her colleges.

In the lateness of her start in modern progress, the South has a certain advantage in being able to profit by the experience of other countries and sections, and to avoid the blunders which they have made. Her people should and will decline to adopt the showy and tawdry features of modern America, and they will strive for the worthier things. Her leaders should study the economic, political, and social history of the South, and guide the South of today to profit both by its former successes and its former failures. The leaders and the people must combine thought and vim and courage, and work for further substantial conservative progress.

5

The Plantation as a Civilizing Factor

AS A FEATURE of the present wave of prosperity in the cotton belt, there is to be noted a movement just beginning for the re-establishment of plantations to replace the small farms in the production of the staple crops.* The origin of the movement is due to the economic motive, and from the economic point of view it seems fully justified. It is a movement for the use of more capital and better implements, for the avoidance of debt and obligations, for the improvement of methods of cultivation, and for the use of skilled management in the superintendence of wage-earning labor. It is therefore a movement of progress from the stagnation of demoralized industry in the recent past toward a more effective system for the future. Together with the recent great upgrowth of cotton factories, it indicates that the South is now becoming more fully alive to the spirit of specialized and systematized industry which is elsewhere prevalent in modern America.

It appears to be fairly beyond denial, in view of the ignorance and improvidence of the great laboring class in the South, that a system for the organization of labor under skilled management is desirable in agriculture as well as in mining, commerce, and manufacturing. From the point of view of the modern economic world, which demands productiveness as a condition of life, the plantation system when thoroughly understood cannot fail to be approved as at least a partial cure for the inefficiency of labor in the South under the present regime of small farmers. The question

* *Sewanee Review*, XII (July, 1904), 257–67.

remains, what will be the effect of the system upon the mental, moral, and industrial development of the negro? And this social aspect of the matter will receive our present attention.

In all inquiries of this sort, theories of abstract right and wrong must give place to considerations of what is wise and advisable in reaching the best future results. The question of the inherent rights of men is in no way involved. The question of the equality of men does not pertain. The vital question is, How can improvement be made in industrial conditions, known to be unsatisfactory, and how is civilization to be promoted among the mass of Southern negroes who are beyond question in need of further and higher development? The clash of the abstract theories of the abolitionist school against the blind resistance of the Bourbons of the South has wrought such terrible havoc in the past that men should be prepared to inquire into conditions and methods of remedy in a broadminded spirit, seeking the truth of today and the policy of wisdom for tomorrow, no matter what pet theories may go to the wall.

The conditions of our problem are as follows: 1. A century or two ago the negroes were savages in the wilds of Africa. 2. Those who were brought to America, and their descendants, have acquired a certain amount of civilization, and are now in some degree fitted for life in modern civilized society. 3. This progress of the negroes has been in very large measure the result of their association with civilized white people. 4. An immense mass of the negroes is sure to remain for an indefinite period in the midst of a civilized white nation. The problem is, How can we best provide for their peaceful residence and their further progress in this nation of white men and how can we best guard against their lapsing back into barbarism? As a possible solution for a large part of the problem, I suggest the plantation system.

Two contrasting types of plantations developed upon American soil through the adapting of European institutions to the new geographical conditions. In the West Indies the policy of the Spaniards was to exploit the land through the forced labor of the subjugated natives.[1] Large gangs of Indian slaves were compelled to

[1] H. C. Lea, "The Indian Policy of Spain," *Yale Review* (VIII), 119.

work in the mines, upon the roads, and in the sugar cane fields. The system of slavery was so extremely harsh that within a few decades the native population of the West Indies had become diminished to within perhaps a tenth of its original numbers. Distressed by this terrible state of things, the Spanish priest Las Casas suggested, about 1518, that negro slaves be imported from Africa to relieve the unbearable hardships of the natives. In quick acceptance of this idea, thousands of negroes were rapidly poured into the West Indies, where they were largely employed in sugar production. When the English settled Barbados, in 1625, and captured Jamaica, in 1655, they borrowed from the Spaniards the system of plantations which the Spaniards had already developed.

These plantations in the English West Indies were of the commercial type, where the predominating purpose of the planter was to get money, and to get it as rapidly as possible. West Indian planters lived in the islands merely for the time being. When they had established their plantations upon a paying basis, they usually left them to overseers and went back to England to spend their income. While the men were making their fortunes in the tropics their mothers and wives and children were mostly at home in England; English families as a rule did not establish English homes upon the West Indian plantations. The proportion of whites in the population of Jamaica and Barbados remained very small; for instance, in 1768 Jamaica had about 17,000 whites and 167,000 negroes. The negroes were not in close enough touch with the whites to be able to adopt their civilization with any degree of rapidity. There were few white families to set examples for the blacks; and in consequence polygamy, paganism, and other savage customs were long continued among the West Indian negroes. Fresh negroes from Africa were so cheap that for pure money-making it appears to have been cheaper to work the slaves to exhaustion and buy new ones, than to make any thorough endeavor to increase the enlightenment and the efficiency of the negroes at hand. And in fact the West Indian conditions were so severe as to require constant importations to prevent the stock of negroes from diminishing.

In 1670 a band of settlers, partly from England and partly from

Barbados, established the colony at Charleston, South Carolina. These settlers brought with them the West Indian system of plantations, and in the following years extended it throughout the sea-island sections of South Carolina and Georgia. Yet certain modifications were introduced. Whereas the Jamaica sugar estates averaged about one hundred and eighty slaves to the plantation,[2] the Carolina rice and indigo plantations were found to be most profitable when there were only about thirty negroes under one manager.[3] Again, the South Carolinians soon came to look upon the colony as their home, and on their estates they established homes upon the English pattern. The planters could live on their estates for only the cooler months of each year; but that residence of even a few months gave the negroes an opportunity to bring their imitative faculties into play and to seize many ideas of civilization. Yet on the whole, the Carolina coast plantation was too nearly of the commercial type for the negro to secure the most rapid progress.

In the colony of Virginia the resort to white indented servants and the discovery of the value of tobacco production caused the development of the system of patriarchal plantations before the negro became a factor in the situation. The plantation there was not borrowed from the Spaniards, but was developed as a modification of the old English institution of the manor. Involuntary labor was used because labor of any sort was profitable, and hired labor was not to be had so long as there was abundance of free land on the outskirts of settlement. The chief desire of the substantial men of Virginia was to live as English gentlemen lived. They soon found that by resorting to indentured white servants, and later to negro slaves, instead of to serfs, hired labor, and manorial tenants they could establish themselves in something very much like the English manor system, and could gain an honest competence as landowners and managers of agricultural labor.

Negroes gradually replaced the white servants in this system, without causing any substantial change in the general organization.

---

[2] Bryan Edwards, *History of the West Indies*, Book 2, Appendix 1.
[3] B. R. Carroll, *Historical Collections of South Carolina*, II, 202. See also the report upon the archives of Georgia, in the forthcoming American Historical Association *Report* for 1903.

The desire of the planters was not so much to make money and vaunt it in England like the nabobs of the Indies, but to live in comfort as English gentlemen. The Virginians early became noted for generosity, hospitality, and kindliness; and their virtues were not shown to their white guests exclusively. The planters and their families were in close personal association with a large proportion of their servants; and these negroes in the Virginia system of patriarchal plantations had an extraordinary opportunity to acquire habits of industry and the forms of English civilization. A very instructive consideration is that, whereas in the West Indies among able-bodied slaves a freshly imported African would bring about the same price as a negro born and reared upon a sugar plantation, in Virginia even before the eighteenth century a home-grown negro was considered nearly twice as valuable as a fresh African. This contrast gives forcible illustration of the efficiency of the Virginia training school.

The Virginia system of plantations was extensively adopted in America before the West Indian system appeared upon the Carolina coast, and it always remained by far the more prevalent of the two. By the time of the American Revolution these patriarchal plantations had become established through Tidewater and Piedmont Virginia, Maryland, and eastern North Carolina. The invention of the cotton gin in 1793 led to the rapid extension of the same system throughout the uplands of the Lower South.

While the cotton belt was being settled society in it was rough, vigorous, and democratic. White men labored hard to earn money to buy slaves, and many of them afterwards worked hard in the cotton furrows alongside their slaves. The indolent, shiftless poor whites were scorned by industrious white men and negroes alike. The slaves, far from the extreme of abjectness, gained self-respect and acquired admirable qualities. When prosperity prevailed and wealth came, the slaves were usually in some degree the beneficiaries from the improvement in their masters' circumstances.

The average size of cotton plantations remained relatively small. The United States census of 1860 shows that a holding of twelve negroes of all ages was decidedly above the average in the cotton belt. It was most common for one white family to own one or two or three negro families, who lived in cabins near by, and were in constant association with their master and mistress and the white children. The aim of the planter was to have his force of laborers reach the greatest possible degree of efficiency. This purpose was to be gained only by training the negroes and guarding their health and strength from injury through overwork or dangerous occupation of any sort. When in the middle of the nineteenth century the price of able-bodied negroes mounted up to about $1,500, it became too great a money risk to require one of them to perform a dangerous or exhausting task. And in fact we find records of many instances where planters hired Irish immigrants to dig ditches and do other straining work in order to protect the negroes from risk of injury. Slaves were too expensive to use in such tasks when Irishmen could be hired. The great majority of planters were kind masters from interest and inclination, looking after the moral and industrial development of their slaves as a matter of business as well as from higher motives. On the other hand, there were doubtless a large number of instances of harsh masters and maltreated slaves. In fact, the dark side of antebellum conditions was somber enough to cast a heavy gloom over the bright; but the evil features were due chiefly to the institution of slavery and not to the system of plantation industry.

The planters of the Old South, within the lifetime of a few generations, developed a fairly efficient body of laborers out of a horde of savages. The negroes became fairly honest, industrious, and intelligent; and even though this may have been at the cost of their sturdiness, initiative, and self-control, the net results were surprisingly good. On the whole, the system of the Old South, with all its limitations, accomplished a good work, which it was perhaps not fitted to carry further. The slavery system had completed its work and was already becoming an anachronism when the Civil War and Reconstruction overthrew it, and with it all system in the South. There followed a period of great social upheaval and industrial demoralization, which was partly remedied by a temporary resort to small farms and tenant cropping.

But none who were well informed have expected that the average negro, with his inevitable shortcomings, would make a successful independent farmer without a large additional amount of training. The plantations were broken up, and the negroes have in name been working for themselves and by themselves. But in truth they have continued to be under the supervision of the landowners and the merchants, who act in some measure as non-resident planters. But this system of absentee control has such serious faults that it cannot permanently stand. The supervision over the so-called negro farmers is unsystematic, and the economic results are lamentably small. And, still worse, the isolation upon their separate farms is proving injurious to the higher development of the negroes themselves.

The civilization which our negroes have now partly acquired is English civilization, gained from association with the English race. They have advanced exclusively by the help and through their imitation of the Anglo-Americans.

Without the continuance of the interracial association there is strong reason to believe that the negroes would gradually lose much of the praiseworthy element in their present attainments. In fact several keen-sighted students have already detected a tendency of the negroes, where segregated in masses in the black belt, to lapse back toward barbarism. Of course, if its prevention is possible, such retrogression must not be allowed to continue. That it has not yet grown more serious is due to the policy pursued by the better element of the white people; for they have followed the traditions of their fathers in practicing the truest charity while letting not their left hands know what their right hands have been doing. Their extreme reticence in publishing their deeds has been a mistake which in future should be avoided. The South has long been held in a false position of hostility to the negro, while in actual truth the conservative, thinking, God-fearing element among the Southern people have been and still remain the most substantial, practical, and valuable friends that their black neighbors have ever had. Before the war their families, dwelling in the midst of their negro quarters, did what we call, in the modern phrase, social settlement work. In later years they have continued that work of guidance, instruction, and inspiration as best they could under the adverse conditions resulting from the work of the carpetbaggers.

For the future, the exceptional negroes may take care of themselves, the Northern negroes and those in the South who yearn for the higher literary education may be provided for by the Northern philanthropists; but the great mass of the black population will for generations remain dependent as before upon the friendship and helpfulness of their best white neighbors.

To secure the best results for all parties, a more sympathetic relationship must be established, which shall include larger numbers of both races. And no system for this purpose has yet been developed which compares in good results with that of the old patriarchal plantation. The patriarchal feature is necessary. The average negro has many of the characteristics of a child, and must be guided and governed, and often guarded against himself, by a sympathetic hand. Non-resident ownership and control of plantations will not do. The absentee system has no redeeming virtue for the purpose at hand. With hired, voluntary labor instead of forced labor, it is the Virginia plantation system and not that of the West Indies which is needed. The presence of the planter and his wife and children and his neighbors is required for example and precept among the negroes. Factory methods and purely business relations will not serve; the tie of personal sympathy and affection is essential to the successful working of the system. The average negro longs for this personal tie. Respect, affection, and obedience for those who earn and encourage his admiration are second nature with him. The negroes are disposed to do their part for securing the general welfare when the proper opportunity is given them. What they most need is friendly guidance and control for themselves, and peace and prosperity for the South as a whole; economic depression will always work to their discouragement and injury, and sectional and racial irritation must in every case check their progress.

It is generally conceded that the concentration of the negroes in cities gives more opportunity for the increase of depravity among them than for their progress in civilization; for it puts the average negroes into close association with the worst element of their own race and with the vicious class of the whites as well. Life in the country offers less glittering but more substantial attractions, and the system there may easily be arranged to meet all the actual needs of the average negroes. As is true with large numbers of whites, but in greater degree, the negroes are in less need of literary education than of practical knowledge and genuine wisdom. They need to become well-developed men and women, and not half-baked scholars. The Southern plantation, with its product of Washington, Jefferson, the Pinckneys, Lowndes, Calhoun, Troup, and Yancey, needs no eulogy as a school of manhood. Under modern conditions, with the negroes possessing their freedom, the plantation should prove a school for black men as well as white.

The exceptional negroes should feel no call to work as hired plow hands; their usefulness lies elsewhere. As the race progresses, more and more of its members will graduate from the school of the plantation and become self-directing units in our general American system. But for many generations there will probably remain a large enough number of "natural born" plow hands to keep a multitude of planters profitably busy with their superintendence.

The exceptional negro is in advance of the average negro because he has acquired a greater amount of the white man's civilization. He is prepared in many cases to educate the average negro up to a somewhat higher plane. But while the exceptional negro has acquired this capability by borrowing and adapting the white man's ways of life, the average and the exceptional white men possess their civilization and their capability as a natural inheritance. To contend that the educated negro is the best source of guidance and enlightenment for the average negro in the American system is to argue that the reflected light of the moon is brighter and more effective than the direct rays of the sun. To urge that the negroes should be sent back to Africa to work out their own salvation is to hold with Rousseau that the state of nature (savagery) is the highest existence for man, and that our own system of law and order and industry and progress is useless as a pattern for any backward race.

From the point of view of morality, industry, intelligence—of everything that civilization means—the segregation of the negroes must work to their detriment. Their concentration in city slums is vicious; their isolation from white neighbors in the black belt of the seacoast cannot cease to mean stagnation, if not retrogression, for them; the race prejudice taught them by the carpetbaggers was and is a positive injury; their general aloofness upon small farms must insulate them in large measure from the best influences for progress in the South of today. The most feasible means of general betterment lies in building up a system of plantations of moderate size, where the negro may take his place in the modern world of specialized and organized industry and yet have the protection from the harsher features of the modern strife, which will be afforded him by the patriarchal character of the system of which he is a part.

The process of building up these modern plantations must needs be in a measure slow and beset with obstacles, but the obstacles can hardly be of insuperable character. A conviction of the shortcomings of the present system of renting and cropping must be brought home to the South as a whole, or at least to the cotton belt which is the heart of the modern agricultural South, and, in truth, this conviction is already prevalent with a large proportion of thinking Southerners. There are surely a large number of men who understand negro management and who can master the best methods of agriculture for the South; and thousands of these men are already at hand, or are prepared to fit themselves for the work, as soon as the movement gains sufficient headway to attract their energies. The mass of the negroes must be taught that good wages on a plantation are better than debt and failure, or even partial success upon their half-independent, ill-tended small farms, and still better than indolence and vice in the towns. A great mass of the white people have already learned of the superior attractiveness of steady wages over their meager and uncertain farm returns, and the teaching of a similar lesson to the negroes should not prove impossible. True, a large amount of capital will be needed for investment in land, houses and stock, ditches and terraces, machinery, wages, and supplies; but the present high price of cotton and the general flow of capital into the South in recent years must soon supply a fund to meet this need. Finally, a substantial beginning is necessary in the movement, and examples must be set of successful enterprise in this line in each district in the South in order to overcome the inherited conservatism of the people. But there are already a number of individual examples being set at various points in the cotton belt, and the system itself has been familiar to the people from days of old.

While a certain class of theorists have been proclaiming the virtues of small farms and independence for the negroes, a scattered handful of practical men of affairs have set to work in building up plantations whereon they may establish themselves in prosperity and at the same time relieve a portion of the mass of negroes from their distress and indecision. The movement thus begun is gathering headway. It is attracting capable white men back to the soil, and must soon begin to draw the surplus negroes out of the towns. The movement should be studied on the ground and encouraged as a solution for many of the difficulties of the racial situation and as a means of progress for a whole tier of the Southern states.

PART TWO

The Slave Plantation
in Economy and Society

6

The Origin and Growth of the Southern Black Belts

IN A FORMER essay[1] I have shown, from a study of slave
prices, that slavery became an economic burden in America,
and that the purchase of the unfree laborers made a great drain
upon the earnings of the community which imported them.*
American slaveholding was essentially industrial in character; and
industry under the slave-using system was essentially capitalistic.
For the sake of controlling the labor, a very large portion of the
capital was invested in the legal ownership of the labor itself. This
system was expensive not only to the individual planter, but to the
whole community. If other sections and periods of the slaveholding South were analyzed, the burdensomeness of slaveholding and
the slave trade, which I have demonstrated for the cotton belt,
would be found to have prevailed as a very general phenomenon.

The present study is concerned with the tendency of slavery as a
system of essentially capitalistic industry to concentrate wealth,
such as there was, within the hands of a single economic class and
within certain distinctive geographical areas. Aside from land,
slaves were in the South by far the principal form of wealth. The
study of the administrative and geographical concentration of slave
property is of course a study of the growth of the plantation system
and of the black belts produced by it.

* *American Historical Review*, XI (July, 1906), 798-816.
[1] "The Economic Cost of Slaveholding in the Cotton Belt," on page 117
of this book. Further studies of a complementary nature, also included in
this volume, are: "The Economics of the Plantation," on page 65 and "The
Plantation as a Civilizing Factor," on page 82.

At any time in any typical district of the South, there were non-slaveholders, small slaveholders, and large slaveholders. Most members of each of these classes were engaged in agriculture. The non-slaveholder tilled his land by the labor of himself and his family. The large slaveholder tilled his by the labor of his slaves under supervision. The small slaveholder often combined the labor of his slaves, his family, and himself in a mixed system. Thus there were small, medium, and large units of industry, which have been distinguished as small farms, large farms, and plantations. In each of these types of organization a more or less definite system of labor and administration was followed. This is a static view of the Southern industrial regime, and with more or less elaboration has been the one nearly always presented by historians and economists alike.

This description should be not the end of the matter, but a mere preface to the study of the dynamic forces at work and of the result which they effected in shaping the economic and social life and in controlling political policies. It is the dynamic view which is essential for the full understanding of the South. An emphasis upon the dynamic phase of Southern conditions and upon the plantation system as a principal factor in the shaping of Southern economy is the chief contribution here attempted.

At the outset in some of the Southern colonies there were experiments with systems of joint labor and paternalism. As soon as these had given place to private enterprise, there began the differentiation of the two chief industrial types, the plantation and the farm, which were thenceforth to be characteristic. In each instance settlement was first made on the seaboard, and prosperity was first achieved where certain staple crops could be raised and exported to market. The great abundance of land available and the short-lived fertility of most of the soil caused a great hunger for land and a rapid extension of settlement to satisfy that hunger. Thus the westward movement set in; and the van of it was made up of small farmers. While actually modified by many complications, which must here with doubtful safety be left out of account, the chief influence shaping the migration was the competition of industrial units.

After a certain period in the production of each staple, whether tobacco, rice, or cotton, the increase of the output caused a reduction of prices and profits, and brought distress to the less efficient of the producers, forcing many of them to abandon the industry. The Southern staples were all excellently adapted to production by the plantation system. The small producers were accordingly at a disadvantage, and were in most cases the first to make a change. The farmers tended to drift to the edge of settlement and to assert some independence of the staples by producing as far as possible the articles which their own families needed to consume. The further the farmer removed from tidewater and markets, the greater his tendency to a self-sufficing economy.

Many of the planters were also on the move. The tide of small farmers advancing toward the frontier in search of new opportunity was followed in many areas by a tide of planters who sought new openings where their capital might be employed more advantageously than in the older areas where the competition was more stringent. Districts which from the lack of the required qualities of soil or climate or of facilities of transportation were not available for the planters could be enjoyed by the farmers alone; but all others were entered by the planters sooner or later, and after more or less conflict were dominated by them.

Some of the non-slaveholders moved away from the encroaching plantations and settled anew as yeomen farmers; others by thrift bought slaves and in time became planters; others simply held their own in spite of the disadvantage of competing with negro labor in the same industry; while still others retrograded in the scale of life, drifted to the barren tracts, and lived from hand to mouth as anemic poor-whites. The planters, meanwhile continued to encroach wherever they could upon the territory already occupied in part by the smaller industrial units. The very nature of the plantation system caused this phenomenon. The case was very much like that of the great commercial and industrial organizations of today, whose nature requires them to encroach wherever possible upon the spheres of their weaker rivals.

The economic history of the Old South in its plantation districts was made up very largely of extensions and repetitions of the same general phenomena. One suitable area after another was occupied by much the same process. The period of occupation was followed by the same strife of industrial systems, which resulted usually in the victory of plantation methods. Then the planters continued to compete among themselves, and wore out such soil as was exhaustible. The final stage, reached in a few districts, was either a change to varied industry to which the plantation system was unsuited, or the partial depopulation of the country through the exodus of all the more energetic producers to new and more attractive lands. Superficially the process worked with a considerable variety in the several districts; but fundamentally the conditions and the development were a simple process, repeated in one area after another.

The theme is one whose treatment is readily aided by the use of statistics. Take for example the county of Crawford, which lies in a good cotton district in middle western Georgia. The state secured this tract from the Indians in 1821, and quickly threw it open to settlement through the agency of that highly democratic institution, the Georgia land lottery. The land was divided into tracts of 202½ acres each, and distributed by lottery among all the citizens of the state who were fortunate in the drawing. Immigrants of various types flowed in apace, and within a few years the population had reached the normal density for the state in that period. Then ensued the usual contest of the systems for domination. We happen to have a census of population and slaveholdings in Crawford county in 1824,[2] just three years after its opening, and another in 1860, when the county had become an undistinguished part of the upland cotton belt. A comparison of the data furnished by the two enumerations will show the effects of the competition of industrial units and systems which we are studying.

The total number of whites in 1824 was 1,781; and in 1860, 3,407; total slaves in 1824, 579; and in 1860, 4,270; free blacks

[2] The census for 1824 was made by the state authorities. The returns are in manuscript in the state capitol at Atlanta. The figures for 1860 are from the *Eighth United States Census*, volume on agriculture, 226.

SLAVEHOLDINGS IN 1824

OWNERS	SLAVES EACH	OWNERS	SLAVES EACH
27	1	6	10
18	2	2	11
17	3	1	12
9	4	2	13
7	5	2	15
9	6	1	20
4	7	1	28
1	8	1	31
5	9	1	42

SLAVEHOLDINGS IN 1860

OWNERS	SLAVES EACH	OWNERS	SLAVES EACH		
51	1	34	10 and under		15
56	2	28	15 "	"	20
30	3	20	20 "	"	30
30	4	18	30 "	"	40
19	5	8	40 "	"	50
19	6	7	50 "	"	70
16	7	1	70 "	"	100
12	8	4	100 "	"	200
16	9				

negligible. The whites in 1824 were enumerated in 230 families, of which 116 had no slaves, and 114 possessed slaveholdings of an average size of five negroes each. In 1860 the white families had increased to about 630, of which 369 had slaveholdings averaging 11.6 in size. The average slaveholding had more than doubled in size. The most marked feature of the contrast is the growth in number and size of the larger slaveholdings—in a word, the passage of the domination of the community from the men of few or no slaves to the men of the planter class.

This was an obvious and normal development. The men with the fewest impedimenta were of course the quickest in their movements.[3] But the large slaveholders, though more slowly, moved surely. They gradually bought up the lands of the drawers in the lottery who did not wish to occupy their lots, and of such of their neighbors as might decide to move farther west. Thus they accumulated large tracts which would justify and maintain the plantation system. As years went on planters continued to come in from the east. Some indeed after a period of residence moved west, but their further westward journey when made at all was usually more deliberate and later than that of the smaller farmers, who moved out in search of new opportunity as easily as they had moved in in search of it.

The plantations grew in number and in size as well. The farms expanded less, if indeed their number and area did not actually decrease. In some other districts which will be considered below, the tendency to the domination by the planters, and in the long run their well-nigh complete possession of the district, was considerably more rapid and sweeping.

We are now ready to consider more fully the dynamic conditions of life and industry. The first form of society in almost every part of the South was that of the normal wilderness-frontier, in which industry was primitive, commerce rudimentary, and society individualistic in notable degree. There was little opportunity for specialization of industry or for any regular routine work.[4] The greater the versatility of the individual settler, when completely isolated, and the less the degree of routine, the greater was his progress in the comforts of his own homely production. So soon as he began to produce a surplus, however, and to establish a commercial connection with the rest of the world, the need of extreme versatility diminished and the value of routine increased.

If a normal development had been followed, these frontier farmers through exporting a specific surplus product would have accu-

[3] The restlessness of the frontier farmers is strikingly illustrated in the so-called "autobiography" of Gideon Lincecum, printed in the *Publications of the Mississippi Historical Society*, VIII, 443-519.

[4] *Cf.* letter of the Reverend John Urmstone to the secretary of the Society for the Propagation of the Gospel, in Francis L. Hawks, *History of North Carolina* (1859), II, 215.

mulated capital, and would have developed an industrial and social system like that of Europe and the American settlements to the northward. But wherever it was possible to produce a marketable surplus through strictly routine industry in agriculture, this normal progress was interrupted in the South by an invasion of the planters, who brought with them a cheaper supply of labor, with a more effective system of routine work.

While the life of the frontiersman, and of every self-sufficing farmer, was a succession of changes from one occupation to another, the economic life on the plantations was made as far as possible a fixed routine. Just as in the case of the factory system, which of course is entirely analogous as regards labor organization, the success of industry depended upon its regularity and the constant repetition of similar tasks.

On the larger plantations some of the weaker negroes were often assigned to spinning, weaving, sewing, and like occupations in the line of domestic manufactures,[5] while slaves of unusual ability were often employed altogether as plantation carpenters, blacksmiths, millers, etc.[6] There was always of course a supply of domestic ser-

[5] For example, the "Worthy Captaine Matthews" with his weavers, his tannery, and his eight shoemakers, as well as his dairy, wheatfields, etc., described in 1649 by the author of "A Perfect Description of Virginia." Reprinted in Force's *Tracts*, II., no. 8, pp. 14–15. Another striking instance is shown incidentally in the papers of Robert Carter of Nomoni Hall (manuscripts in possession of Virginia Historical Society). In 1782 Carter, a great Virginia planter, was operating a "Woolen and Linen Factory" at Aires, with six negro weavers and four negro winders, under the management of Daniel Sullivan. But apparently the profits did not justify the use of slave labor, and the enterprise was given up.

[6] This practice had its disadvantages. Witness the following extract from a letter of Colonel J. B. Lamar, a large Georgia planter, to his sister, Mrs. Howell Cobb, in 1846 (manuscript in possession of Mrs. A. S. Erwin of Athens, Georgia): "My man Ned the carpenter is idle or nearly so at the plantation. He is fixing gates and like the idle groom in Pickwick trying to fool himself into the belief that he is doing something . . . . While I was gone I had him in town and on returning found that he had been drunk and fighting, and misbehaving in every way, so that I have banished him to rural life. He is an eye servant. If I was with him I could have the work done soon and cheap, but I am afraid to trust him off where there is no one he fears. . . . I shall sell the rascal the first chance I get."

vants in each well-to-do planter's household. Occasion also frequently arose for detaching part of the force of field hands for sundry small tasks, whether for the benefit of the one plantation alone or in some joint undertaking of the neighborhood. But by far the greater part of the available labor supply was used for the routine work in the fields, under the direction of either the master, the overseer, or a foreman.

On most estates the laborers were divided into two or more groups for the better adjustment of the strength of the laborers to the needs of their tasks. For example, in the upland cotton districts it was customary to set apart the strongest laborers as plowhands, while the rest used the hoe, and each group worked under its own supervisor.[7] Upon many estates of small dimensions the owner would lead the plow-gang, making his own furrow, and requiring the negroes to keep pace with him, while his son would do likewise with the hoe-gang. Or if the planter spared himself from the manual labor, he would oversee the work either in person or through a hired overseer, or in many cases through a reliable slave whom he constituted foreman or "driver" and vested with authority subordinate to his own. In some localities, as in most of the Carolina rice district, the negroes instead of being worked strictly in gangs were given tasks of hoeing or plowing a specified area for each day.

Whether the method followed was the task system or the gang system, the great characteristic feature and the strength of the plantation method was in its division of labor and above all in its

[7] The gang system on the great sugar estates in Jamaica in the eighteenth century was described by Bryan Edwards in his *History, Civil and Commercial, of the British Colonies in the West Indies*, bk. 4, chap. 5 (first edition, London, 1793, II, 128–29). The negroes were there worked in three sets, or gangs, he says. The first set, comprising most of the robust men and women, was employed in clearing the land, digging the holes, planting the cane, and in croptime tending the mill. On the average plantation it included about one-third of the whole number of slaves, exclusive of domestics. The second set, composed of boys and girls, women in pregnancy, and convalescents, was employed in weeding the canes and other light work. The third set was of young children, attended by an old woman. They gathered feed for the pigs, weeded the gardens, etc., with the purpose mainly of being kept from idleness and learning habits of industry.

arrangement for the performance by the negroes of a labor nearly always of routine character. The routine system was the only system by which the unintelligent, involuntary negro labor could be employed to distinct advantage; and, other things being equal, the most successful planter was always he who arranged the most thorough and effective routine.

The saving of time and effort, together with the protection of the life, health, and strength of the laborers, were the essential requirements of success in the profitable use of slave labor under American conditions.[8] That success was heightened, of course, when by fostering a sentiment of affection and loyalty, or by means of a system of inexpensive rewards, zeal was made to replace fear as a motive to labor.

Where the above-named features were present, the plantation system was probably the most efficient method ever devised for the use of stupid labor in agriculture on a large scale. Its efficiency was so great in the antebellum South that when slave labor became scarce and dear the planters were the only ones who could afford to buy it as a steady practice. It is true that a few corporations owned slaves for their service. For example, the Athens (Georgia) Manufacturing Company owned eight slaves in 1850;[9] the South

[8] The road to the fullest success is pointed out by Richard Corbin, a great Virginia planter, in a letter of instruction and advice, January 1, 1759, to James Semple, who was to be his agent during his protracted absence from home. He writes: "The care of [the] negroes is the first thing to be recommended that you give me timely notice of all their wants that they may be provided with all necessarys. . . . Observe a prudent and a watchful conduct over the overseers that they attend to their business with diligence, keep the negroes in good order, and enforce obedience by the example of their own industry, which is a more effectual method in every respect of succeeding and making good crops than Hurry and Severity; the ways of industry are constant and regular, not to be in a hurry at one time and do nothing at another, but to be always usefully and steadily employed. A man who carries on business in this manner will be prepared for every incident that happens. He will see what work may be proper at the distance of some time and be gradually and leisurely providing for it, by this foresight he will never be in confusion himself and his business instead of a labor will be a pleasure to him . . . ." (manuscript in Virginia Historical Society Library, Richmond, Virginia)

[9] Manuscript tax digest, Clarke County, Georgia, 1850.

Carolina Railroad Company bought seventy-eight slaves for its service between 1845 and 1860;[10] and for a period prior to 1834 the state of Georgia attempted to use state-owned slaves for developing her roads and waterways.[11] But as a rule corporations found it more advantageous to use free labor wherever possible; and when the use of slaves was necessary they preferred to hire them from their owners rather than to buy them and run the risk of loss from their illness, death, or escape.[12] Where possible, indeed, it was frequently much preferred to avoid either the purchase or hiring of slaves in such enterprises as the building of railways, by letting out the work on contract to the planters who lived near by and could use their own slaves under their own personal superintendence.

[10] At prices ranging from $400 to $1,500. List printed, with names, dates, and prices, in *Report of the President* of the South Carolina Railroad Company for 1864. Copy in the Charleston Library, Charleston, South Carolina.

[11] William C. Dawson, *A Compilation of the Laws of Georgia, 1819 to 1829* (Milledgeville, 1831), 399. Act appropriating $50,000 for the purchase of additional able-bodied negroes in number sufficient to make a total of 190 when added to those already owned by the state. *Federal Union* (a newspaper published at Milledgeville, Georgia), January 29, 1834. Advertisement by W. C. Lyman, superintendent of roads for the eastern division of Georgia, giving notice that he will sell at auction on stated days in March and April 118 slaves belonging to the state of Georgia and attached to the several road-tending stations in his division.

[12] E.g., the *Palladium* (Frankfort, Kentucky), December 1, 1868. Advertisement: "Negro Men Wanted. The subscribers wish to hire three or four Negro Men, to work in their Factory in Frankfort. They will be taught Weaving, and liberal wages will be paid for their services. Apply immediately to Danl Weisiger and Co."

Cf. also *Report of the Macon and Western R. R.* (Georgia) for 1859. Under the heading of repairs to the road, the superintendent lists the "labor of 100 negroes [i.e., slaves] with overseer and supervisor, an average of $200 each (including food and clothing), $20,000."

Cf. also the *Southern Banner* (Athens, Georgia), January 12, 1854: "High price of Hands.—The *Norfolk Argus* says it has never known the demand for slaves greater than at the present season, nor that description of labor scarcer or higher than at the present season. Many farmers, rather than engage at the present rates, consider it more prudent to curtail their agricultural establishments. Ordinary field hands have commanded as high as one hundred and fifty dollars, and No. 1 laborers have readily brought $225, accompanied with a life insurance for the value of the slave. The great demand for laborers proceeds from the turpentine regions in North and South Carolina, as well as the works of railroad improvements which are soon to commence."

Paternal attention was necessary as a safeguard against serious losses and disaster. Its necessity was recognized increasingly as the cost of slave labor mounted higher and higher in the nineteenth century. The competition of planters became keener; and the preservation of the health, happiness, and vigor of the laborers, as well as the maintenance of firm control over them, became more essential than ever for success in plantation industry.[13] When planters were absentees, there was pressing need of securing overseers of qualifications not alone of honesty, but of carefulness, forcefulness, knowledge, industry, and tact.[14] Where these qualities were lacking in the director, the enterprise often went to wreck.

[13] *Cf.* Frederick Law Olmsted, A *Journey in the Seaboard Slave States* (1859), 45.

[14] The overseer problem was a difficult and vital one in the conduct of the large estates, particularly when a planter had more than one plantation. The following narrative will illustrate. It is taken from the plantation records of Louis Manigault, Esq., of Charleston, South Carolina, who owned the two adjacent rice plantations "Gowrie" and "East Hermitage" on the Savannah River, operating them as a single large establishment. The records were made year by year in a continuous account. The manuscripts are now in the possession of Mrs. Hawkins Jenkins, of Pinopolis, South Carolina. The narrative for 1855 relates that the death of his overseer on December 7, 1855, left Mr. Manigault alone on the plantation. After refusing many applications for the place, he employed Leonard F. Venters, a young man of twenty-four years who had had experience near Georgetown, South Carolina, and was well recommended. Early in May Manigault left the plantation, as usual, for the summer. "Venters", he says in the account of operations, "made two great and fatal mistakes. He drew off his 'Sprout Water' too rapidly, prostrating his rice to the ground, and again he left his fields dry too long before he could get at them to give first hoeing. His rice was all stunted, sickly, and grass took him. We have made one half a crop. He says 'he will do better another year that now he sees into it', and as is well known, 'never change an overseer if you can help it', we try him once (but only once) more. We have purchased 19 [additional] negroes, amongst them 13 prime hands, costing in all $11,850. Also 771 acres High Land on Georgia Main for Cholera Camps, Children's summer residence, etc. costing $2,195 . . . ." At the end of the next year he wrote: "My expectations with regard to the overseer improving upon his last year's sad experience were vain. Mr. Venters did do a little better than before, as far as an increase in the crop was concerned, but very little; moreover elated by a strong and very false religious feeling he began to injure the plantation a vast deal, placing himself on a par with the negroes, by even joining in with them at their prayer meetings, breaking down long established discipline, which in every case is so *difficult* to preserve, favouring and siding in any difficulty with the people, against the Drivers, besides causing numerous grievances which I now have

Where these qualities of strength, resourcefulness, and devotion to affairs were present, there was a decided tendency to an increase in the size of the plantation thus advantaged. This tendency was held somewhat in check by the force of conservative custom against the sale and purchase of slaves except in emergencies; but in the newly developing sections, and especially when times were flush and credit easily obtained, the rapid growth of slaveholdings in the hands of men of personal strength was a marked phenomenon.

Incapable owners, on the other hand, often lost part or all of their slave property. Perhaps this was less frequent with large holdings than with small ones, for the large estates could afford to employ capable overseers during the minority of heirs, and in similar contingencies, while the small ones could not. While some slaveholdings, then, were handed down from generation to generation unchanged in number except through births and deaths, by far the most of them were occasionally altered in size by purchase and sale; and the law of the survival of the stronger in the competition brought it about that there should be a growth in the size of those slaveholdings which were controlled by the most capable managers, and an increase in their number and size in the districts where negro labor could be used to the best advantage. Economy of effort and expense in administration, economy in the purchase of supplies, and perhaps also economy in the marketing of the product all worked toward strengthening the advantage of the large

---

every reason to suppose my Neighbours knew; and perhaps I was laughed at and ridiculed for keeping in my employ such a man. I discharged Mr. Venters, and on 8th January, 1858, engaged Mr. Wm. H. Bryan . . . . He is very highly recommended by Dr. King, and spoken of as a good planter and a man of character. I give him $800 for the year 1858 . . . ." At the end of the next crop-year the record runs: "The crop of 1858, W. H. Bryan Overseer, has turned out wretchedly. From what I can learn since my return from Europe and after spending the entire of '58-'59 on the plantation, there has been gross neglect and great want of attention on the part of the Overseer . . . . On 8th April, 1859, Mr. Wm. Capers Jr., an Overseer of high rank and standing, . . . takes charge at the rate of One thousand dollars per annum, the highest salary we have yet paid . . . ." Capers proved efficient, brought things to rights, and made a very good crop. But Mr. Manigault expresses in his observations for 1859 the well-founded belief: "The truth is, on a plantation, to attend to things properly it requires *both Master and Overseer.*"

holder over the small one, and of the strong man over the weak. The concentration of slaveholdings was an inevitable tendency.

Yet there were hindrances and limitations to this process. In the first place, the whole body of the negro population was tremendously inert, and of course made no migration or progress of any sort of its own accord. Its labor as a rule was good only in a routine, and any change was difficult and problematical. Many of the whites also fell into a routine and were disposed to let good enough alone and put off changes till the morrow. After the American Revolution there were no entails or primogeniture, and estates once accumulated were liable to be divided in inheritance. Plantations, furthermore, might easily become too large and the fields too scattered for effective administration. The standard of maximum efficiency varied in the different staple regions and even on different soils within the same belt; but in every case such a maximum existed, and any growth beyond it decreased the profits of the establishment. Undue cumbrousness might be avoided by dividing one plantation into two or three; but that was not fully satisfactory, for overseers were expensive and they could never adequately fill the place of the master. There was a current adage, "The master's footprints are fertilizer to his soil." [15] In colonial times the limitations on the size of plantation estates were less cogent; but when slave prices mounted and when, in the later period, the margin of profit became small, it became more advis-

[15] The force of this is illustrated by the following description by a cotton-planter of his troubles and resolutions: "I have discharged Harvey, the overseer at the Hurricane, for getting drunk, neglecting business and not paying attention to that important branch of planting, viz. raising hogs. I have employed a man named Bagly in his place, a man of some reputation as an overseer . . . . I was in Baldwin [County] yesterday, trying to infuse new energy into everybody, and I think my turning off the late overseer has aided me in my exertion, as both overseers seem to understand that retaining their places depends on their energy and industry, and when they flag they must find a home elsewhere. I am kept busy and intend they shall be too, as long as my health lasts . . . . I have opened a regular set of books like a merchant. I found my business getting so confused I was forced to do it, and I am very glad I was, as I now keep all my accounts as easily and clearly as I could wish." Extracts from a letter from Colonel John B. Lamar, Macon, Georgia, January 5, 1846, to Hon. Howell Cobb. Manuscript in possession of Mrs. A. S. Erwin, Athens, Georgia.

able to invest profits in bank-stock and the like and avoid too great cumbrousness of land and slave property. The actual size of the average slaveholding, indeed, was very much smaller than the layman has been led to believe.

There was, in the second place, a limitation of habitat. No cereals nor any other crops but the four or five Southern staples could be cultivated as a main product with the system of full routine which plantation industry required. That system was always confined, accordingly, within the staple areas and within the districts where economical transportation could be had, and where public policy was friendly.

The friendliness or unfriendliness of a given region toward the plantation system might undergo decisive change. For example, the invention of the cotton gin and the improvement of transportation made the Piedmont available for planters; while, on the other hand, the exhaustion of soils in parts of Maryland and Virginia and the rise of tobacco production at a smaller cost in the West, drove out the plantation system from some of the Tidewater counties there.

The actual development as regards slavery in any given locality, whether in the South or the North, was the resultant of the interplay of these forces working for and against the plantation system. There were large parts of the South which, like the whole North, failed at any time to attract planters. The area, on the other hand, which invited them in large numbers may be divided into several distinct staple-producing sections, and may best be studied statistically through inquiry into the growth of the industrial units in selected counties which possess the type-features of the section.

For the colonial period, hardly any reliable statistics in this connection are available for study; but in view of the fairly complete repetition of processes in the successive settlement of similar areas in the plantation districts, it will here suffice to use the data for the period from 1790 to 1860, which is covered by the United States censuses and by certain local tax returns which we may use to supplement the census enumerations. The United States Census Bureau has never printed any local statistics of slaveholdings except for the year 1860, and many of the manuscript census returns for the early decades have been irretrievably lost; for example, those for Virginia and Kentucky to 1810, for Tennessee and Georgia to 1820, and for Alabama to 1830. But counties in Maryland may be taken as typical of the black belt of the whole Virginia-Maryland region, and a South Carolina coast district as an example for the Georgia lowlands also. There is no trouble in securing tables for the Mississippi-Louisiana region; and as for the Georgia-Carolina upland cotton belt, the summaries here presented from the manuscript tax returns in selected counties are preferable to those of the decennial censuses, because they were made much more frequently, and a series of returns for closely adjacent years is available for the study of the effects of particular economic crises, and the like.

These upland Georgia counties which we have selected, Oglethorpe, Hancock, and Clarke, all lying in the older part of the cotton belt, are probably the most instructive of all for which we have data; for in the period covered by these statistics these counties went through the full development from practically frontier and colonial organization, through and past their agricultural prime, and in turn came to furnish numerous emigrants to colonize the lands farther west.

GROWTH OF SLAVEHOLDINGS IN SELECTED COUNTIES OF THE GEORGIA COTTON BELT.

(Statistics compiled from county tax digests.)

Year	Numbers of Slaveholders and Slaves						Largest Holding	Total Owners	Total Slaves	Average Holding
	I 1–3	II 4–9	III 10–19	IV 20–49	V 50–99	VI over 99				

OGLETHORPE COUNTY.

Year	I 1–3	II 4–9	III 10–19	IV 20–49	V 50–99	VI over 99	Largest Holding	Total Owners	Total Slaves	Average Holding
1794	215	114	60	10	0	0	26	389	1,980	5.1
1800	272	163	69	17	0	0	31	521	2,788	5.32
1805	295	234	79	22	1	0	76	631	3,598	5.7
1810	316	262	139	37	3	0	73	757	5,255	7.07
1815	286	230	138	50	5	0	77	709	5,457	7.73
1820	280	258	130	82	8	0	77	758	6,444	8.5
1835	219	203	142	89	12	0	80	655	6,689	10.2
1850	183	153	131	103	17	0	90	587	7,111	12.1
1860	165	151	112	96	16	1	130	541	6,589	12.2

HANCOCK COUNTY.

1802	368	288	135	26	2	0	53	819	4,823	5.9
1807	378	323	185	45	3	0	65	934	6,424	6.9
1813	227	222	136	64	4	0	77	653	5,612	8.6
1821	229	208	145	88	8	0	93	678	6,331	9.34
1825	197	147	107	86	13	2	152	552	6,315	11.44
1835	145	132	107	77	17	2	180	480	5,680	11.84
1844	123	133	113	53	21	2	205	445	5,787	13.0
1856	144	112	106	95	27	3	146	487	7,516	17.45

CLARKE COUNTY.

1805	205	117	31	9	0	0	45	362	1,758	4.86
1810	191	123	57	10	1	0	51	382	2,124	5.55
1815	137	129	61	17	1	0	51	345	2,167	6.4
1818	164	152	83	24	0	0	46	413	2,997	7.02
1820	181	141	97	29	0	0	44	448	3,139	7.0
1830	206	154	91	55	3	1	120	510	4,529	8.9
1837	159	158	88	53	8	6	208	472	5,303	11.3
1840	130	161	73	59	5	4	209	432	4,358	10.16
1845	177	146	101	56	9	2	247	491	5,231	10.6
1850	177	163	103	73	4	1	102	521	5,217	10.13
1855	152	161	116	60	7	2	135	498	5,166	10.36
1864	167	175	111	73	8	1	150	535	5,420	10.13

By study of these tables[16] and charts, which date from the time when cotton production began in the upland district, the effect of the growth of the cotton industry may be watched and measured. The tables deal with both the number and the size of the slave-holdings. Studying them with the chronology of prosperity and depressions in the cotton belt in mind,[17] we find the following facts:

1. The *average size* of slaveholdings tended to increase with moderation in ordinary periods, while in periods of either marked prosperity or severe depression there was nearly always a stimulated growth of the larger slaveholdings and a thinning out of the small ones, and hence a quickened growth in the size of the average slaveholding.

2. The *aggregate number* of slaveholdings tended to increase or decrease according to the stage of development which the community had reached. That is, so long as population was scanty and

[16] The manuscript returns from which these summaries were made are to be found in the courthouses at the respective county seats.

[17] Cf. *Political Science Quarterly* (XX), 267.

Movement of Average Slaveholdings in Typical Counties

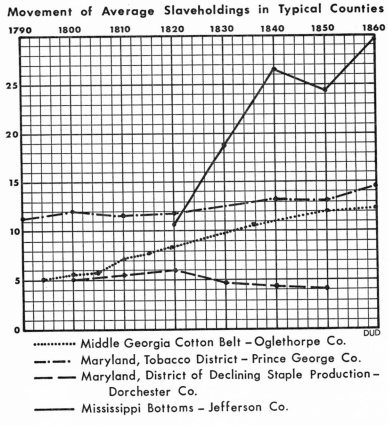

.... Middle Georgia Cotton Belt – Oglethorpe Co.

—.—. Maryland, Tobacco District – Prince George Co.

—— —— Maryland, District of Declining Staple Production –
Dorchester Co.

———— Mississippi Bottoms – Jefferson Co.

opportunity abundant, the small producers as well as the large ones flowed in. But when the land had become more completely occupied and opportunity restricted, an outflow would begin, and the smallest units would lead the exodus. Both flush times and hard times quickened this fluctuation of the total of units, merely hastening movements which were already in progress. These tendencies are illustrated more fully in Oglethorpe and Hancock counties than in Clarke, for in Clarke County there lay the considerable town of Athens. A town, of course, contributed to the

Movement of Slave and White Population in Typical Counties

Total Slaves

Total Whites

Movement of Slaveholding and Non-Slaveholding Families in Typical Counties

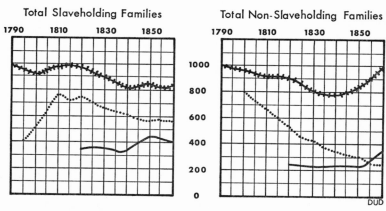

Total Slaveholding Families

Total Non-Slaveholding Families

.... Middle Georgia – Oglethorpe County
— — Maryland – Dorchester County
++++++ Maryland – Prince George County
———— Mississippi Bottoms – Jefferson County

total of slaves a large number of domestic servants, who were not affected by the laws controlling the units in agriculture.

For the sake of clearness in the accompanying charts, Oglethorpe is used as a single type county for the upland cotton belt. In the respective charts, the line for Oglethorpe County shows: (1) a moderate and steady growth in the average size of slaveholdings; (2) a fluctuating but almost continuous rise in the total number of slaves; and (3) a decline in the total of whites after about 1810; (4) that the number of slaveholdings increased until 1810, held its own to 1820, when the aggregate population reached its highest point, and decreased thereafter through the lessening of the number of small slaveholders; (5) that the non-slaveholders, throughout the period covered, decreased continuously, though with diminishing speed in the later decades. The number of non-slaveholders for the several periods has been roughly ascertained by comparing the number of slaveholding families in a given year with the total number of families, as stated in the federal censuses.

MOVEMENT OF SLAVEHOLDINGS IN OTHER TYPICAL AREAS.
(Statistics compiled from the United States Census Returns.)

Year	Numbers of Slaveholders and Slaves						Largest Holding	Total Owners	Total Slaves	Average Holding
	I 1–3	II 4–9	III 10–19	IV 20–49	V 50–99	VI over 99				

JEFFERSON COUNTY, MISSISSIPPI.

Year	I 1–3	II 4–9	III 10–19	IV 20–49	V 50–99	VI over 99	Largest Holding	Total Owners	Total Slaves	Average Holding
1820	125	97	75	40	6	2	158	345	3,665	10.6
1830	66	107	78	88	18	6	251	363	6,700	18.4
1840	72	74	58	95	39	11	456	349	9,176	26.3
1850	99	86	68	108	63	7	374	431	10,493	24.3
1860	81	87	70	99	71	17	above 300	425	12,396	29.2

BEAUFORT DISTRICT, SOUTH CAROLINA.

Year	I 1–3	II 4–9	III 10–19	IV 20–49	V 50–99	VI over 99	Largest Holding	Total Owners	Total Slaves	Average Holding
1790	143	110	88	153	67	24	607 (next, 265)	585	14,236	24.3
1800	107	127	115	152	70	26	300	600	16,031	26.7
1850	148	189	174	184	131	83	610 (next, 480)	909	32,279	35.5
1860	202	253	188	216	142	69	above 500	1,070	32,530	30.4

PRINCE GEORGE COUNTY, MARYLAND.

1790	358	272	202	124	24	6	265	986	11,176	11.2
1800	294	294	180	117	31	5	155	921	11,067	12.0
1810	330	284	206	135	32	3	125	990	11,760	11.6
1820	315	290	199	132	34	3	117	973	11,484	11.7
1840	257	229	148	154	23	3	202	814	10,636	13.1
1850	256	241	164	166	28	5	198	860	11,510	13.0
1860	269	199	170	162	40	7	under 200	847	12,479	14.7

DORCHESTER COUNTY, MARYLAND.

1800	465	304	85	28	1	1	121	884	4,596	5.0
1810	478	353	92	29	2	1	151	955	5,063	5.3
1820	560	382	100	21	1	1	200	1,065	5,198	4.9
1830	585	379	96	19	0	1	116	1,080	5,005	4.7
1840	531	355	81	8	1	0	65	976	4,222	4.3
1850	613	351	78	8	1	0	56	1,051	4,281	4.0

The data for Beaufort District, South Carolina, and Jefferson County, Mississippi, illustrate the movements for those parts of the black belts in which the proportion of negroes was particularly great, and show that while there was a larger unit of maximum efficiency in the alluvial areas, the same general influences held good which prevailed in Middle Georgia. Beaufort is cited as an old plantation area, and Jefferson as a new and rapidly developing one. The statistical picture in these cases is slightly disturbed by the fact that stretches of pine-barrens alternated with the fertile bottomlands, and offered a haven to a number of poor whites who were too low in the scale of industry to be affected by the competition of the staple producers. The movement in the fertile areas was well described by Messrs. Simons and Alston in their speeches in the South Carolina legislature at the beginning of the nineteenth century, on the subject of the slave trade. Their description, as reported, was as follow: "As one man grows wealthy and thereby increases his stock of negroes, he wants more land to employ them on: and being fully able, he bids a high price for his less opulent neighbor's plantation, who by selling advantageously here, can raise money enough to go into the back country, where he can be more on a level with the most forehanded, can get lands cheaper, and speculate or grow rich by industry as he pleases." [18]

[18] "Diary of Edward Hooker," American Historical Association *Report* for 1896, p. 878.

The two Maryland counties analyzed are typical of the longest settled areas, in their two partly contrasting portions: the portion which maintained the plantation system, and the portion which had replaced its staple by varied industry and had abandoned plantation methods. The first of these is illustrated by Prince George, which was in 1860 the chief tobacco county in Maryland; the second by Dorchester, which by 1860 had altogether ceased producing the staple. In each of them the population, both whites and slaves, tended to remain fairly stationary. In Prince George the number of the small holdings diminished and that of the larger ones increased as time went on, while in Dorchester just the opposite movement was usually in progress. Where plantation methods were no longer followed, there was little incentive to the concentration of slaves. In such cases the negroes were wanted rather as "help" than as gang labor.

The districts which did not ever produce any of the staples in appreciable quantity lie beyond the scope of this essay. Suffice it to say that in them there was little or no importation of negroes except possibly in rare periods of particular local prosperity; and when, after such importation, slave prices reached high levels in the country at large it was often found more advisable to sell the slaves than to employ them in the non-staple industries.

To summarize: the plantation system was the master feature in the regime of American slaveholding. In the prevalence of industrial competition, that system controlled in large measure the migration and the activity of both races. It tended to segregate the races; and, except for domestic service, it tended under limitations, in the long run, to eliminate the small slaveowner and to constitute the industrial system entirely of the two types, the paternalistic plantation and the democratic small farm, the one devoted always primarily to the staples, the other as a rule depending little upon staple production.

The dynamic view is full of significance; industry and society while apparently static were really in continuous motion and change. Affairs proceeded much in a routine; but no repetition of process was ever quite identical with its preceding occurrence. The routine itself was essentially dynamic. Impelled by the force of competition and directed by the requirements of capitalized industry, the plantation regime promoted the growth of slaveholding accretions and extended the black belts wherever gang labor could be made the most effective system.

7

The Economic Cost of Slaveholding in the Cotton Belt

APART from mere surface politics, the antebellum South is largely an unknown country to American historians.* The conditions, the life, the spirit of its people were so different from those which prevailed and still prevail in the North that it is difficult for Northern investigators to interpret correctly the facts which they are able to find. From the South itself they have received little assistance; for before the war Southerners were content, as a rule, to transmit traditions without writing books and since the war they have been too seriously engrossed in adapting themselves to new conditions to feel any strong impulse towards a scientific reconstruction of the former environment. When the South shall have been interpreted to the world by its own writers, it will be highly useful for students of other sections and other countries to criticize and correct, utilize and supplement the Southern historical literature. At the present time, however, the great need seems to be that of interpretation of developments in the South by men who have inherited Southern traditions. This consideration will perhaps justify the following incomplete study.

Whether negro slavery was an advantage in the early colonies and whether it became a burden in the later period, and, if so, how the change occurred, and why the people did not relieve themselves of the incubus—these are a few of the fundamental problems to which the student must address himself. The present essay, based on a study of slave prices, deals with the general economic

* *Political Science Quarterly*, **XX** (June, 1905), 257-75.

conditions of slaveholding, and shows the great transformation caused by the opening of the cotton belt and the closing of the African slave trade.

As regards the labor supply, the conditions at the outset in the new world of America were unlike those of modern Europe, but similar to those of Asia and Europe in primitive times. The ancient labor problem rose afresh in the plantation colonies, for land was plentiful and free, and men would not work as voluntary wage-earners in other men's employ when they might as readily work for themselves in independence. There was a great demand for labor upon the colonial estates, and when it became clear that freemen would not come and work for hire, a demand developed for servile labor. At first recourse was had to white men and women who bound themselves to serve three or four years to pay for their transportation across the sea, and to English criminals who were sent to the colonies and bound to labor for longer terms, frequently for five or seven years. Indian slaves were tried, but proved useless. Finally the negroes were discovered to be cheap and useful laborers for domestic service and plantation work.

For above half a century after the first negroes were brought to Virginia in 1620, this labor was considered a doubtful experiment; and their numbers increased very slowly until after the beginning of the golden age of the colony toward the end of the reign of Charles II. But the planters learned at length that the negroes could be employed to very good advantage in the plantation system; and after about 1680 the import of slaves grew steadily larger.[1]

In the West Indies the system of plantations worked by slaves had been borrowed by the English settlers from the Spaniards; and when the South Carolina coast was colonized, some of the West India planters immigrated and brought this system with them. In view of the climate and the crops on the Carolina coast, negro slave labor was thought to be a *sine qua non* of successful colonizing. The use of the slaves was confined always to the lowlands, until after Whitney invented the cotton gin; but in the early years

[1] For statistics of the increase of slaves in Virginia, see J. C. Ballagh, *History of Slavery in Virginia*, 10–25, *et passim.*

of the nineteenth century the rapid opening of the great inland cotton belt created a new and very strong demand for labor. The white farming population already in the uplands was by far too small to do the work; the lowland planters began to move thither with their slaves; the Northern and European laboring classes were not attracted by the prospect of working alongside the negroes; and accordingly the demand for labor in the cotton belt was translated into an unprecedented demand for negro slave labor.

Negro slavery was established in the South, as elsewhere, because the white people were seeking their own welfare and comfort. It was maintained for the same economic reason, and also because it was thought to be essential for safety. As soon as the negroes were on hand in large numbers, the problem was to keep their savage instincts from breaking forth, and to utilize them in civilized industry. The plantation system solved the problem of organization, while the discipline and control obtained through the institution of slavery were considered necessary to preserve the peace and to secure the welfare of both races. Private gain and public safety were secured for the time being; but in the long run, as we shall see, these ends were attained at the expense of private and public wealth and of progress.

This peculiar labor system failed to gain strength in the North, because there was there no work which negro slaves could perform with notable profit to their masters. In certain parts of the South the system flourished because the work required was simple, the returns were large, and the shortcomings of negro slave labor were partially offset by the ease with which it could be organized.

Once developed, the system was of course maintained so long as it appeared profitable to any important part of the community. Wherever the immediate profits from slave labor were found to be large, the number of slaves tended to increase, not only through the birth of children, but by importations. Thus the staple-producing areas became "black belts," where most of the labor was done by slaves. With large amounts of capital invested in slaves, the system would be maintained even in times of depression, when the plantations were running at something of a loss; for, just as in a factory, the capital was fixed, and operations could not be stopped without a still greater loss. When property in slaves had become important, the conservative element in politics became devoted, as a rule, to the preservation of this vested interest. The very force of inertia tended to maintain the established system, and a convulsion or crisis of some sort was necessary for its disestablishment in any region.

As a matter of fact it was only in special industries, and only in times of special prosperity, that negro slave labor was of such decided profit as to escape condemnation for its inherent disadvantages. But at certain periods in Virginia and in the Lower South, the conditions were unusual: all labor was profitable; hired labor was not to be had so long as land was free; indentured white servants were in various ways unsatisfactory, and negro slaves were therefore found to be of decided profit to their masters. The price of Africans in colonial times was so low that, when crops and prices were good, the labor of those imported repaid their original cost in a few years, and the planters felt a constant temptation to increase their holdings of land and of slaves in the hope of still greater profits.

Thus in Virginia there was a vicious circle: planters bought fresh lands and more slaves to make more tobacco, and with the profits from tobacco they bought more land and slaves to make more tobacco with which to buy yet more land and slaves. The situation in the Lower South was similar to that in Virginia, with rice and indigo, or sugar, or in latter times cotton, substituted for tobacco. In either case the process involved a heavy export of wealth in the acquisition of every new laborer. The Yankee skipper had a corresponding circle of his own: he carried rum to Guinea to exchange for slaves, slaves to the plantation colonies to exchange for molasses, molasses to New England to exchange for more rum, and this rum again to Guinea to exchange for more slaves. The difference was that the Yankee made a genuine profit on every exchange and thriftily laid up his savings, while the southern planter, as a rule, invested all his profits in a fictitious form of wealth and never accumulated a surplus for any other sort of investment.

From an economic point of view the American system of slavery was a system of firmly controlling the unintelligent negro laborers, and of capitalizing the prospective value of the labor of each work-man for the whole of his life. An essential feature of that system was the practice of buying and selling the control over the slave's labor, and one of the indexes to the economic situation at any time may be found in the quotations of slave prices.

The slave trade had no particular local home or "exchange," but it extended throughout all the slaveholding districts of America. Though the number and frequency of slave sales was relatively small, the traffic when once developed had many of the features of modern stock or produce markets. It cannot be forgotten, of course, that the slave trade involved questions of humanity and social organization as well as the mere money problem; but from the financial point of view the slave traffic constituted simply an extensive commodity market, where the article dealt in was life-time labor. As in any other market, the operations in the slave trade were controlled by economic laws or tendencies. There were bull influences and bear influences, and occasional speculative campaigns. And when at times the supply was subjected to mo-nopoly control, the prices tended to go wild and disturb the general system of finance in the whole region.

In the general slave market there was constant competition among those wishing to sell, and among those wishing to buy. The volume of the colonial slave trade and the rate of slave prices tended to fluctuate to some extent with the tides of prosperity in the respective staple-producing areas; but during the colonial period the plantations in the different regions were of such varied interests, producing tobacco, rice, indigo, cotton, sugar and coffee, that depression in one of these industries was usually offset, so far as concerned the slave trader, by high profits in another. Barbados was the information station. The slave ships touched there and gathered news of where their "ebony" was to be sold the highest.[2] The Royal African Company had the best system of intelligence, and about 1770 and 1780 it sold its cargoes at a fairly uniform price of £18 to £22 per head,[3] while the independent traders appear to

[2] D. McKinnon, *Tour Through the British West Indies*, 8.
[3] *Virginia Magazine*, III, 167. Calendar of State Papers, Colonial Series, America and West Indies, 1775–76, p. 155 *et passim*.

have obtained from £15 to £25, according to the chances of the market. American-born slaves, when sold, brought higher prices than fresh Africans, because their training in plantation labor and domestic service rendered them more valuable. The prices of the home-raised slaves varied considerably, but so long as the African trade was kept open, the price of field hands of all sorts was kept reasonably near to the price of the savage African imports.

In the very early period the sellers in the slave market were more eager than the buyers, and the prices ranged nearly as low as the cost of purchasing slaves in Africa and transporting them to America; but great prosperity in all the different groups of plantations at the same period soon greatly increased the demand, and the ships in the traffic proving too few, prices rapidly advanced. After this, however, there came a decline in tobacco profits; then the war of revolt from Great Britain depressed all the staple industries simultaneously, and following that the American production of indigo was ruined by foreign competition. Thus in 1790–95 slave prices reached the bottom of a twenty years' decline.[4]

[4] The depression of industry in the staple districts toward the close of the eighteenth century is illustrated by several contemporary writers. Samuel Du-Bose, in his reminiscences of St. Stephen's parish, describes conditions in low-land South Carolina in the period after the close of the American Revolution:

"When peace was restored every planter was in debt. . . . Ruin stared many in the face. Besides, with the exception of rice, the country had no staple crop; for since the bounty, which as colonists they had enjoyed on the export of indigo and naval stores, had been discontinued, these products ceased to have any value, and negroes fell in price. Prime gangs were not unfrequently sold for less than two hundred dollars per head. . . . The people however . . . were sanguine respecting the future. . . . They strove to reduce their expenses to the lowest possible point; they manufactured clothing for themselves and their slaves; raised abundant supplies of poultry and stock of various kinds, and with these contrived to live in plenty. . . . [At length] the Santee Canal was projected and constructed within their neighborhood. Everyone availed himself to a greater or less extent of this opportunity of hiring their negroes; for men they received thirty and for women twenty pounds sterling per annum, besides their food. At times a thousand laborers were employed on this work, which was seven years in being completed. The enterprise, which was disastrous to those who had embarked in it, rescued a large number of planters from ruin. It was commenced in 1792, and finished in 1800. Two or three years after it had been commenced, a few planters in the neighborhood tried the cultivation of cotton on a small scale, but the progress of this enterprise was slow and irreso-

The developments following Whitney's invention of the cotton gin revolutionized the situation. Slave prices entered upon a steady advance, which was quickened by the prohibition of the African trade in 1808. They were then held stationary by the restrictions upon commerce, and were thrown backward by the outbreak of war in 1812. But with the peace of Ghent the results of the new cotton industry and of the cessation of African imports became strikingly manifest. The inland fields of the Lower South proved to be peculiarly adapted for the production of cotton. The simplicity of the work and the even distribution of the tasks through the seasons made negro slave labor peculiarly available. With the increasing demand of the world for cotton, there was built up in the South perhaps the greatest staple monopoly the world had ever seen. The result was an enormous demand for slaves in the cotton belt. American ports, however, were now closed to the foreign slave trade. The number of slaves available in America was now fixed, the rate of increase was limited, and the old "tobacco South" had a monopoly of the only supply which could meet the demand of the new "cotton South."

Till 1815 "colonial" conditions prevailed, and the market for slave labor was relatively quiet and steady. In 1815 began the "antebellum" regime, in which the whole economy of the South was governed by the apparently capricious play of the compound

lute, in consequence of the difficulty of preparing it for market. With the improvement of the gins, the cotton culture increased and was extended, until 1799, when Capt. James Sinkler planted three hundred acres at his plantation Belvidere, on Eutaw Creek, and reaped from each acre two hundred and sixteen pounds, which he sold for from fifty to seventy-five cents per pound." This pamphlet of DuBose's is *reprinted* in T. G. Thomas' *History of the Huguenots in South Carolina*, (N. Y., 1887), 66–68. The accuracy of the statements quoted is borne out by the very interesting manuscript records of the Porcher-Ravenel family, which are now in the possession of members of the family at Pinopolis, St. John Parish, Berkeley, South Carolina.

Virginia conditions are indicated in a letter of George Washington to Alexander Spotswood, Nov. 23, 1794, which is published in the *New York Public Library Bulletin*, III, 14, 15. Spotswood had written that he intended moving west, and asked advice as to selling his lands and slaves. Washington replied that he believed that before many years had passed slaves would become a very troublesome sort of property, and that, except for his principles against selling negroes, he himself would not by the end of twelve months be possessed of a single one as a slave.

monopoly of cotton and slave labor. The price of cotton was governed by the American output and its relation to the European demand. And the price of slaves was governed by the profits in cotton and the relation of the labor demand to the monopolized labor supply.[5]

For an understanding of slaveholding economics, a careful study of the history of slave prices is essential. Prior to the middle of the eighteenth century, the scarcity of data, the changing value of gold, the multiplicity of coinage systems, and the use of paper money with irregular depreciations unfortunately present so many obstacles that any effort to determine the fluctuation of slave prices would be of very doubtful success. For the following periods the study is feasible, although under the best of existing circumstances slave prices are hard to collect and hard to compare. The proportion of the slave population on the market at any time was very much smaller than the student of prices could wish for the purpose of his study; and many of the sales which were made are not to be found in the records. The market classification of the slaves was flexible and irregular; and, except in Louisiana, most of the documents in the public archives do not indicate the classification. To make thoroughly accurate comparison of slave prices at different times and places, we should need to know, among other things, the sex, age, strength and nativity of the slaves; the purity or mixture of blood of the negroes, mulattoes, quadroons, mestizoes, etc.; and their special training or lack of it. For such statistical purposes, however, the records have many shortcomings. In many cases they state simply that the slave Matt or Congo or Martha, belonging to the estate of William Jones, deceased, was sold on the date given to Thomas Smith, for, say, $300, on twelve months' credit. Such an item indicates the sex and states the price, but gives little else. In other instances the slaves are classed as infants, boys, men (or fellows) and old men; girls, wenches and old women. Whole families were often sold as a lot, with no individual quotations given. Women were hardly ever sold separate from their young children. In the dearth of separate sale quota-

[5] *Cf.* De Toqueville, *Democracy in America*, II, 233.

tions, any study of the prices of female slaves would have to be based chiefly upon appraisal values, which of course were much less accurate than actual market prices.

The sales made by the professional slave traders were generally recorded each in a bill of sale; but in most of the localities these were not transcribed into the formal books of record, and the originals have mostly disappeared. The majority of the sales of which records are to be found were those of the slaves in the estates of deceased persons. These sales were at auction; and except in abnormal cases, which may often be distinguished, they may be taken as fairly representative of slave prices for the time and place.

There was always a great difference between the values of individual slaves. When the average price of negroes ranged about $500, prime field hands brought, say, $1,000, and skilled artisans still more. At that rate, an infant would be valued at about $100, a boy of twelve years and a man of fifty at about $500 each, and a prime wench for field work at $800 or $900.

The most feasible comparison of prices is that of prime field hands, who may be defined as well-grown, able-bodied fellows, with average training and between eighteen and thirty years of age. To find the current price of prime field hands in lists where no classification is given, we take the average of the highest ordinary prices. We ignore any scattering extreme quotations, as applying probably to specially valuable artisans, overseers, or domestic servants, and not to field hands. Where ages are given, we take the average of the prices paid for grown fellows too young to have received special training. We leave aside, on the other hand, the exceptionally low quotations as being due to infirmities which exclude the slave from the prime grade. The professional slave traders in the domestic traffic dealt mostly in "likely young fellows and wenches." In the quotations of the sales by these traders, when no details are recorded, we may assume that the average, except for children, will range just a little below the current rate for prime field hands.

In view of all the hindrances, the production of a perfectly accurate table of prices cannot be hoped for, even from the exercise of the utmost care and discrimination. The table which follows is simply an approximation of averages made in a careful study of several thousand quotations in the state of Georgia.[6]

The parallel quotations of cotton prices[7] afford a basis for the study of slave-labor capitalization. In examining these quotations it will be noticed that during many brief periods the prices of slaves and cotton rose and fell somewhat in harmony; but that in the whole period under review the price of cotton underwent a heavy net decline, while slave prices had an extremely strong upward movement. The change which took place in the relative slave and cotton prices was really astonishing. In 1800 a prime field hand was worth in the market about 1,500 pounds of ginned cotton; in 1809, about 3,000 pounds; in 1818, about 3,500; in 1826, about 5,400; in 1837, about 10,000; in 1845, about 12,000; in 1860, 15,000 to 18,000. In his capacity for work, a prime negro in 1800 was worth nearly or quite as much as a similar slave in 1860; and a pound of cotton in 1860 was not essentially different from a pound of cotton in 1800. But our table shows that within that epoch of three-score years there was an advance of some 1,000 or 1,200 per cent in the price of slaves as measured in cotton.

The decline in the price of cotton was due in some measure to a lessening of cost, through improvements in cultivating, ginning and marketing. The advance in slave prices was due in part to the increasing intelligence and ability of the negroes and to improvements in the system of directing their work on the plantations, and also in part to the decline in the value of money. But the tenfold or twelvefold multiplication of the price of slaves, when quoted in terms of the product of their labor, was too great to be explained

[6] The sources used for this tabulation are the documents in the Georgia state archives and the records of Baldwin, Oglethorpe, Clarke and Troup counties, all lying in the Georgia cotton belt, together with bills of sale in private hands, travelers' accounts, and articles in the newspapers of the period. Instances of sudden rise or fall in slave prices and sales of large and noted estates were often reported in the local press, with comments. There is no printed collection of any large number of slave-price quotations.

[7] The cotton price averages are made from the tables given by E. J. Donnell in his *Chronological and Statistical History of Cotton*, New York, 1872, with the aid of the summaries published by G. L. Watkins, *Production and Price of Cotton for One Hundred Years*, U. S. Department of Agriculture, Washington, 1895.

SLAVE AND COTTON PRICES IN GEORGIA

Year	Average Price of Prime Field Hands	Economic Situation and the Chief Determinant Factors	Average N. Y. Price of Upland Cotton	Years
1755......	£55...			
1773......	60			
1776–1783.	....	War and depression in industry and commerce.		
1784......	70	Peace and returning prosperity.		
1792......	$300	Depression due to Great Britain's attitude toward American commerce.		
1793......	....	Cotton gin invented.		
1800[8].....	450	....	30 cents.	1795–1805
1808......	....	African slave trade prohibited.		
1809......	600	Embargo moderates rise in prices.	19 cents.	1805–1810
1813......	450	War with Great Britain..	12 cents.	1813
1818......	1000	Inflation...............	29 cents.	1816–1818
1819......	....	Financial crisis.........	16 cents.	1819
1821......	700	Recovery from panic.....	14 cents.	1821
1826......	800	Moderate prosperity....	15 cents.	1824–1827
1827......	....	Depression.		
1828......	700	....	10 cents.	1827–1828
1835......	900	Flush times...........	17½ cents.	1835
1837......	1300	Inflation—crash........	13½ cents.	1837
1839......	1000	Cotton crisis..........	13½ cents.	1839
1840......	700	Cotton crisis; acute distress................	9 cents.	1840
1844......	600	Depression.............	7½ cents.	1844
1845......	....	Severe depression.......	5½ cents.	1845
1848......	900	Recovery in cotton prices. Texas demand for slaves...............	9½ cents.	1847–1848
1851......	1050	Prosperity.............	12 cents.	1851
1853......	1200	Expansion of cotton industry and simultaneous rise in tobacco prices.[10].............	11 cents.	1850–1860
1859......	1650			
1860[9].....	1800			

[8] The quotations down to this point are lowland quotations. There were very few slaves in the uplands before 1800.

[9] In the later fifties there were numerous local flurries in slave valuations. In central Georgia prime negroes brought $2,000 in 1860, while in western Georgia and central Alabama the prices appear not to have run much above $1,500. For prices in the other parts of the South in that decade, see G. W. Weston,

except by reference to the severe competition of the planters in selling cotton and in buying slaves. Their system of capitalized labor was out of place in the modern competitive world, and burdened with that system all the competition of the cotton planters was bound to be of a cut-throat nature. In other words, when capital and labor were combined, as in the American slaveholding system, there was an irresistible tendency to overvalue and overcapitalize slave labor, and to carry it to the point where the financial equilibrium was unsafe, and any crisis threatened complete bankruptcy.

Aside from the expense of food, clothing and shelter, the cost of slave labor for any given period of time was made up of several elements:

1. Interest upon the capital invested in the slave.

2. Economic insurance against (a) his death, (b) his illness or accidental injury, and (c) his flight from service.[11] Of course, insurance policies were seldom taken out to cover these risks, but the cost of insurance against them must be reckoned in the cost of slave labor for any given period.

3. The diminishing value of every mature slave by reason of increasing age. Because of the "wear and tear" of his years and his diminishing prospect of life and usefulness, the average slave of fifty-five years of age would be worth only half as much as one of twenty-five years, and after fifty-five the valuation decreased still more rapidly. In computing the cost of any group of slaves it will be necessary to set over against this depreciation the value of the

---

Who are and who may be slaves in the United States, a pamphlet published in 1856. See also Brackett, *The Negro in Maryland;* Ingle, *Southern Sidelights;* Hammond, *The Cotton Industry,* and *De Bow's Review,* XXVI, 647.

[10] The rise in tobacco prices and the revival of prosperity in Virginia in this decade tended to diminish the volume of the slave trade and contributed to raising slave prices. W. H. Collins, *The Domestic Slave Trade in the Southern States* (New York, 1904), p. 57.

[11] Physicians' and attorneys' fees should perhaps be included under the head of insurance. It may be noted that doctors' charges were generally the same for slaves as for white persons. To illustrate how expensive this charge often was, we may cite an instance given in the records of Troup county, Georgia, where Dr. Ware collected from Col. Truitt's estate $130.50 for medicine and daily visits to a negro child, from November 29, 1858, to January 5, 1859.

children born; but, on the other hand, the cost by groups would be increased by the need of supporting the disabled negroes who were not in the working gangs.

4. Taxation assessed upon the capitalized value of the slaves. In the slaveholding region as a whole, in the later antebellum period, the total assessed value of slave property was at least as great as that of all the other sorts of property combined.

The rate of slave hire would furnish a good index of the current price of slave labor year by year, if sufficient quotations on a stable basis could be obtained. But on account of the special needs or wishes of the parties to the individual bargains, there were such opportunities for higgling the rate in individual cases that the current rate is very elusive. The following averages, computed from a limited number of quotations for the hire of men slaves in middle Georgia, are illustrative: In 1800, $100 per year; in 1816, $110; in 1818, $140; in 1833, $140; in 1836, $155; in 1841, $140; in 1860, $150. These were in most cases the years of maximum quotations in the respective periods. The local fluctuations in short periods were often very pronounced; but in the long run the rate followed a gradual upward movement.

The relation between the price of slaves and the rate of their hire should theoretically have borne, in quiet periods, a definite relation to the rate of interest upon capital; but the truth is that in the matter of slave prices there was, through the whole period after the closing of the African trade, a tendency to "frenzied finance" in the cotton belt. Slave prices were largely controlled by speculation, while slave hire was regulated more largely by the current rate of wages for labor in general. The whole subject of these relations is one for which authentic data are perhaps too scanty to permit of thorough analysis.

Negro slave labor was expensive, not so much because it was unwilling as because it was overcapitalized and inelastic. The negro of himself, by reason of his inherited inaptitude, was inefficient as a self-directing laborer in civilized industry. The whole system of civilized life was novel and artificial to him; and to make him play a valuable part in it, strict guidance and supervision were essential. Without the plantation system, the mass of the negroes would have been an unbearable burden in America; and except in slavery they could never have been utilized, in the beginning, for plantation work. The negro had no love of work for work's sake; and he had little appreciation of future goods when set over against present exemption from toil. That is to say, he lacked the economic motive without which voluntary civilized industry is impossible. It is a mistake to apply the general philosophy of slavery to the American situation without very serious modification.[12] A slave among the Greeks or Romans was generally a relatively civilized person, whose voluntary labor would have been far more productive than his labor under compulsion. But the negro slave was a negro first, last and always, and a slave incidentally. Mr. Cairnes and others make a great mistake when they attribute his inefficiency and expensiveness altogether to the one incident of regulation. Regulation actually remedied in large degree the disadvantages of using negro labor, though it failed to make it as cheap, in most employments, as free white labor would have been. The cotton planter found the negro already a part of the situation. To render him useful, firm regulation was necessary. The forcible control of the negro was in the beginning a necessity, and was not of itself a burden at any time.[13]

In American slaveholding, however, the capitalization of labor-value and the sale and purchase of labor-control were permanent features; and when the supply was "cornered" it was unavoidable that the price should be bid up to the point of overvaluation.[14]

---

[12] Palgrave's *Dictionary of Political Economy* contains an excellent article upon slavery, in which it is indicated that harshness and compulsion were not always essential in slave labor; that the motive force was often a sort of feudal devotion to the master; and, further, that negro slave labor was practically essential for developing the resources of the hot malarial swamp regions.

[13] The current rate of hire today for negro workmen in agriculture in Georgia is from $8 to $12 per month; but for the year 1904, the state of Georgia leased out its able-bodied convicts at an average rate of $225 per year. When under strict discipline, the average negro even today, it appears, is worth twice as much as when left to his own devices.

[14] In the periods of high slave prices employers found that slave labor was too expensive to be used with profit except in plantation industry under the most favorable circumstances. Striking proof of this is to be seen in the eager employment wherever they could be had, of Irish and German immigrants for canal and railway building, ditching and any other labor which might prove

And this brings us to the main economic disadvantage of the system.

In employing free labor, wages are paid from time to time as the work is done, and the employer can count upon receiving from the products of that labor an income which will enable him to continue to pay its wages in the future, while his working capital is left free for other uses. He may invest a portion of his capital in lands and buildings, and use most of the remainder as circulating capital for special purposes, retaining only a small percentage as a reserve fund. But to secure a working force of slaves, the ante-bellum planter had to invest all the capital that he owned or could borrow in the purchase of slaves and lands;[15] for the larger his plantation was, within certain limits, the more economies he could introduce. The temptation was very strong for him to trim down to the lowest possible limit the fund for supplies and reserve. The slaveholding system thus absorbed the planter's earnings; and for such absorption it had unlimited capacity, for the greater the profits of the planters the more slaves they wanted and the higher the slave prices mounted. Individual profits, as fast as made, went into the purchase of labor, and not into modern implements or land improvements.[16] Circulating capital was at once converted

---

injurious to a negro's health and strength. Slaves were growing too dear to be used. W. H. Russell (*My Diary North and South*, Boston, 1863, p. 272) writing of the Louisiana sugar district in 1860, says: "The labor of ditching, trenching, cleaning the waste lands and hewing down the forests, is generally done by Irish laborers, who travel about the country under contractors, or are engaged by resident gangsmen for the task. Mr. Seal lamented the high prices for this work; but then, as he said, 'It was much better to have Irish do it, who cost nothing to the planter, if they died, than to use up good field hands in such severe employment.'" The documentary evidence in regard to the competition and rather extensive substitution of immigrant labor for that of slaves in the times of high slave prices is quite conclusive, in spite of its fugitive character. Further data may be found in *De Bow's Review*, XI, 400; *Harper's Magazine*, VII, 752 *et seq.*; Sir Chas. Lyell, *Second Visit to the United States*, II, 127; Waddell, *Annals of Augusta County, Virginia*, 272, 273; and the James River and Kanawha Canal Company's fourth annual report, Richmond, 1839.

[15] *Cf.* F. L. Olmsted, *A Journey to Texas*, 8–10.

[16] This was lamented by many planters, especially in times of low staple prices. *Cf. Southern Agriculturist*, published at Charleston, 1828, II, 1 *et passim*; and especially an address by Dr. Manly before the Alabama State Agricultural Society, Dec. 7, 1841, published in the Tuscaloosa *Monitor*, April 13, 1842. (File in the Alabama State Department of Archives and History.)

into fixed capital; while for their annual supplies of food, implements and luxuries the planters continued to rely upon their credit with the local merchants, and the local merchants to rely upon their credit with northern merchants and bankers.

Thus there was a never-ending private loss through the continual payment of interest and the enhancement of prices; and, further, there was a continuous public loss by the draining of wealth out of the cotton belt by the slave trade.[17] With the stopping of the African slave trade, the drain of wealth from the lower South was not checked at all, but merely diverted from England and New England to the upper tier of Southern states; and there it did little but demoralize industry and postpone to a later generation the agricultural revival.

The capitalization of labor lessened its elasticity and its ver-

[17] This injurious effect of the slave traffic is strikingly illustrated on the account by a Charleston bookseller, E. S. Thomas, of the misfortunes which befell his business by the reopening of the South Carolina ports to the foreign slave trade in 1803. Thomas had found the business opportunities in Charleston exceedingly good; and for some years he had been annually doubling his capital. But in November, 1803, he had just opened a new importation of fifty thousand volumes, when news came from Columbia that the legislature had opened the ports to the slave trade. "The news had not been five hours in the city," he writes, "before two large British Guineamen, that had been lying on and off the port for several days expecting it, came up to town; and from that day my business began to decline. . . . A great change at once took place in everything. Vessels were fitted out in numbers for the coast of Africa, and as fast as they returned their cargoes were bought up with avidity, not only consuming the large funds that had been accumulating but all that could be procured, and finally exhausting credit and mortgaging the slaves for payment. . . . For myself, I was upwards of five years disposing of my large stock, at a sacrifice of more than a half, in all the principal towns, from Augusta, in Georgia, to Boston." E. S. Thomas, *Reminiscences*, II, 35, 36.

The same general phenomena were observed in various other parts of the South, as is shown by the following extract from a letter written August 22, 1774, by one John Brown, a citizen of Virginia, to William Preston: "Some time ago you told me that you intended to enter the servant trade, and desire[d] me to tell if there was any encouragement our way for the sale of them. I think there is none, for these reasons: (1) the scarcity of money; (2) servants are plenty and everyone has as many as they want; besides, the country is sunk in debt by them already. If you have not as yet engaged, I think it not prudent for you to do it at the present juncture; you have business enough upon hand, but these things you can better think of than I can." Original MS. in Wisconsin Historical Society, Draper Collection, series QQ, vol. III, no. 81.

satility; it tended to fix labor rigidly in one line of employment. There was little or no floating labor in the plantation districts; and the planter was obliged to plan in detail a whole year's work before the year began. If he should plant a larger acreage than his "force" could cultivate and harvest, a part of the crop would have to be abandoned, unless by chance some free negro or stray Irishman could be found for the odd job. As an illustration of the financial hardships which might befall the slaveholder, it may be noted that in 1839 William Lowndes Yancey happened to lose his whole force of slaves through poisoning in the midst of the working season. The disaster involved his absolute ruin as a planter, and forced him to seek some other opening which did not require the possession of capital.[18]

In the operations of cotton production, where fluctuating and highly uncertain returns demanded the greatest flexibility, the slaveholding system was rigid. When by overproduction the price of cotton was depressed, it could be raised again only by curtailing the output in the American cotton belt, which had the monopoly. But the planter, owning cotton lands and slaves trained in the cotton field alone, found it hard to devote his fields with success to other crops or to sell or lease his negroes to any one else, for no one else wanted them for any other purpose than cotton production. In fact, the proportion of the southern resources devoted to cotton production tended always to increase. To diminish the cotton output required the most heroic efforts. As a rule, the chances of heavy gains from cotton planting outweighed those of loss, in the popular estimation; and the strong and constant tendency was to spoil the market by over-supply.

There were uncertain returns in cotton raising, and great risks in slaveowning. The crop might be heavy or light in any year, according to the acreage and the weather, and prices might be away up or away down. A prime slave might be killed by a rattlesnake or crippled in a log-rolling or hanged for murder or spirited away by the underground railroad. All these uncertainties fostered extravagance and speculation.

[18] G. W. DuBose, *Life of William L. Yancey*, 39.

In the cotton belt inflation and depression followed each other in rapid succession; but the times of prosperity brought less real advantage and periods of depression caused greater hardship in the slaveholding South than in any normally organized community. For by the capitalizing of labor, profits were generally absorbed through the purchasing of additional slaves at higher prices, while in time of need the cotton planter found it impossible to realize upon his investment because his neighbors were involved in the same difficulties which embarrassed him, and when he would sell they could not buy.

When after the peace in 1815 the system of industry and finance of the antebellum South had fully developed itself, the South and its leaders were seized in the grip of social and economic forces which were rendered irresistible by the imperious laws of monopoly. The cotton planters controlled the South, and for some decades they dominated the policy of the federal government; but the cotton planters themselves were hurried hither and thither by their two inanimate but arbitrary masters, cotton and slavery.

Cotton and slavery were peculiar to the South, and their requirements were often in conflict with the interests and ideas prevailing in the other parts of the United States. As that conflict of interests and sentiments was accentuated, it became apparent that the South was in a congressional minority, likely to be overridden at any time by a Northern majority. Ruin was threatening the vested interests and the social order in the South; and the force of circumstances drove the Southern politicians into the policy of resistance. To the leaders in the South, with their ever-present view of the possibility of negro uprisings, the regulations of slavery seemed essential for safety and prosperity. And when they found themselves about to become powerless to check any legislation hostile to the established order in the South, they adopted the policy of secession, seeking, as they saw it, the lesser of the evils confronting them.

Because they were blinded by the abolition agitation in the North and other historical developments which we cannot here discuss, most of the later generation of antebellum planters could not see that slaveholding was essentially burdensome. But that which was partly hidden from their vision is clear to us today. In the great system of Southern industry and commerce, working with seeming smoothness, the negro laborers were inefficient in spite of discipline, and slavery was an obstacle to all progress. The system may be likened to an engine, with slavery as its great fly-wheel—a fly-wheel indispensable for safe running at first, perhaps, but later rendered less useful by improvements in the machinery, and finally becoming a burden instead of a benefit. Yet it was retained, because it was still considered essential in securing the adjustment and regular working of the complex mechanism. This great rigid wheel of slavery was so awkward and burdensome that it absorbed the momentum and retarded the movement of the whole machine without rendering any service of great value. The capitalization of labor and the export of earnings in exchange for more workmen, always of a low degree of efficiency, together with the extreme lack of versatility, deprived the South of the natural advantage which the cotton monopoly should have given. To be rid of the capitalization of labor as a part of the slaveholding system was a great requisite for the material progress of the South.

8

The Economics of Slave Labor
in the South

THE United States census returns of 1860 and 1900 show
that in the two main products, cotton and corn, the per
capita output was smaller by at least 40 per cent in the
latter year than in the former, in the states of Alabama, Mississippi, and Louisiana.* The same observation holds true for such typical black-belt counties in these states as Lowndes and Marengo in
the first, Yazoo and Bolivar in the second, and Madison and
Rapides parishes in the third. In these communities agriculture
had not been revolutionized in the interim by the introduction of
commercial fertilizers as it had been in the Atlantic states, and the
situation had not been affected by a great influx of white laborers
as in Texas. These Alabama, Mississippi, and Louisiana statistics
probably furnish the most accurate available test of average negro
efficiency in the slavery regime as compared with average negro
efficiency in the present-day regime of wage labor and peasant
farming. The experience of recent employers of Southern convict
labor tends to the same conclusion that in tasks where gang work
is feasible, average negroes when under compulsion are nearly
twice as productive as when left to the control of their own im-
pulses. Slave labor, it should be said, was usually not under as
severe compulsion as convict labor is; but any loss due to laxity of
coercion was probably more than offset on the average by virtue of
the systematic appeal made by very many masters to the loyalty

* *The South in the Building of the Nation* (13 vols.; Richmond, 1909-
13), V, 121-24.

of one type of their slaves and to the pecuniary self-interest of another. Great numbers of domestic servants were more stimulated by personal devotion and pride of service than by fear of punishment. On the other hand, a large proportion of the specially eager and provident slaves, particularly artisans, shopkeepers and jobworkers in the towns, were allowed to hire their own time from their masters and to retain for themselves all earnings above the amount agreed upon for their hire. By this means some slaves bought their manumission. Others preferred a heightened standard of conduct as slaves to the doubtful benefits of legal freedom. On the whole, negro slave labor was probably not as productive as free white labor among modern industrial nations; yet in view of its being negro labor, first, last and always, and slave labor incidentally, it was brought in the antebellum regime to have a distinctly high degree of efficiency.

Nevertheless, slave labor proved to be a type of labor peculiarly unprofitable to its employers in a multitude of cases, and peculiarly burdensome in the long run to nearly all the communities which maintained the system. This was because the institution of slavery involved the capitalization of labor-control, caused the exportation of wealth from the prosperous districts for the purchase of recruits to the labor supply, and excluded or discouraged most of the population save masters and slaves from sharing or endeavoring to share in large-scale industrial affairs. Furthermore, slavery as an inseparable element of the plantation system tended to devote the great bulk of negro labor incessantly to the production of the staple crops. This fixed the community in a rut and deprived it of the great benefits of industrial diversification. The strong upward tendency of slave prices in the whole period following the close of the African slave trade[1] caused a constant increase of the financial investment in slaves as compared with the investment in all other sorts of property; it reduced the resources available for equipment and current expenses; and it increased the liability of great damage to the community resulting from any financial crises which might

[1] See "The Economics of the Slave Trade," on page 140 of this volume.

occur.[2] This rise of prices led to a distinct overvaluation of slaves in the closing decades of the antebellum period. There are records of numerous instances where slaveholders employed Irish and German gangs for ditching, levee building, and other heavy and dangerous work, in order to safeguard the life and health of their precious slaves. When unskilled able-bodied field hands were quoted in the market at from $1,200 to $1,800 per head, as they occasionally were, between 1835 and 1860, they were too dear for economic employment in any but the most profitable tasks and those affording the least risk of disease and accident. The employment of slave labor in factory work was relatively slight, partly because negro aptitudes were not well suited for it, and partly because their labor at the market rates usually prevailing for slaves was too dear for the purpose.

The plantation slave-labor regime, by force of circumstances which they could not control, involved the planters in a severe competition with one another in the purchase of labor and in the sale of crops. This competition carried the price of labor so high and the price of the staples so low that there tended to be no margin of real profits for any but the greatest and most efficient planters. Usually scarcely one-fourth of the Southern white population belonged to slaveholding families; and in 1860 the number of persons owing ten slaves or more was returned at 107,957 in a total white population in the Southern states of 8,099,760 souls. In the slaveholding communities, accordingly, the advantages of the slave-labor system were confined to the negroes themselves and to a small proportion of the whites. And those whom it did not benefit, it in many cases positively injured. By reason of its lower standard of comfort and the ability of its employers to tide over crises, slave labor tended, like penitentiary labor does, to drive away the competition of free labor and restrict its opportunity. The deprivation of opportunity from free laborers was a vice of the regime to which its capitalistic absorption of earnings alone is comparable. Slave labor was, therefore, on the whole, productive but less profitable to the communities employing it than to the outside world.

[2] See "Financial Crises in the Antebellum South," on page 145 of this volume.

BIBLIOGRAPHY.—Cairnes, J. E.: *The Slave Power* (London, 1863, 2d ed. enl., London, 1863); DeBow, J. D. B. (ed.): *The Industrial Resources, etc., of the Southern and Western States* (New Orleans, 1852–53); Fitzhugh, George: *Sociology for the South, or the Failure of Free Society* (Richmond, 1854); Goodloe, D. R.: *Inquiry Into the Causes Which Have Retarded the Accumulation of Wealth and Increase of Population in the Southern States* (Washington, 1846); Helper, H. R.: *The Impending Crisis of the South* (New York, 1857); Loria, Achille: *La Constitutione Economical Odierno* (Turin, 1899); Olmsted, F. L.: *A Journey in the Seaboard Slave States* (New york, 1856); Phillips, Ulrich B. (ed.): *Plantation and Frontier Documents* (Cleveland, Ohio, 1909); "The Economic Cost of Slaveholding in the Cotton Belt" (in the *Political Science Quarterly*, 1905); "The Slave Labor Problem in the Charlestown District" (in *ibid.*, 1907); *The Pro-Slavery Argument* (Charlestown, 1852); Weston, G. M.: *The Progress of Slavery in the United States* (Washington, 1857).

9

The Economics of the Slave
Trade, Foreign and Domestic*

A DIFFERENCE between serfdom and slavery is that in the former there is no regular agency for the distribution of labor, while in the latter there is necessarily a system of labor exchange. Serfdom was a mediaeval institution for controlling labor in a society almost devoid of money and desirous of checking its own retrogression in the arts and comforts of life. The American slave-labor regime was developed, under a money ecconomy, to enable European settlers and capitalists to exploit American resources with the aid of African labor. Any fixing of laborers to the soil as in serfdom, would have hindered the purpose in America. Success in the early task of conquering the wilderness and developing the varied opportunities required that those who controlled labor should be able to carry it from district to district, change it from occupation to occupation, and transfer it at will to fresh employers. Accordingly, in the colonial regime, which was inherited and further elaborated by the antebellum South, the laboring force was organized for quick response to either the regional or occupational call of industrial opportunity. By reason of the slave-labor system the expansion of settlement in the South was actually far more rapid than in the North; and the development of new industries for which the regime was suited, cotton and sugar production, for example, was accomplished with great speed. This mobility of labor was secured in part by the migration

* *The South in the Building of the Nation* (13 vols.; Richmond, 1909–13), V, 124–29.

of planters and their shifting the employment of their slaves from staple to staple or from agriculture to handicrafts as the case might be. In very considerable part also it was attained through the services of the slave trade.

The slave market was in a sense the prototype of the more modern employment bureau, but its operations and their economic bearings were considerably more intricate. The earnings of the slave traders were sometimes in the form of commissions, but usually in the form of profits. In the foreign branch of the trade the expenses of transportation and sustenance were heavy and the risk of loss considerable, but the first cost of the slave cargoes in Africa was so slight (ranging from a string of beads to a hundred gallons of rum per head), that in general there was a fairly steady opportunity for very substantial profits. The price of prime youths from Africa rose by gradual stages from about £15 sterling per head in 1660 to about £50 in 1770, and thence to about $500 in 1807. In the Spanish, French, and Portuguese colonies the prices were similar, and the volume of the trans-Atlantic trade was enormous.[1] In the domestic trade the expenses were lighter and the transactions were more rapidly completed, but the difference between prices in the slave-selling and the slave-buying areas fluctuated so actively that at times the margin of profit upon which the trader had counted was completely wiped out before the completion of his southwestern journey, and he had to sell at a sacrifice or march his coffle back to Virginia. Furthermore, the volume of the interstate traffic was probably far smaller than that of the foreign slave trade in its heyday. On the whole, numerous traders accumulated fortunes in the business, the larger number of them by far, it would seem, in the foreign branch.

A significant news item is the following, written by a correspondent at Charleston, South Carolina, and published in the Boston *Chronicle*, March 27, 1769: "A calculation having been made of the amount of purchase money of slaves expected here the present year, it is computed at £270,000 sterling, which sum

[1] For this see *The South in the Building of the Nation*, IV, 211, 223.

will by that means be drained off from this province." Every importation from any distant quarter, whether Africa, Connecticut, or Virginia, involved an exportation from the community concerned of money or produce or the incurring of debt, to the amount of the slaves' market value. It tended also to put the community upon the slave-labor basis and to discourage the immigration of wage-earning whites. Instead of being able to hire laborers of assorted talents at reasonable wages to be paid from current earnings, the community became almost utterly dependent upon crude labor bought for lifetime and paid for from permanent capital at a capitalized, fluctuating, and oftentimes inordinate, valuation. The prevalence of banking and commercial credits, with their liability to recurrent expansion and contraction, tended to increase the frequency and degree of slave-price fluctuations and to increase the evils of using capitalized labor in competitive industry.

The range of slave prices at various times and places in the antebellum South may be gathered from the accompanying table, which has been made after extensive research by the present writer

AVERAGE PRICES OF PRIME FIELD HANDS

(Young slave men, able-bodied but unskilled)

	1800	1808	1813	1818	1828	1837	1843	1848	1853	1856	1860
	$	$	$	$	$	$	$	$	$	$	$
Washington, Richmond, and Norfolk	350	500	400	700	.....	900	.....	.....	1,250	1,300	.....
Charleston, S. C.	500	550	450	850	450	1,200	500	700	900	.....	1,200
Louisville, Ky.	400	.....	550	800	500	1,200	.....	.....	.....	1,000	1,400
Middle Georgia	450	650	450	1,000	700	1,300	600	900	1,200	.....	1,800
Montgomery, Ala.	.....	.....	.....	800	600	1,200	650	800	.....	.....	1,600
New Orleans, La.	500	600	.....	1,000	700	1,300	600	900	1,250	1,500	1,800

among the archives in the vicinities indicated. The prices given in the table are average prices of "prime field hands," or able-bodied young male slaves of no special training. The averages are only approximate; but they are sufficiently positive to demonstrate, among other things, that the differences in slave prices from period to period were much wider than those at different places in the same year. That is to say, the regime not only gave opportunities for slave trading from region to region, but it promoted speculation in slaves by planters as well as by slave traders. It, in fact, involved most owners of slaves, willy nilly, in a more or less speculative commerce in slave property. One serious limitation of the general system in this connection was that it could not normally supply labor for short periods. Its commodity was lifetime labor, and its units were not easily divisible. Many slaves, it is true, were hired out by their owners, but the necessity of red-tape to provide for the liability of lessor or lessee in case of the death, flight, or incapacity of the slaves during the term of lease hampered such recourse. The extensive hiring of slaves which actually prevailed was a demonstration of the slave trade's limitations as a labor distribution agency. Employers with large capital, it is true, might buy slaves with a view to their temporary employment and their sale at the end of it. But in view of the oscillations in slave prices, the slave-trading risks assumed in such cases would dwarf the industrial earnings. The regime put a premium upon permanence and steadiness of employment. At the same time, it put a premium upon the readiness of masters to sell slaves whenever their market value was greater than the prospective industrial value of their labor. The stigma which society put upon slave trading appears in the light of this to have been uneconomic; but the conservatism which it promoted tended to mitigate the fevers of slave speculation.

Among the positive economic effects of the domestic branch of the slave trade were the following: It made a passive laboring population extremely mobile, and carried the negroes into the districts where since the abolition of slavery they have sluggishly remained. The current of the trade flowed southwestward and westward from Virginia and the Carolinas.[2] It transferred many slaves to severer task masters, and many to masters who could and did provide them with better food, clothing and shelter—that is, it increased the vigor and efficiency of slave labor. It drained earnings out of the developing districts for the benefit of the older com-

[2] For the volume of the domestic trade see *The South in the Building of the Nation*, IV, 219-223.

munities where industry was decadent, and thereby made it to the interest of the border states to maintain the institution of slavery. On the whole the slave trade was inseparably a part of the slave-labor regime as it actually prevailed, and the problems of the economic value and vice of the slave trade cannot be divorced from the economic problem of slavery in general nor from the question whether the negroes were fit for industrial and legal freedom in the American community.

BIBLIOGRAPHY.—Ball, Charles: *Narrative of Life and Adventures* (Philadelphia, 1854); Ballagh, J. C.: *A History of Slavery in Virginia* (Baltimore, 1902); Blake, W. O.: *History of Slavery and the Slave Trade* (Columbus, Ohio, 1858); Buxton, T. F.: *The African Slave Trade and its Remedy* (London, 1840); Carey, H. C.: *The Slave Trade, Domestic and Foreign* (Philadelphia, 1856); Chambers, William: *Things as they are in America* (London, 1854); Collins, W. H.: *The Domestic Slave-Trade of the Southern States* (New York, 1894); DeBow, J. D. B. (ed.): *The Industrial Resources, etc., of the Southern and Western States* (New Orleans, 1852-53); DuBois, W. E. B.: *The Suppression of the African Slave-Trade to the United States* (New York, 1896); Phillips, Ulrich B. (ed.): *Plantation and Frontier Documents* (Cleveland, Ohio, 1909).

10

Financial Crises in the Antebellum South

S PARSELY settled agricultural communities usually tend to be out of touch with money markets and to be undisturbed by crises, because their industry is usually democratic and their employment of capital and credit slight.* But in the antebellum South, or at least in the plantation districts which largely determined financial conditions for the whole South, the reverse was the case. Relatively little capital, it is true, was invested in buildings, drainage, and machinery; but the investment in land was large, and, more notably, the ownership of labor itself in the slavery regime involved the use of very great amounts of capital and very extensive dependence upon credit. When to these considerations it is added that industry was devoted to the production of staples, mainly cotton, in which the crops and prices were subject to wide and frequent fluctuations, the factors begin to appear which made the antebellum South one of the most sensitive of all modern communities to the movements of money and credit.

Slave labor "possessed the power of labor and the mobility of capital." It was to be had by the highest bidder, no matter how remote his plantation; and a heightened valuation of slave labor by any group of substantial employers who wished to increase the scale of their plantations would force a heightened valuation on the part of all of their effective competitors and a heightened capitalization of slave-labor industry in general. When credit was

* *The South in the Building of the Nation* (13 vols.; Richmond, 1909–13), V, 435–41.

easy and prospects promising, thousands of planters would be eager to buy slaves, and their continued competition in the market would force up slave prices by successive stages until the straining of credit or the decline of agricultural prospects checked the progress. Meanwhile the cotton-belt planters would have been sending great remittances both northward and eastward, through the slave traders, and abstaining from appyling their earnings to any tangible forms of investment save bare lands and slaves. The process here indicated was at times moderate in volume; at other times it waxed into a veritable speculative mania, a "negro fever" as it was called, and was usually accompanied by a rage for speculation in lands as well. Floods of paper money and public credit offered to private borrowers by populistic governments often intensified the speculation and aided in carrying land and slave prices to irrationally high levels. Every bubble, of course, must burst. Usually the immediate occasion for a financial reaction in the South was a contraction of credits in London or New York. If this affected credits only and not commodity prices in which the South was concerned, the Southern reaction would be moderate. But if it caused, or was by any chance accompanied by, a considerable fall in cotton prices, woe to the plantation community. The blight upon the prospects of planters' earnings would prompt creditors to force the settlement of accounts. Simultaneous attempts by hundreds of planters to sell part of their lands and slaves in order to pay their debts and save the rest, would cause a rapid decline of land and slave prices. If the worst came to worst, no planter had "quick assets," and property was liable to severe sacrifice under the sheriff's hammer. Stay-laws and paper money, though often tried, were nearly always futile in checking the disaster; the panic must run its course. At its end, much property would have changed hands, and the valuation of lands and slaves would have been substantially diminished. Within a twelvemonth or two afterward, however, the same process as before would have begun again, of planters increasing the size of their gangs by buying slaves, first for cash and then more of them on credit. Prices of land and slaves would rise, at first slowly, then faster, and then with speculative acceleration, until another furor of speculation would be upon the community.

The chronology of the antebellum South, like that of every other modern capitalistic community, is filled with a succession of industrial expansions and contractions, reflected in the money market by alternating inflations and panics. The prosperity near the end of the colonial period was succeeded by severe depression during the war for independence, and this depression was prolonged by the ruin of the indigo industry which the arrival of peace revealed. Washington, for example, intimated in 1794 that he thought slave property had poor prospects of profits in the coming years. The invention of the cotton gin, however, altogether changed the outlook, and the first decade of the nineteenth century saw flush times in the slaveholding communities. These were ended by the War of 1812 but renewed promptly on a greater scale upon the arrival of peace and unhampered trade in 1815. A mania for land and slave speculation ensuing, focusing in the Alabama–Mississippi region, was punished by the panic of 1819, and the decade of the twenties was taken up with a series of similar oscillations on a smaller scale. Peter Baugh, of Talbotton, Georgia, afterward wrote of his own experiences as typical in this period. In one of the boom years about 1820, he bought for $5,000 a tract of land five times as large as he needed for cultivation, bought or hired hands to work it who failed to earn their hire, and borrowed money at 16 per cent to pay for provisions to feed his expensive laborers. In 1824 he was forced to close out. His land sold for $1,600; a slave for whom he had previously refused an offer of $1,100 brought $480. After realizing on all his assets, Baugh says he started life anew with a debt of $1,000. The early thirties brought an accelerating wave of speculation, culminating in 1837 with average field hands bringing the unheard of price of $1,300, lands high in proportion, credit universally relied on and dealt in on a huge scale by a multitude of flimsy banks. The world-wide panic of 1837 brought acute distress in the South, as elsewhere, but its ruinous force in the cotton belt was partly checked by the relative firmness and early recuperation of cotton prices, and partly postponed by virtue of the fact that the several state governments, in the southwest particularly, having loaned the public credit on a prodigious scale, were the chief creditors of their own citizens and were less urgent in pressing for settlement than private creditors would have been.

But this postponement of the day of reckoning only made it the more severe when it came at last in 1839–40. Meanwhile a widely advertised bull movement in the cotton market in 1838–39, led by Nicholas Biddle and his bank at Philadelphia, diverted cotton-belt attention from slaves to cotton for commodity speculation. A great chain of Southern banks in the spring of 1839 offered loans freely on cotton to the extent of about fourteen cents per pound, and loaned enormous sums on that basis to planters who wished to keep their crop off the market. The maximum price of middling cotton at New York in these months was fifteen or sixteen cents. In the summer prices sagged; in September they went below fourteen cents; and they continued relentlessly to decline until in April, 1840, middling was at seven and eight cents. Then after a slight improvement, the downward course was resumed until the spring and summer of 1842 when middling was steadily between six and seven cents at New York, and about two cents below these prices in the interior of the cotton belt. The market was a little more satisfactory during the crop years of 1842–43 and 1843–44, but throughout the autumn of 1844 it ranged below even the record low prices of 1842. With the spring of 1845, at last, a steady advance was begun which carried the price above twelve cents in 1846. Then for the first time did the country substantially recuperate. The panic in the autumn of 1839 had carried cotton below the value at which great quantities of it had been pledged for loans. When the time of settlement came, the planter had to make good the deficit or go bankrupt, and in the latter case the bank which had made the loan would have to assume the loss. Slave and land prices fell in sympathy with cotton prices; and throughout the half-decade duration of the hard times it was almost impossible to settle any considerable debt without excessive loss in the process. Dozens of banks and thousands of planters were absolutely bankrupted, and even some of the state governments were driven to repudiate their bonds. The focus of the distress was in the Mississippi bottoms and adjacent districts, as usual. Among the descriptions of the state of affairs extant is the following, written by W.

H. Wills of North Carolina in a diary of a trip through Mississippi in 1840, published in the Southern History Association *Publications*, VIII, 35:

I find through this country some of the finest lands I have ever seen and calculated to yield as much as any lands in the United States. But alas! to such conditions are the people reduced in money affairs.— Speculation, speculation, has been making poor men rich and rich men princes; men of no capital, in three years have become wealthy, and those of some have grown to hundreds of thousands. But as great as are the resources of Miss.; and as valuable as are her lands, yet there were limits to both and these limits have been passed, lost sight of and forgotten as things having no existence. A revulsion has taken place, Miss. is ruined, her rich men are poor and her poor men beggars. Millions on millions have been speculated on and gambled away by banking, by luxury, and too much prosperity, until of all the States in the Union she has become much the worst. We have seen hard times in North Carolina; hard times in the east, hard times everywhere, but Miss. exceeds them all. Some of the finest lands in Madison and Hinds Counties may now be had for comparatively nothing. Those that once commanded from thirty to fifty dollars per acre may now be bought for three or five dollars and that with considerable improvements, while many have been sold at sheffs. Sales at fifty cents that were considered worth ten to Twenty dolls. The people too are running their negroes to Texas & to Alabama, and leaving their real est. & perishable property to be sold or rather sacrificed. In the community where I am, it may probably be said that *not one man in fifty* are solvent and probably less a number than this, but what are more or less involved. So great is the panic and so dreadful the distress that there are a great many farms prepared to receive Crops & some of them actually planted, and yet deserted, not a human being to be found upon them. I had prepared myself to see hard times here, but unlike most Cases, the actual condition of affairs is much worse than the report.

The crisis of 1839–44 was the last painful stringency in the experience of the antebellum South. Cotton prices were maintained so steadily at the prosperous level of from ten to twelve cents during the whole decade of the fifties that even the panic of 1857 failed to bring a severe convulsion. Nevertheless, during that decade speculation in slaves again waxed so strong and carried slave prices so high at its end that a severe financial crisis could not have been far off, had the great war of secession not intervened with its own overwhelming one.

Every community dependent upon capitalistic industry experiences much the same succession of ups and downs. It is the price which, with the world's present imperfect adjustments, must be paid for the benefits of capital. But the antebellum plantation communities, it must be said, gained less solid advantages in their prosperous periods and lost more in their periods of adversity than do normally constituted capitalistic communities employing free labor. In American panics Wall Street may export to Lombard Street the stocks and bonds which have fallen abnormally low in the American market, and thereby relieve itself of part of its stress; but the cotton belt in crises could not re-export the slaves which it had bought in flush times. The regime, which the individual slaveholders were practically as powerless as the slaves to remodel, impelled the investment of earnings in prosperous times in low-grade laborers at high prices; and it intensified the loss from panics because of its lack of fluid securities.

BIBLIOGRAPHY.—Baldwin, J. G.: *The Flush Times of Alabama and Mississippi* (New York, 1853); Callender, G. S.: "The Early Transportation and Banking Enterprises of the States in Relation to the Growth of Corporations" (in *Quarterly Journal of Economics*, XVII, 111–62); Catterall, R. C. H.: *The Second Bank of the United States* (Chicago, 1903); Debouchel, V.: *Histoire de la Louisiane* (New Orleans, 1841); Dewey, D. R.: *Financial History of the United States* (New York, 1903); Donnell, E. J.: *Chronological and Statistical History of Cotton* (New York, 1872); Emerick, C. F.: "The Credit System and the Public Domain" (in *Vanderbilt Southern History Publications*, No. 3, Nashville, 1899); Niles, H. (ed.): *The Weekly Register* (Baltimore, 1811–49); Sumner, W. G.: *A History of Banking in all the Leading Nations* (Vol. I, New York, 1896); Wills, W. H.: "Diary" (in *Publications of the Southern History Association*, VII and VIII, Washington, 1903, 1904).

PART THREE

Industrial
and Urban Problems

11

Transportation in the Antebellum South:
An Economic Analysis

EVER since the resort to tobacco culture at Jamestown and
to rice in Carolina, the South has been mainly a group of
staple-producing areas, requiring means of exporting their
products and seeking the greater part of their miscellaneous supplies from beyond their own limits.* The principal transportation
problem has always been that of sending the staples to markets
abroad, and obtaining food supplies and manufactures whenceso-
ever they might best be secured. The specific problems differed
somewhat in the various localities and periods, and certain other
considerations had at times some degree of importance; but the
predominating and fundamental purpose remained ever the same.
Feeling little desire to possess a carrying trade, and leaving to outside agents the external commerce between its own ports and the
rest of the world, the South was chiefly concerned in developing a
system of internal transportation and commerce, by providing
communication between the several staple areas and their gate-
ways.

When fully developed in its staple system of the antebellum
period, the South comprised the following great economic provinces, more or less distinguished by their staples and their natural
facilities for transportation:

1. Lowland and Piedmont Virginia, a tobacco region, gradually
encroached upon by the cereals. The transportation problem was
simply that of getting products to the navigable rivers and the

* *Quarterly Journal of Economics*, XIX (May, 1905), 434–51.

great Chesapeake. Most of Maryland was an annex to this province, and the Albemarle district in North Carolina was a sub-province tributary to it.

2. The Charleston-Savannah coast district, with a multitude of shallow waterways to transport the crops of rice and sea-island cotton to the deep-water harbors at Charleston, Beaufort, Savannah, and Brunswick. This alluvial area was fertile and prosperous from early times; but its people were not content with their narrow bounds, and sought energetically in the later period a means to overthrow the obstacle of the pine-barrens which shut them in.

3. The Eastern cotton belt, stretching from the southern edge of Virginia to central Alabama. This province was mainly confined to the Piedmont region, a country of many hills and rapid streams. Its outer edge could be reached by navigation upon a few of the larger rivers, but easy natural means of transportation within the belt itself were wholly lacking. The problem was to send cotton to the coast and to get supplies from across the pine-barrens, on the one hand, or the mountains, on the other. The first system was that of using as main stems the rivers which crossed the barrens, and supplementing them with a network of country roads radiating from the heads of navigation. As regards intercourse with the Northwest, the resort was either to caravans across the mountains or to the circuitous water route of the Mississippi, the Gulf, the Atlantic, and the Carolina and Georgia rivers. The eastern cotton belt confronted by far the most difficult transportation problem in the South; and not only the local planters, but all the world of commerce, were much concerned in its solution.

4. The Western cotton belt, reaching from Alabama to Texas and sweeping as far north along the Mississippi bottoms as the southern edge of Kentucky, was quite similar to the eastern belt in its all-important product of short-staple cotton; but it was in contrast in point of transportation advantages, for its great reaches of navigable stream extended to nearly every district where the best cotton lands were located. The planters had only to haul their cotton to the river, tumble it over the cliff, and let it await the coming of a boat bound for Mobile or New Orleans. The building of artificial avenues was a later and less pressing need than in the

eastern cotton belt. The sugar district of southern Louisiana was a part of this province.

5. The region of Kentucky and middle Tennessee, with its products of tobacco, livestock, and grain, had a water outlet by way of the Ohio or the Cumberland and the Mississippi to New Orleans; but it needed an equipment of direct routes to the Atlantic seaboard and to the eastern cotton belt, as well as a local system to supplement the rivers.

6. The Tennessee-Shenandoah range of connecting valleys, with their fertile limestone soil, producing much the same commodities as the great basin to the northwest, but deprived of their natural advantage of vicinity to the staple belts by the forbidding Blue Ridge, until at length, after many plans and efforts, the mountains were pierced, and a system of railways brought the great wave of prosperity which had so long been awaited.

7. The peninsula of Florida, afflicted with a barren soil, and leading nowhither, is negligible as a part of the economic South. It it is more to be noted, perhaps, as an obstacle in the coasting trade than as an economic province.

These several provinces in some cases shaded into one another; but, as a rule, they were separated by pronounced obstacles, among which the most important were the belt of pine-barrens, and the Blue Ridge and the Cumberland Mountains. The pine-barrens were a stretch of sandy, infertile, pine-grown country, intervening between the coast and the cotton belt throughout most of the latter's extent. The population in the barrens was sparse and self-sufficing, producing no staple for export, and making little effective demand for articles from without. The transportation problem was not that of putting the region itself into communication with the rest of the world, but that of crossing the barrier and connecting the coast with the inland cotton areas. The obvious method in the railway period was to build a single trunk line from each seaport across the barrens, and then to lay out a system of radiating lines in the cotton belt which would gather freight and serve as feeders to the main stem. With the completion of the main stem, remunerative business began, and the extension of the road was then a matter of comparative ease.

The Blue Ridge and Cumberland mountains, running in great parallel ridges from Pennsylvania to Alabama, sharply divided off the economic provinces in their neighborhood. The flanks of these ranges were turned by the Potomac and Tennessee rivers; but the one was hardly navigable at all in the uplands, and the other was broken in two by the great obstruction at the Muscle Shoals in northern Alabama. And, even if these rivers had been more easily navigable, they would still have been inadequate to meet the needs of the situation, for their courses lay in the wrong directions. What was most needed were direct routes connecting the grain and live stock producing intramontane valleys, and the Ohio basin beyond, with the cotton belt which consumed much of this product of grain and livestock. And no one was content until that direct communication was at length established by the building of south–east and north–west railway systems.

In other regions where there were no such conspicuous barriers the factor of mere distance was of considerable importance in causing and directing a demand for transportation facilities. Social, political, and military needs, as well as economic considerations, required that these facilities, wherever established, should be of the greatest efficiency feasible.

The lay of the land directed the currents of transportation and commerce; for those currents, of course, followed the lines of least resistance. The provinces of the South demanded intercourse with one another, with England, Europe, and the West Indies, with Pennsylvania, New York, and New England, and with the great American Northwest. The particular channels through which the volume of commerce should flow were chosen and developed by the activity of the people under the general conditions of their environment. There was in some instances a choice of routes, but in no case was the range of alternatives a wide one. Physical geography was imperative in dictating the routes; and, even after nature had apparently been conquered by the steam railway, it still continued to play pranks with the fortunes of the cities along the routes. More was needed than a railroad and the survey of town lots before a city would arise. And the land-lookers were frequently at fault in their efforts to found commercial cities.

The strategic points, or centres of trade, as finally developed, had always two features in common: (1) access to the outside world; (2) a tributary area around or behind them. These trade centres in the South were of several classes. First, of course, there was an equipment of seaports. There were Baltimore, Norfolk, Wilmington, Charleston, Savannah, Mobile, and New Orleans, and potentially Galveston, in the first rank, each with an adequate harbor, and each with an important hinterland. Inferior to these were Beaufort, North Carolina, Beaufort, South Carolina, Brunswick, Georgia, St. Augustine and Pensacola, Florida, Bay St. Louis, Mississippi, which possessed good harbors, but were cut off from the great hinterland by the unrelieved pine barrens; and another group, comprising Georgetown, South Carolina, Darien, Georgia, and Appalachicola, Florida, which possessed a river communication with the interior, but lacked harbor facilities.

In the interior the principal group of trade centres, in the older parts of the South at least, were those located at the head of navigation, or "fall line," on the larger rivers. To these points the planters and farmers brought their output for shipment, and there they procured their varied supplies. If the boats which carried the freight down stream could return against the current, they would fetch cargoes of manufactures, groceries, and salt to the merchants of the fall-line towns. And even if the river craft could not ascend the stream—and this was generally the case before the days of steamboats—the goods would be brought by pack train or by wagon to the point whence the staples had been shipped. It was a great convenience to the producer to be able to sell his crop and buy his goods in the same market. Thus the towns at the heads of navigation grew into marked importance as collecting points for produce and distributing points for supplies of all sorts. Some of the great planters, it is true, gave their business to factors at the seaports or even in England; but that practice was customary only among those planters who lived below the fall line. For the upland producers, before the coming of railroads, the transit of produce to the coast had to be broken at the nearest point where the freight could be transferred from wagon to boat; and this was generally at the head of the river navigation. These points where the rivers crossed the fall line were therefore strategic points which had access to the sea, and had each a productive tributary area: the growth of commercial towns there was inevitable. On the Atlantic slope the fall-line towns were Alexandria, Fredericksburg, Richmond, Petersburg, Fayetteville, Columbia, Augusta, Milledgeville, and Macon. On the rivers that flow to the Gulf were Columbus, Montgomery, Shreveport, Nashville, and Knoxville.

In the case of mighty rivers flowing in their navigable course not only from, but through fertile districts, there was occasion for subsidiary towns along their courses. Where no one spot upon the river bank had any distinct advantage over any other, as, for example, on the Tombigbee, the tendency was hostile to towns. But upon the Mississippi and its branches the physiographic conditions favored Natchez, Vicksburg, Memphis, Louisville, and St. Louis in their commercial growth even more than if they had been at the fall lines of smaller streams.

A fourth group of towns owed their origin to the penetration of the mountain barriers, and owed their growth to the development of the direct trade in food supplies. Thus by the building of railroads Atlanta became the gateway to the eastern cotton belt from the Northwest, and Chattanooga sprang up at an important crossing of the routes, and the trade of Nashville and Knoxville and Louisville and Cincinnati was much increased.

Aside from physiography there were certain features of social economics which strongly influenced the development of transportation and commerce. 1. Population in the South was widely scattered, and nowhere in compact masses. Passenger traffic must therefore be relatively light. 2. In each great economic province nearly every locality was issuing the same sort of output; and there was little interchange of products between neighboring districts. No traffic of volume between way stations might therefore be expected. 3. But the demand for transportation of staples outward and supplies inward was urgent, and offered opportunities for profit to common carriers. The principal staples, however, were relatively light and precious, the producers had their teams at leisure in marketing season, and the rivers always kept flowing to the sea. That is to say, the planters could, if need arose, assert their independence of even the railroads, and thus could always keep the freight rates within bounds. 4. Another awkward feature for the common carrier was the great rush of business in the marketing season and the lean months following in spring and summer. On the cotton railroads the whole year's profits had to be gained practically between September and January.

And there were still greater difficulties, affecting the building as well as the operation of canals, railroads, etc. 5. The institution of slavery involved the investment of wealth in slave labor, and tended strongly against the presence of floating capital. The slave trade, whether domestic or foreign, drained capital out of the districts where it had been earned, and tended to make all the people debtors seeking money to borrow instead of capitalists seeking openings for investment. 6. The universal inclination towards agriculture diminished the available supply of native white labor for any other purpose; the presence of negroes and slavery reduced the number of European immigrants; and the plantation form of organization for staple production almost completely monopolized the supply of negro laborers. There was thus a singular dearth of floating labor—a dearth which discouraged, crippled, or ruined many undertakings. 7. The plantation system, dominating the whole industrial life of the South, attracted nearly all the men of capacity into agricultural management, and caused a shortage of efficient promoters and managers in other industries. Many of the men who were active in plans of river improvement, railway building, and the like, had more enthusiasm than judgment, while men of greater wisdom and poise often contented themselves with merely stating their opinions, and refrained from active part in the battle of ideas. More than one bubble was blown in spite of the moderate remonstrance of the conservative planters, and more than one bubble burst as they had said it would burst. 8. Individualism and conservatism prevailed in the South to a marked degree, and operated against joint undertakings and new enterprises. Many a project failed on this account, and those which succeeded had in every case to earn their victory.

As might have been expected, when such were the conditions, the initiative came mostly from the cities, and the cities furnished the greater part of the capital employed.

In methods of transportation there was, of course, greater development in the civilized world during the first half of the nineteenth century than in any other period. Experiments were made in the South with nearly or quite all of the transportation devices which were being discussed and applied in the Northern states and Europe. Some of these methods were wholly unsuccessful when used to meet the Southern conditions; some of them were successful for certain localities, but failed in others. The general system, as it came to be developed in the South at large, was, of course, made up of heterogeneous parts, working together with more or less efficiency for the common end.

There was first, of course, the ocean highway, which needs no discussion here, except perhaps a jotting that the resort to ocean steamships after about 1820 freed the traffic from dependence upon currents of wind and water, and enabled mariners to use the shortest transatlantic route, thereby building up the northern ports at the expense of those of the South. Closely akin was the navigation of inlets and sounds and such so-called rivers as the Potomac and the James in their lower courses, and the bayous of Louisiana, in which there was no appreciable current. Here the possession merely of primitive boats would make the planter independent of costly mechanism. On the more rapid streams there was usually a long navigable stretch, which accommodated descending freight; but these rivers had to be supplemented by roads to serve the returning voyagers. Even in the Piedmont country the rivers could be used in flood season to transport small boats with light cargoes, but, of course, could not be used at all for the upward journey. The introduction of steamboats provided the means for the upward navigation as far as the fall line, but they hardly affected the river problem within the Piedmont.

Across country and away from the streams, recourse was first had to buffalo paths and Indian trails, and then to roads which were cleared to permit the wagon traffic. Then came the need of ferries, causeways, and bridges, and the resort to the toll system or to public ownership.

The rapid increase of settlement in the uplands in the later eighteenth, and especially its rapid growth in importance in the early nineteenth century, brought a demand for something more than local roads with county officials in charge. And yet that demand, so far as the planters and farmers were concerned, was often more apparent than real. Canals were projected in many regions, and in some cases were actually built; but in general they were found to be unsuited to the physical conditions, except for certain concrete cases in special localities. The rivers in the South flow mostly in deep valleys or even gorges, which furnish many obstacles to the building of canals along or across their courses, while the very heavy and irregular rainfall and the frequency of freshets and floods, especially after the extensive clearing away of the Piedmont forests, caused great danger of destruction of works, and exerted a deterring influence when canals were considered. Furthermore, the soil in some places was so porous that the water would seep through and leave a canal bed dry; and in other places there was so much rock that canal digging was too costly. Canals, on the whole, were clearly not the solution of the problem, except for such special localities as, for example, that of the Dismal Swamp.

Efforts were made at systems of turnpike roads, and in Kentucky and Tennessee they were built with considerable success. But in the cotton belt the case was peculiar, and hostile to the prosperity of a toll system. The cotton producers harvested and marketed their cotton in the fall and winter season, when there was little other work demanding attention with men or mules or wagons. The crop was precious enough, though somewhat bulky, to justify its transportation for even long distances by wagon, even on bad roads. In fact, with the journey once begun, it did not matter particularly—since it was the leisure season on the farm—whether the team returned from market in three days or three weeks. Therefore, paved roads which quickened speed were, in the eyes of the cotton producers, who were their own carriers, a smaller consideration than the tolls which must be charged upon them. It is not surprising, therefore, that when a system of turnpikes was built in South Carolina in the twenties, it was permitted by the planters to fall into absolute neglect and decay. Plank roads were the subject of experiment in Alabama in the forties, with the same lack of success as the Carolina turnpikes had had.

Realizing the insufficiency of all these earlier inventions to the needs of their case, those who were looking to the final solution of the general problem were satisfied with nothing short of railroads. Railroads with steam locomotion, when once invented, were speedily recognized as dwarfing in importance all that had gone before; and nowhere was their acceptance more eager than in the staple regions of the South. The press and the people in the later twenties and the thirties were all agog with the new invention, which, it was thought, would carry cotton to the coast for a song, and bring groceries and manufactures and the mail, and perhaps immigrants, with marvellous speed and cheapness. The building of a system of railways was a far more costly and difficult undertaking than the early projectors had imagined; yet the building of that system did actually bring the solution of the Southern problem of transportation, and the story of its progress and its work is a most important part of the economic history of the South in the later antebellum period. But with railroads in contemplation, the pressing question became one of finance.

In early times there had been a general reliance upon individual enterprise for transportation, whether by boat, pack train, wagon, or stage. But private means were not adequate to the later and larger problems. There had been stage lines and canals and turnpikes established by private stock companies, and the device of joint stocks was now relied upon in large part for railway building. But capital was scarce and timid, and though in some cases the hope of profit, together with patriotism for the South in its race with the North for population and wealth, led to the enlistment of considerable sums from private sources, public activity of some sort was generally an essential requirement for success. The federal government had a practice of building federal roads to and through the territories; and when Gallatin was Secretary of the Treasury he had planned a system of transportation to be built by the federal government throughout the whole country. But in the succeeding decades the hope of federal railroads practically vanished. And the South, being mainly a stronghold of strict construction, furnished little advocacy of such a system. The idea of state ownership was more popular; but there were many individualists who opposed it on principle, and many others opposed particular propositions of that sort because they objected to the levying of taxes upon their own localities for the building of roads which would not reach their own districts. In fact, the agitation for state railroads was not successful except in special instances. In general, the sentiment of individualism was too strong.

For most of the railroads for which the demand was efficient, the resources were these: a number of individuals were willing to invest a portion of their fortunes in the enterprises; the state governments were friendly and anxious to facilitate the projects; the states could do this by granting charters giving permission to build, by subscribing to stock with state funds, and by granting special money-making privileges, such as banking and issuing bank-notes;[1] capitalists at the North or abroad were willing to aid Southern railway projects indirectly by the purchase of state bonds, and later, when some of the roads had proven financially successful, they even subscribed directly for railroad stock; and, last in this enumeration, but not least in practical effect, the city governments in the South were among the parties most keenly interested in the building of transportation lines which would increase and extend the commerce of their own cities.

In the actual progress of road, canal, and railway building these several resources were utilized in varying combinations. In South Carolina, for example, the state subscribed for stock on an equal footing with other shareholders; in Tennessee the state pledged itself to provide funds to pay for rails when enough other subscriptions had been secured to build the road-beds; in Georgia the state

[1] The issuing of lottery privileges had gone out of fashion. Some of the newer states held in trust a fund from the United States derived from the sale of public lands, to be devoted to the improvement of transportation. In 1837 all of the states received a windfall in the distribution of surplus revenue; and this was used in many instances as an additional resource for internal improvements.

made no subscriptions to the stock of the company roads, but pledged a great assistance to them in the building of a railway at state expense to connect their termini with the Tennessee River and the projected railways beyond; some of the shorter lines were built entirely with private capital; and at least one short road in North Carolina, begun in 1847, owed its establishment to the subscription of a Northern syndicate.

Thus, by one means or another or by a combination of several, the Southern transportation system grew. Its broad outlines only can here be indicated.

The first noteworthy enterprises of internal improvement begun in the South were the Chesapeake and Ohio and the James River and Kanawha canals, chartered in 1785, and the Dismal Swamp and the Santee canals, chartered in 1790. The two former were intended to serve not only the Virginia-Maryland uplands, but ultimately the Ohio Valley as well. The economic conditions which led to the beginning of these undertakings continued without material change for a number of years, and work on the canals, beset with financial difficulties, was slowly pushed forward, at times hopefully, at times despondently; but they were finally eclipsed by railroads, and were never completed. The Dismal Swamp Canal, intended to connect Albemarle Sound with Norfolk and the sea, was carried forward haltingly, and not completed, short as it was, until 1822. Thereafter it proved of considerable utility for several decades, until partly replaced by improved avenues. The Santee Canal was undertaken with a vim, and quickly completed by the lowland Carolinians under the lead of Charleston. Its purpose was by connecting Charleston with the Santee River to institute a direct trade between the inland foodstuff producers and the staple producers of the coast, thus affording the one a ready market and the other cheaper supplies, and fostering a greater unity in the state. The canal was soon completed; but its great number of locks hampered transit, and, the principal need of it in connection with the food supply of the lowlands having disappeared with the invention of the cotton gin and the resort to staple production in the interior, the canal was left in neglect. In the same period a number of river improvements were under way in the Carolina uplands; but the overwhelming impetus to cotton planting engrossed the attention of the people, and projects recently held to be important were completely neglected.

For twenty or thirty years after the invention of the gin, in 1793, the one great economic phenomenon in the lower South was the development of the cotton industry. Cotton prices were high, and profits on the output were phenomenal. There was a rush of people to the cotton belt, and every one was anxious to become a producer on a large scale. The result of this was a tremendous demand for negro slave labor. But the negroes must, of course, be bought and paid for, and this required the expenditure of all the money at command. People were so eager to utilize their resources to this end that they were impatient of all other suggestions. The consequence was that internal improvements were quite neglected.

But after about 1817, when the development of the western part of the cotton belt began to have effect in reducing the price of cotton and diminishing profits in the older fields, the Carolina planters began to cry out for cheaper access to market. Hence the resort to turnpikes; but the turnpikes were a demonstrated failure almost before they were built. The westward progress of the centre of cotton production continued remorselessly, and Charleston, with grief, perceived that Savannah, Mobile, and New Orleans were waxing prosperous at her own expense. Then came the authentic news of the successful operation of railroads in England. At once the city, the state, and the people combined their resources, and built their railroad from Charleston to Augusta. The purpose was partly to accommodate the planters in the interior of the state, but it was principally to divert the trade of Augusta from Savannah to Charleston, thus depriving Savannah of the natural advantage which its river had afforded. Towns and citizens in middle Georgia soon after combined in the Georgia Railroad Company to build a railway west from Augusta, which was expected to serve as an extension of the South Carolina Railroad.

Savannah now became alarmed. Enlisting the aid of the town of Macon and of many private citizens, and securing the indirect aid of the state of Georgia, a group of Savannah promoters, with the backing of the city corporation, instituted the Central of Georgia Railroad Company, and built the road to Macon. A continuation of that road to the northward of Macon was undertaken by other companies; and the state government determined to insure the success of both the Georgia and the Central of Georgia lines by building a state-owned road to the Chattanooga, expecting connections to be provided in Tennessee by other parties. The building and operation of these lines in Georgia, with others supplementing them, resulted in diminishing the cotton receipts and the commerce of Mobile and New Orleans, and spurred those cities to railroad enterprise.

All of the chief ports of the Lower South, as well as several inferior ones, were thus reaching out with railroads for the trade of the cotton belt. And, with still greater ambition, they began to strive further for the trade of the great Northwest. Baltimore, Richmond, and Norfolk, each with its special road, as well as Philadelphia and New York, were also ere this in the race for the West; and eventually all of them reached it, but with differing results. Charleston especially was disappointed in her hopes of Western traffic, for her great scheme in the later thirties for a direct road to Cincinnati fell through, and as regards Western trade the South Carolina railroad proved to be merely an annex to the Georgia system. In fact, all of the ports of the Lower South had built their hopes of Northwestern traffic much too high; for when the lines were completed, and freight began to flow southward, most of the Western commodities of course found their market in the cotton belt, and never reached the Southern seaboard. Atlanta arose, and throve upon the adversity of the ports.

Contemporaneous with this building of railroads perpendicular to the coast, another system parallel to the coast was gradually extending its length from Washington through Richmond, Raleigh, Augusta, Montgomery, and Mobile to New Orleans, and also a system connecting the Shenandoah-Tennessee valley with the Northeast, the Virginia coast, the South, and the Southwest. In addition, a moderate number of branch lines were being built from the main stems, and a few short roads were in progress in the West to supplement the rivers.

Not every project was destined to succeed, not every demand was proved to be efficient. The panic of 1837, and the long and severe depression from 1839 to 1845, killed many a flimsy railroad company as well as many a bubble bank. After that trying-out period the projects were brought to a more common-sense basis, and the less urgent and less efficient demands were relegated to the distant future.

After the main lines had been built, in large degree independently of one another, the process began of building connecting links, providing transfer facilities, and integrating the system of roads. And by 1860 every province of the South east of the Mississippi had been put in railway communication with every other province and with the outside world.

By the end of the antebellum period the South had come to be equipped with at least the skeleton of a well-planned railway system, reaching throughout nearly all of its extent and answering all the principal needs of transportation. And yet, in the larger aspect, that system was a source of weakness and a failure. Transportation is not an end in itself, but, when rightly used, is a means to the end of increasing wealth, developing resources, and strengthening society. And in the South these greater purposes were not accomplished. The building of railroads led to little else but the extension and the intensifying of the plantation system and the increase of the staple output. Specialization and commerce were extended, when just the opposite development towards diversification of products and economic self-sufficiency was the real need. In their actual effects the Southern railroads increased the competition in staple production, diminished the prices of the exports, and thus inured to a certain extent to the injury of the Southern producers, though to the benefit of the outside world.

12

Railroads in the South

I N THE two decades following the War of 1812 the opening of the Southwest for prosperous settlement by planters caused a radical shifting of the territorial balance in the South as a whole, and forced the eastern half of the South into drastic readjustment in its economic regime.* The lands of the West were fresher and very much more fertile. The soil and climate of its several zones were splendidly suited to tobacco and cotton; its districts of greatest fertility were all penetrated by great rivers giving easy though slow carriage of crops to the sea; and some of these same rivers brought cheap foodstuffs in abundance from the cereal states on the north. Farmers, planters, and slaves moved west by hundreds of thousands in these decades, until it became an acute problem in all the older seaboard states, from Maryland to Georgia, how to check the outward flow, and save their region from severe and permanent depression. Tobacco and cotton prices ranged so low from 1818 to the early thirties that profits were almost unknown in the Piedmont industry, and commerce was very slack in the adjacent seaports. Casting about for reforms, the husbandmen instituted a great improvement in tillage by the introduction of horizontal plowing and terracing on the hillsides, and some attempt was made at restoring the fertility of worn lands by marling or other fertilizing. But the most crucial economic problem facing planters, merchants, and indeed the whole community, was that of improving and cheapening transportation. The existing equipment

* *The South in the Building of the Nation* (13 vols.; Richmond, 1909–13), V, 358–67.

of dirt roads and narrow, rapid, shallow, and obstructed rivers made both the marketing of crops and the securing of supplies heavily expensive and distressingly burdensome in the competition with the more fortunate Southwest. Accordingly, the people of the Southeast were on the alert for some invention which would solve the transportation problem and bring them economic salvation. Canals and turnpikes were experimented with, but because of cost and engineering difficulties found wanting. In 1822 a patent railway was brought to Charleston for exhibition, but proved unavailable, probably from the lack of a motive power suitable to it. Finally, about 1827, came the news that railroads with steam locomotives were proving successful in England. Promptly in 1827 and 1828, respectively, companies were chartered to build railroads from Baltimore and Charleston into the interior. The Baltimore and Ohio Company was the first in America to break ground. The South Carolina Company was more prompt in its constructive work, however, and by 1833 had finished its road, which, with its 136 miles, was then the longest railroad in the world. After delays in the progress of the Baltimore and Ohio, thirteen miles of its track were opened for traffic in 1830, and 135 miles in 1835. Traffic, both passenger and freight, was steadily handled on both of these roads by steam locomotives from the time that their first sections of track were opened. No sooner were these successes demonstrated than multitudinous projects were launched and a thousand localities began to clamor for railroad connections. A legislative charter was required for each company launched, and only strong interests could carry bills through the assemblies. Furthermore, the difficulty of enlisting the great amounts of capital required prevented many companies from fulfilling their charter requirements and from beginning actual construction. The scarcity of private capital caused many corporations and promoters to appeal for state aid. This carried many of the roads into politics and caused some of them, the North Carolina Central, for instance, to be located (for political expediency) in districts or directions of poorer traffic-strategy than they should have been.

The railroads launched and constructed in the Southeast in the thirties and forties fall mainly into two groups: (1) Lines parallel to the seacoast, to facilitate the transit of mails, passengers, and freight between the South and the North. Thus between 1830 and 1836 there were chartered four companies which by 1840 had completed a series of connecting railroads reaching from Alexandria on the Potomac to Wilmington, North Carolina, and connecting at Wilmington with a line of steam packets running to Charleston and Savannah. (2) More important for freight traffic and more vital in their economic service were a number of roads built in directions perpendicular to the coast. Among these, in addition to the Baltimore and Ohio and the South Carolina companies, were the Louisa Railroad, later known as the Virginia Central, running west from Richmond; the Southside Railroad, running west from Petersburg; several petty roads in North Carolina, superseded in 1849 by the state-controlled North Carolina Central Railroad; in South Carolina various branches to the original stem from Charleston, radiating to Camden, Columbia, Spartanburg, Greenville, and Anderson; and in Georgia a group of roads which in the fifties became the keystone of the Southern railroad system. In the one year, 1833, were chartered the Georgia, the Central of Georgia, and the Monroe (soon reorganized as the Macon and Western) companies, which with great zeal built their roads respectively from Augusta westward, from Savannah north of west to Macon, and from Macon westward of north. In 1836 the Georgia legislature resolved to build with public moneys the Western and Atlantic Railroad from a point now known as Atlanta to Ross' Landing on the Tennessee River, now known as Chattanooga. After a distressing interruption during the hard times of the early forties, this road was pushed to completion in 1851. Meanwhile, its launching had converged the two lines already in progress from Augusta and Savannah to a common terminus in order that they might share in the grain trade which the Western and Atlantic was to bring from Tennessee and the Northwest. The Nashville and Chattanooga Road, chartered in 1845 and opened in 1854, completed this connection with the river and rail system of the Northwest, and promptly made Atlanta the "gate city," the distributing point for Western grain and meats for the whole cotton belt. The connection of the Western and Atlantic with East Tennessee was made, after the failure of the Hiwassee Company, by the East Tennessee and Georgia Company, chartered in 1848 and completing its road in 1856.

Meanwhile the Southwestern Company of Georgia, chartered in 1845, was building a branchwork of roads from Macon westward and southwestward to Columbus, Americus, Albany, and other towns; and the allied Atlanta and West Point, and Montgomery and West Point companies were building from Atlanta to Montgomery. In northern Alabama an early company chartered in 1830 built a railroad along the Muscle Shoals to serve as a portage, forty-four miles long, between the upper and lower reaches of the Tennessee River. In 1846, this company was merged into the Memphis and Charleston Company, which never opened its track farther than from Memphis to Stevenson on the Nashville and Chattanooga line. In the further Southwest, a New Orleans project of the thirties for a railroad to Nashville prospered for several years but was utterly wrecked by the panic of 1839. Several less pretentious undertakings, intended to connect inland towns like Clinton, Jackson, and Brandon, Mississippi, with the river highway near by, were carried through in the thirties and early forties. The Southwest was not spurred into the efforts necessary to success in more ambitious enterprises until the late forties and early fifties, when the tapping of the Tennessee region by the Georgia roads caused a drain of traffic southeastward which had formerly flowed through Memphis, New Orleans, and Mobile. Then at length Southwestern activity began by which these cities and their tributary regions were to make giant strides. In 1850 the total extent of railroads in the South was about 2,400 miles, of which all but two or three hundred miles, lay eastward of Alabama and the Appalachian Mountains. In 1860 the mileage had increased to above 11,000, of which nearly one-half lay in the transmontane and Southwestern regions. The conspicuous roads of the period in the region between the Ohio river and the Gulf of Mexico were the Mobile and Ohio, chartered in 1848 and opened from Mobile to Cairo in 1859; the New Orleans, Jackson and Northern, chartered in 1850 and opened from New Orleans to Canton in 1859; the Mississippi Central, or Memphis and New Orleans, continuing the line of the New Orleans, Jackson and Northern to Memphis; the Memphis and Chicago, running northeastward from Memphis; the Louisville and Nashville; the Tennessee and Alabama, building southward from Nashville; the Alabama and Mississippi, or Southern Railroad as it was called for some years, filling in the gaps between Montgomery and Vicksburg, and the Montgomery and Mobile. In the middle region and among the mountains, the East Tennessee and Virginia was opened in 1855, connecting with the East Tennessee and Georgia at one end and the Southside Railroad at the other, and forming a long intramontane line parallel with the coast. In the eastern half of the South in the fifties the principal achievements were the extension of the Baltimore and Ohio, the Virginia Central, the Southside, and the North Carolina Central; the building of the Orange and Alexandria; the beginning of the Richmond and Danville; the building of lines from Wilmington, North Carolina, through Florence to Charleston, from Charleston to Savannah, from Savannah to southwest Georgia, and from Jacksonville to Tallahassee and St. Marks. In addition, on the map of 1860 several dozen minor roads appear, scattered through many districts and serving as feeders either to main lines of railway or to the rivers. Beyond the Mississippi there was a continuous railroad across the state of Missouri and other roads radiating from St. Louis; and there were several short lines, the beginnings of larger projects, in Texas and Louisiana. In Arkansas the people heard no locomotive whistles before the war.

As to the cost and capitalization of the railroads, no authentic general tabulations appear to have been made for the antebellum South, and complete data for tabulation are not now extant. In general, few roads had large bonded debts except where state aid had been granted. For example, the Georgia Railroad, with a length of 213 miles, had a capital stock in 1847 of $2,289,200 and no bonded debt; while in 1860, with 231 miles of road, its capital stock was $4,156,000 and its bonded debt $312,500, to offset which it owned stocks and bonds of other roads to the amount of $1,003,650. The Southwestern Railroad of Georgia in 1860, with 206 miles of road, had a capital stock of $3,318,279 and a bonded debt of $396,500; and its neighbor, the Macon and Western Railroad, running 103 miles from Macon to Atlanta, had in 1860 a capital stock of $1,500,000 and no bonded debt. The original cost of constructing the Georgia and Central of Georgia roads, completed in the middle forties, averaged from $13,000 per mile, and at least half that amount per mile additional was expended before 1860 in re-laying with heavier rail and in other betterments. The Western and Atlantic Railroad, 137 miles long, was built by the state of Georgia through rough territory at an initial cost, ending in 1851, of $24,000 per mile, with an added cost for betterments in the next decade of $16,000 per mile.

The affairs of state-aided roads are illustrated by a committee report to the Tennessee legislature made at the end of 1859, describing the status of the railroads lying in whole or in part within that state. There were ten roads reported as completed, with a total length of 1,180 miles, of which 748 miles lay in Tennessee and 100 miles remained yet to be built. The aggregate cost of constructing these roads is given at $27,078,545, and the cost of equipment at $2,149,350; their capital stock aggregated $11,390,606, all paid in, their bonded debt was $11,050,449, including $8,979,000 of state aid from Tennessee, and doubtless additional amounts from neighboring states, and their floating debt was $2,033,605. Seven other roads were reported as in course of construction, with 463 miles built out of a total intended of 949 miles; their cost of construction to the date of the report was $14,649,455, and of equipment $1,011,014, their capital stock aggregated $8,625,425, of which $5,410,653 had been paid in, their funded debt $6,684,786, including $2,961,000 of state aid from Tennessee, and their floating debt was $985,908. On the whole, the cost of construction upon Southern railroads to 1850 averaged probably about $17,000 per mile, and to 1860 about $25,000 per mile. This was little more than half the average cost of Northern roads in the periods. The capitalization of most of the Southern companies approximated rather closely the cost of their roads and equipment. In the case of a few powerful companies only had the corporations begun to increase their stocks or bonds for the purpose of acquiring the securities of connecting roads; and practically none had resorted to stock manipulation nor in any considerable degree to stock-watering. These practices were more common in the North, but none of the important Southern roads had fallen under Wall Street control in the antebellum period.

By 1860 the South was equipped with a good skeleton railroad system, reaching all vital parts of the territory east of the Mississippi River, and handling with fair efficiency the relatively light traffic of the sparsely settled country. The year 1861, replacing peace with tremendous war, radically transformed the railroad situation. The blockade by land and sea promptly stopped the outward and inward flow of commerce, and showed that the several parts of the South customarily did little business with one another. On many roads freight traffic in the first year of the war fell to a tithe of its former volume. Beginning in 1862, however, the movement and counter-movement of troops to and from the threatened points on all the frontiers of the South, and the movement of non-combatant refugees from the danger zones to the interior began to tax the passenger-carrying capacity of the roads. By 1863 the depletion of supplies in the battle zones caused the roads leading from the centre to the periphery of the South to become more busy in handling corn than they had formerly been in handling cotton. As Confederate money depreciated, freight and passenger rates were raised, but not as rapidly as prices of things in general. Meanwhile rails and rolling-stock were becoming dilapidated and could be repaired or replaced only at great expense, if at all. The Confederate government, as a military necessity, took control of the rolling-mills and machine shops and impressed most of the material in reach, using the cast iron for ordnance instead of car wheels, and the wrought iron for wagon and cannon tires instead of for rails. The government made money payment for the supplies and services it received, but strive as it might, it could not avoid the crippling of the roads. Trains, bridges, tracks, and depots were occasionally destroyed by the enemy or even by retreating Confederate armies, and rolling-stock was sometimes marooned by the destruction of the track at either end of a line. The books of many companies showed large nominal net earnings from 1862 to 1864, and dividends of handsome nominal percentage were in some cases distributed; but there was no pretense of prosperity. Current expenses were light only because supplies could not be bought nor repairs be made. Huge sums would have been written off for depreciation of roads and equipment, and earnings carried to reserve to replace the wear and tear when peace should return, except that Confederate money was depreciating with such velocity that no one could afford to keep it, and the country offered no safe investments of any sort. At the end of the war the Southern railroads were in a condition of almost complete physical wreck; but the comparative freedom of the companies from bonded debts enabled them to rehabilitate their properties in the following years with considerable speed. Meanwhile during the war, whereas the rivers in the South proved to be lines of weakness and disaster in the Confederate defence, the railroads nearly all proved to be lines of strength, of the utmost service in supplying men, munitions, and sustenance to the threatened districts on all the borders.

BIBLIOGRAPHY.—De Bow, J. D. B. (ed.): *The Industrial Resources, etc., of the Southern and Western States* (4 vols., New Orleans, 1852–53); Ingle, Edward: *Southern Sidelights* (New York, 1896); Martin, W. E.: *Early History of Internal Improvements in Alabama* (in Johns Hopkins University *Studies*, series XX, iv, Baltimore, 1902); Phillips, Ulrich B.: A *History of Transportation in the Eastern Cotton Belt to 1860* (New York, 1908); Reizenstein, M.: *Economic History of the Baltimore and Ohio Railroad* (in Johns Hopkins University *Studies*, XV, vii–viii, Baltimore, 1897); Weaver, C. C.: *Internal Improvements in North Carolina Previous to 1860* (in Johns Hopkins University *Studies*, XXI, iii–iv, Baltimore, 1903).

13

Historical Notes of
Milledgeville, Ga.

MILLEDGEVILLE was a fairly typical unprogressive village in Middle Georgia; a town in the midst of a region where town life was overshadowed by the prominence of the plantation system.* The merchants and the innkeepers and perchance the lawyers twirled their thumbs or whittled soft pine throughout the spring and summer, until with the arrival of autumn the neighboring planters began to drop in and market their cotton, and the politicians began to arrive from all directions to spend a month or two and make the laws of the land.

Milledgeville owed its existence to a state enactment of 1803, which ordered its survey as a town and gave it its cumbrous name, when its site was still a wilderness but recently surrendered by the Indians. It owed such commercial importance as it came to have to its location at the head of navigation upon the Oconee River. It was a collecting point for cotton bound for the sea, and a distributing point for manufactures from Europe and the North. But the Savannah and the Ocmulgee were greater streams, with better navigation, and the merchants of Augusta and later of Macon were more enterprising. The commerce of Milledgeville, when once developed, remained purely local and almost stationary.

The town owed its political importance to an act of the legislature in 1804, which selected it as the seat of the state government before a dozen cabins had been built within its limits. But in 1868 the capital was removed to Atlanta, and Milledgeville lost its polit-

* *Gulf States Historical Magazine,* II (November, 1903), 161–71.

ical prop. The building of railroads, which put an end to the river traffic, had already destroyed the commercial advantage which its location on the river bank had secured in the early period. The town accordingly stagnated through Reconstruction and the following decades. Within very recent years Milledgeville has unexpectedly taken a firm hold upon itself and has done surprising things—surprising, at least, for Milledgeville.

Eli Whitney's invention of the cotton gin, in 1793, moulded the subsequent history of Middle Georgia. The early settlers had lived as small farmers, raising corn and wheat and a little tobacco. But from 1800 the production of cotton grew so rapidly in importance that within a decade it overshadowed all other forms of industry. The tide of immigration was changed in character. Virginia and North Carolina planters left their tobacco lands for the more inviting cotton belt. They brought their slaves with them, and slave traders brought still others from the older states and the sea coast and sold them in the cotton region. By 1810 the number of blacks in the vicinity of Milledgeville was about equal to that of the whites. As late as 1821 the Indian country was only a day's march to the west. Society in this region near the frontier was in the main primitive and rough; but a sprinkling of great planters gave here and there some atmosphere of distinction and culture.

Except for the great export staple there would have been little use for merchants or towns. But cotton had to be marketed, and Milledgeville was one of the centres. From the treaty of peace with England in 1815 to the great panic of 1837 there were flush times in the cotton belt. Planters and farmers and slaves fared well, and commercial towns grew with some rapidity; but the plantation advantages attracted the chief attention. Merchants and lawyers were fond of investing their earnings in lands and slaves; for the profits in cotton were heavy, and, moreover, it was deemed more honorable to be a planter than to follow any other calling. The towns could barely hold their own against the attractions of the country. Some of the townsmen who turned planters continued to live in town; but the ideal site for a home was thought to be in the midst of a grove upon the crest of a hill an hour or two's drive outside the town.

The town, however, was on Saturdays and court days and throughout the autumn the scene of much activity. Its streets and shops and courthouse were places for the dissemination of news and the forming of public opinion. The interaction between town and country sentiment and institutions was very close. And any insight into town conditions is to be valued as giving a glimpse of the life of the Old South, now so difficult for the student to reconstruct with faithfulness.

Milledgeville was incorporated by a legislative act of 1810. The town records, to be found in the town clerk's office in a state of neglect, extend from 1816, with a few breaks, to the present. They afford an excellent view of the range of the official action of the town authorities, and here and there they throw unexpected light upon the customs and circumstances of the people. Among these records the town census of 1828 is a treasure, for it not only gives the number of inhabitants but also indicates the occupations of the people, and shows the number of slaves held by each family.

The total population in 1828 is given at 1,599. Total whites, 831, of which 197 were males below 18 years of age; 288 were males above 18 years, and 346 were females. Of male slaves under 18 years old there were 176; above 18 years, 159; total male slaves, 335; female slaves, 413; total slaves, 748; free persons of color, 20; of which 8 were males and 12 females.

Of 167 white families, 41 had no slaves; 12 had 1 each, 17 had 2 each, 25 had 3 each, 9 had 4 each, 13 had 5 each, 10 had 6 each, 11 had 7 each, 6 had 8 each, 5 had 9 each, 6 had 10 each, 3 had 11 each, 2 had 12 each, 2 had 13 each, 1 had 14, 1 had 15, 1 had 17, 1 had 18, 1 had 19, 1 had 21.

Among the whites, 12 were attorneys, 6 physicians, 21 merchants, 16 shopkeepers, 9 innkeepers, 21 printers, 26 house carpenters, 2 joiners, 5 blacksmiths, 6 boot and shoe makers, 4 silversmiths and 8 tailors.

The fact that the town was the state capital accounts for the large number of innkeepers and printers. The white households of the innkeepers were large, and they were, as a class, the largest slaveholders in the town. They had slaveholdings of 5, 5, 6, 12, 12, 14, 17, 19 and 21, respectively. The printers, a few merchants, and several attorneys also had relatively large numbers of slaves. But, of course, the great mass of the slaves was upon the plantations and beyond the reach of this census taker's inquiries. Eighty per cent of the white families in the town had slaves for domestic service. John Marlow is listed with 3 white men and 7 slaves, all of whom were carpenters. James Camak had 6 slaves, among whom one or two are apparently listed as printers. William Y. Hansell had 10 slaves, among whom one was a carpenter, one a blacksmith, and one a cobbler. All free negroes are listed under the names of their white guardians. Their occupations are not stated.

The census taker, who was also the town marshal, possessed an inquisitive turn of mind. Though it was not set down in his instructions, he made jottings of fifteen prostitutes, all of whom appear to have been white women. Of course there was, in addition, a considerable number of occasional prostitutes among the negroes and mulattoes; but the police regulations over the slaves were too strict to permit any of them to be openly professionals. The large number of the women of the town was due to the residence of the host of legislators and other politicians in the town during the annual sessions of the General Assembly.

The minutes of the corporation of Milledgeville extend through nearly the whole lifetime of the town. They contain a record of the enactment and the enforcement of town ordinances, and the conduct of the town's finances and general administration. Here and there they give glimpses of the course of public opinion. The following notes are illustrative:

Item, July 30, 1822. An ordinance. (1.) No slave may live off the lot inhabited by his owner or employer. (2.) No slave may hire his own time from his master or contract to labor for any other person. (3.) No person of color may keep spirituous liquors for sale, and none may keep any horse, cow or hog for his own use. (4.) No free person of color may live in Milledgeville except with a guardian living in the town and a certificate of character and a bond for good behavior. Not exceeding four washerwomen at one time shall be exempt from the provisions of this ordinance, and they only when specially licensed.

Item, August 22, 1822. An ordinance. Articles (1) and (2) of the above ordinance of July 30 are suspended until December 15 in the case of slaves provided with certificate of character and covered by bonds for good behavior.

Item, February 1, 1823. An ordinance for a patrol. Ordered that the marshal divide the whole list of citizens subject to patrol duty into thirty squads, and that each squad do patrol duty for one night in each month. Exemption from patrol duty may be purchased at $6 per year.

Item, March 22, 1823. Fines of $1 each are imposed upon fifteen citizens for failure to perform patrol duty.

Item, January 7, 1824. Treasurer's report. Amount received in 1823 in fines for failure to do patrol duty, $40.50.

Item, January 12, 1824. An ordinance repealing the above ordinance of February 1, 1823.

Item, January 31, 1831. An ordinance providing a new system of patrol. Ordered that the marshal and three sargeants with salaries of $100 a year shall command the patrol in succession. Five citizens are to serve each night. The patrol is to continue from 9 P.M. to 3 A.M. Persons failing to patrol or furnish substitutes are subject to fine from $1 to $5.

Item, February 2, 1825. An ordinance for organizing a town guard to replace the former patrol system. Citizens are permitted to volunteer and receive payment for services. The duty of the guard is to apprehend every slave between ten and sixty years of age found off his master's premises without a pass after the ringing of the market bell at night. Slaves apprehended are to be kept in the guard house till morning, and their owners notified. Each slave is to be released after twenty-five lashes on the bare back and the payment of $1 by the owner.

Item, June 14, 1825. An ordinance amending the above ordinance by exempting slaves from whipping for the first offense.

Item, April 22, 1831. Ordered that the Secretary serve a citation on Edward Cary and that the marshal be directed to bring before this board a negro slave named Nathan belonging to the said Cary, on Monday next, to answer the charge of assault and battery, on one of the patrol of the town and show cause why punishment should not be inflicted.

Item, April 24, 1831. In response to the above citation, Edward Cary appeared without the negro. He alleged that Richard Mayhorn had violated the ordinance of the town by transcending his authority as a Patrol. The evidence of witnesses was introduced to substantiate Cary's statement. The Board ordered that Richard Mayhorn be discharged from the service of the corporation.

Item, July 13, 1831. A patrol reported riotous conduct on the part of a negro named Hubbard, and charged Hubbard with cursing, assaulting, and bruising Billy Woodliff (a slave of Seaborn Jones?) at the door of Billy's shop. Billy Woodliff, being sworn, related how Hubbard abused and bruised him with a rock. Robert Mercer and Mr. Winter also testified. The fact was brought to light that Hubbard's attack upon Billy had been brought about by Billy having taken Hubbard's wife away from him. "The testimoney being concluded, Mr. Wiggins addressed the Board in a speech containing some *lengthy, strengthy,* and *depthy* argument. Whereupon the Board *Ordered* that the negro man Hubbard receive from the Marshal *Ten* lashes moderately laid on, and be discharged."

Item, February 12, 1830. Whereas, the Board has received information that Elijah H. Burritt has violated the statute of the last Georgia legislature by the introduction of certain insurrectionary pamphlets, resolved that the town marshal be directed to enter his name as prosecutor in the case, and that this Board will pay all expenses necessary to bring the offender to punishment.

Item, September 13, 1831. Ordered that the marshal and deputies use increased vigilance with regard to our black population, and particularly that they do not fail to visit every place at which there is an assembly of negroes, and in the event of religious meetings to treat them as the law directs for unlawful meetings, unless there is present at least one white person accepted by the church to which the society belongs.

The rise of the abolition agitation in the North in 1829 and 1831, and the Nat Turner insurrection in Virginia, account, of course, for the policy of the Board as indicated in the two items last noted above.

Item, October 5, 1831. The negro man Nathan belonging to W. B. Hepburn, was brought before the board and examined relative to a suspected insurrection among the blacks. Whereupon, after due consideration of all the circumstances, it was ordered that, as nothing criminal has been proved against him, he be immediately discharged. The yellow man Richard Rogers, a Preacher, was examined and likewise discharged. So also Aleck Reynolds, the Blacksmith, and Casewell, a blacksmith belonging to Peyton Pitts. The Board ordered that, whereas, there has been considerable danger in the late excitement and alarm of an intention at insurrection, by firing guns "by persons carrying arms that were intoxicated," and by boys unable to bear arms, it be ordained that the marshal and patrols take away arms from intoxicated persons and boys and enforce the ordinance against firing arms in the streets.

The examination of these negroes suspected of conspiracy in 1831 and the trials of Nathan and Hubbard, noted above under dates of April 22 and 24 and July 13, 1831, appear to be the only instances recorded of negroes having been tried by the Milledgeville authorities for crimes or misdemeanors prior to the outbreak of the Civil War.

Item, January 5, 1839. "On motion of Alderman Cook, Resolved, That the Marshal be and he is hereby required to pay over to the Council immediately after the passage of this Resolution, all monies received by him for superintending the Balls given by the colored people during the Christmas holidays, and that he be instructed not to receive in future any compensation for such services."

Item, December 19, 1839. Resolved, That the Board deem it improper to grant negroes the privilege of having balls at any other time than during the Christmas holidays, and then in the day time, and that no consent shall be granted except upon the application of the owners or guardians of the negroes.

Item, January 21, 1841. Resolved, Upon petition, that the band of musicians composed of colored persons be allowed to practise in the old theatre not later than 10 o'clock, until further ordered by the Board, provided they obtain the services of some suitable white person to accompany them.

Item, July 15, 1841. An ordinance. It shall be the duty of the marshal and deputy to report any white person disturbing the peace. (Elsewhere the marshal and deputy are directed to patrol and prevent negro disturbances and to report and bring to trial all white persons breaking the peace. The repetition of this ordinance in July, 1841, indicates that an element among the whites had become especially troublesome about that time.)

Item, September 18, 1854. The Board resolves that the petition before them asking the privilege for the negroes of the city of erecting a church for their separate use upon the lands of the city, cannot be entertained unless it be signed by a majority of the citizens of Milledgeville.

Item, January 10, 1840. The Board resolves to order the engraving of bills of the denominations of $3, $2, $1, $.50 and $.25 to the total amount of $14,440.

Item, April 2, 1840. The Change Bills have arrived from Washington to the amount of $7,357.50. The cost of engraving is $200.

Item, April 4, 1840. The Board resolves that these change bills be signed up and put into circulation as rapidly as possible, in exchange for bank notes. Ordered that no notes shall be issued unless a fund for their redemption is on hand equal to at least one-third of the amount proposed to be issued.

In this period of financial depression in the cotton belt, bills of credit were issued by numerous town corporations. In the *Southern Recorder*, January 16, 1842 (a newspaper printed at Milledgeville), a table of the rate of exchange is given. The notes of the Augusta City Council are quoted at par, while those of Columbus, Macon and Milledgeville are quoted at 15 per cent discount. For Savannah scrip, 1840, see Thomas Gamble, Jr., *History of the City Government of Savannah, Ga., from 1790 to 1901*, pages 173-74.

Item, February 23, 1841. "The Street Committee reported that they had hired for the present year the following named hands, from the persons whose names are thereunto annexed, viz.:

Antoinette, of T. F. Greene, trustee .... $ 100.00
Isaac, of C. J. McDonald 150.00

Monday & Sam, of M. J. Kenan	250.00
Prince, Andrew & Prince, of Sarah Davis'	375.00
Henry & Bill, of Emmon Bails	120.00
Andrew, of I. S. Wright	120.00
Joe, of James Smith	120.00
	$1,355.00

"Ordered that notes be executed by the Mayor to the owners of said hands for the several amounts above stated."

Item, January 2, 1840. Rations of negroes hired by the town of Milledgeville: Each week, one peck of meal, six pounds of bacon and one pint of molasses, in season.

Mention is made here and there, also, of potatoes, rice and beef, seemingly for the negro hands. Corn was worth about 50 cents per bushel, bacon 13 cents per pound. The town fed, clothed and sheltered the negroes it hired. One pair pantaloons cost $3.00, one round jacket, $3.00; one shirt, $1.00; one pair shoes, $1.25 to $1.50. The support of the hands and four mules in 1840 cost $897.93. [*Minutes, December 3, 1840.*]

The digest of taxes for 1859 gives a total of 335 taxpayers, of which eight were free negroes. One of these had property assessed at $440, and two others at $75 each. The remainder paid poll tax alone. The real estate was valued at $317,000 and the slaves at $318,600. Taxes were levied as follows: On white males between 18 and 45 years of age, a poll tax of $2.00; on white males between 16 and 18 and between 45 and 60, a poll tax of $1.00; on free male persons of color, between 16 and 60, a poll tax of $10; on free female persons of color between 15 and 50, a poll tax of $5.00; on slaves between 10 and 60 years of age, 40 cents for every $100 of the returned valuation; on real estate and personal property, 40 cents on $100; on merchandise, 50 cents on $100; on money at interest, 30 cents on $100; on peddlers, 10 per cent of their sales; on liquor shops, $50 each; on billiard tables, $25 each; on bagatelle tables, $20 each; on ten-pin alleys, $25 each; on bakers, $10 each; on forges, $10 each; on printing offices, $40 each; on bank agencies, $100 each.

The cash book of the Town Treasurer has an entry under date of November 26, 1864:

"By amount on hand, captured by the Yankees, $1,032.30."

Numerous entries show the depreciation of Confederate money; for instance, under date of March 3, 1863:

"By amount paid for 8 candles, $8.00. By amount paid for pair of shoes, $35.00."

The Record of the Police Court of Milledgeville, 1854 to 1870, contains the records of some 480 misdemeanor cases tried in the mayor's court. Of these none appear to have been against slaves or free persons of color before 1862.

Item, February 15, 1862. "The State vs. Wm., a slave of Doct. G. D. Case. Disorderly & Disobedient Conduct. After hearing the testimony in the above case [it] is ordered and adjudged that Doct. G .D. Case pay the cost and that the boy William receive Ten Lashes by the hand of the Marshal, and then be discharged."

Item, December 8, 1862. The State vs. Hamilton, a slave. Retailing spirituous liquors. Pleaded guilty. Sentenced to thirty-nine lashes.

Item, May 14, 1864. The State vs. Viney, a slave. Using opprobrious and impudent language to a white person. Sentenced to thirty-nine lashes.

Item, July 26, 1865. The State vs. Jarratt (Freedman). Petit larceny. Sentences to ten days imprisonment in the guard house, to be fed on bread and water.

Item, August 17, 1865. The State vs. Charles Harris (Freedman). Malicious mischief. Sentenced to a fine of $25 or in default to be kept in jail until the meeting of the superior court. The sentence was commuted to the wearing of ball and chain and working on the streets for fifteen days.

Item, August 28, 1865. The State vs. Anderson McComb, a freedman. Fighting. Sentenced to fine of $5 or five days work on streets.

Item, August 28, 1865. Three cases of vagrancy against freedmen. Sentenced each to five days work on the streets.

Item, September 15, 1869. The State vs. Joseph Young, colored. Drunkenness. Sentenced to $5 fine or six days in jail.

From 1865 to 1869 the court followed the custom of sentencing white persons to fine or imprisonment in jail, while it sentenced negroes to fine or labor in the chain gang on the streets. After 1869 that distinction apparently ceased to be made.

For a complete view of the life of the community, the town records must be supplemented with the county archives, the state documents, the newspaper files, travelers' accounts, and private correspondence.

The Ordinary's office in the court house at Milledgeville contains a valuable record on wills, inventories, appraisals, and sales of estates. From these we may gather that Jesse Sanford at his death in 1827 possessed 25 domestic servants besides 228 field hands distributed upon his six plantations, and that his personal property embraced mahogany furniture, silver plate, and cut glass decanters. But we may learn on the other hand, that in dozens of cases a featherbed or two was inventoried as the most valuable item in the estate aside from the lands, houses, and slaves. For one great nabob there were scores or even hundreds of very plain farmers, shopkeepers, and the like.

The state archives contain a record of the routine affairs which were attended to in the capitol and the executive mansion. The newspaper files, of which there are unusually good sets in Milledgeville, tell of the course of party politics, of the great speeches, the price of cotton, and the state of the crops. Their editorials and news items are supplemented by a great number of anonymous letters which give all sorts of views upon current questions. But as the years passed, there came to be one subject upon which unfavorable views were not printed. In the early period criticisms and expressions of disapproval of slavery were fairly common; but after the rise of the abolition agitation opinions of that sort were no longer published. This silence was eloquent—and sinister.

The purpose of this rambling article has been partly to give a glimpse of conditions as shown by the indisputable sources, but mainly to indicate that the materials exist for a complete political, social, and economic history of any given community and of the South as a whole. The material can be discovered only by diligent search, and it can be wrought into history only by intelligent and persevering interpretative study. The difficulty of the work has heretofore prevented its accomplishment upon any large scale, but the rewards awaiting the patriotic historian who sets forth the clear and convincing truth about the South will be great enough to blot out the memory of his tedious labor.[1]

[1] There has just appeared from the press of McGowan & Cooke, of Chattanooga, a volume of *Memoirs of the Fort and Fannin Families,* edited by Kate Haynes Fort. This book contains an excellent biography of Dr. Tomlinson Fort, long a prominent citizen of Milledgeville, and gives a good account of family life in the community. As an accurate and attractive history of a typical, well-to-do family, it is a valuable contribution to the social history of the South.

14

State and Local Public Regulation
of Industry in the South

IN Virginia, Georgia, and Louisiana, in the very early stages of the colonization, the governments conducted and regulated industries in a highly paternalistic manner.* In all three colonies the authorities employed indentured servants in general industry on public account, as well as using them specially for iron and glass making in the case of Virginia, and for silk and wine growing in the case of Georgia. But all of these projects of government participation in industry proved so quickly and so completely disastrous, that a highly individualistic regime promptly supervened and came to prevail upon the whole throughout the South. The community ownership of land so characteristic in the New England colonies, and the official cowherds and fence-viewers met with in New England town records, were completely alien to the South. The Southern planting and farming families were rarely settled in groups; and the thinly scattered population felt relatively few needs for government activity in or detailed regulation of industry or commerce. Such needs as did arise in this connection, nevertheless, were promptly met by the provision of whatever machinery for public action the occasion was deemed to require. The legislatures, for example, established a uniform toll rate of one-eighth at all grist and flouring mills, and required the millers to abide by the maxim of "first come, first served" among their patrons. More conspicuously, all the tobacco-producing colonies

* _The South in the Building of the Nation_ (13 vols.; Richmond, 1909–13), V, 475–78.

and states, beginning with Virginia in an act of 1619, maintained more or less constantly some system of regulating the production and marketing of that staple. In some cases the number of plants and leaves to be grown by each laborer was restricted, but more generally the regulation was confined to the inspection of the harvested crop and the confiscation and destruction of the lowest grades. Another instance of regulation, which at the present day, when by-products are so generally utilized, has a peculiarly antiquated appearance, affected the disposition of cotton-seed by the ginners.[1]

Public regulation of wages on any considerable scale seems to have been attempted only in the colonial period and in times of special stress. An instance is an act of the South Carolina legislature, passed in December, 1740, just after a fire had swept the city of Charleston. The act prescribed for a period of ten years maximum rates of wages in all of the building trades. Incidentally, it also fixed maximum prices for brick per thousand, quoted in colonial currency which was then at the depreciated value of seven for one sterling. The prices were for English brick, £6; for New England brick, £3, 10s; for South Carolina brick, £5.

The town regulation of produce markets and bakeries was much more generally customary. Most of the towns maintained public markets; and the rules of some of them, of Augusta, Ga., in 1818 for example, were quite mediaeval in their emphatic prohibition of engrossing, forestalling, and regrating. The bakers in the towns

---

[1] The following enactment by the Georgia legislature in 1803 is typical for the period:

"Be it enacted, * * * That from and after the first day of January next, it shall be the duty of all owners or occupiers of cotton machines for the picking of cotton [i.e., cotton gins], in all villages, or immediately in the vicinity of any town or village within this state, to enclose the seed in such manner as will effectually prevent all stock, especially hogs, from eating them.

And be it further enacted, That all owners or occupiers of such machines as aforesaid, shall secure and keep the seed dry, or remove them at least once every week from said machine, to such a distance from such city, town, village or vicinity thereof, so as to prevent all the unwholesome effects resulting from the stench and vapours arising from the seed, in their putrid state; and it shall be the duty of such owners or occupiers of such machines to enclose the seed in the place to which the same shall be removed, so as to prevent his, her or their neighbors' stock from feeding thereon."

were quite generally required by ordinances to sell loaves of specified weights made of specified qualities of flour, at specified prices. The minimum weights of the loaves to be sold at the standard prices were made to vary according to the price of flour; and as a rule the town clerk would have the duty of publishing the "assize of bread," stating the current price of flour per barrel and the prescribed minimum weights of loaves for the week. In some cases the bakers resisted and defeated the attempts at public regulation; and in Augusta, in 1808, a municipal bakery was proposed to save the public from spoliation through the greed of the bakers. But it seems that nothing came of the plan.

In the latter part of the antebellum period, the most striking items in the line of public regulation of industry were the efforts by state enactment or city ordinance to diminish the opportunity of negro artisans, whether slave or free, for the benefit of their white competitors in the trade. Particularly in cities like Atlanta where white workingmen were numerous, they were disposed to use their ballot-box privilege in bringing pressure for class advantage. They secured numerous laws and ordinances aimed at driving away free negroes altogether and at prohibiting non-resident slaveowners from sending their slaves into the towns, or resident slaveowners from hiring artisan slaves to any other employers. Most of these restrictions, however, like the earlier limitations of wages, were rendered dead-letters, because the interests of the slaveowners and the employers of labor were generally of more influence in determining city routine than were the combined alertness of the white artisans and the zeal of the public functionaries.

BIBLIOGRAPHY.—Bruce, P. A.: *Economic History of Virginia in the Seventeenth Century* (2 vols., New York, 1896); Clayton, A. S.: *Compilation of the Laws of Georgia Passed between 1800 and 1810* (Augusta, 1813); Cooper, Thomas, and McCord, D. J.: *Statutes at Large of South Carolina* (Columbia, 1836-49); Hening, W. W.: *Statutes at Large of Virginia* (13 vols., New York, 1823); Marbury, H., and Crawford, W. H.: *Compilation of the Laws of Georgia* (Savannah, 1802); Phillips, Ulrich B. (ed.): *Plantation and Frontier Documents* (Cleveland, 1908), and "The Slave Labor Problem in the Charleston District" (in the *Political Science Quarterly*, XXII, 416–39).

15

The Slave Labor Problem in the
Charleston District

THE essential features and tendencies of a regime can best be analyzed in those instances in which it has been most fully developed and most persistently maintained.* Isolated phases of American negro slavery may be studied with some success in many places and periods, but its complex working and far-reaching effects can perhaps be learned with relative completeness only from a study of some long settled and very black portion of the Southern black belts. The best example for our purpose is the low-lying coast region of South Carolina and Georgia, which had its focus at Charleston and may well be called the Charleston district. There as elsewhere the establishment of slavery was due entirely to the desire for a labor supply, and its patent effects were chiefly of an economic sort; but the system had also deep and inevitable influences and effects of a social character, and of course developed conspicuous outcroppings in national politics. For all these things the material which can be found for the Charleston district is eloquent.

The physical features of the district, so different from most other parts of North America, invited the early introduction of the plantation system, with negro labor. The heat, dampness and malaria retarded the growth of the white population and promoted the relative increase of the negroes. The development of rice, indigo, and sea-island cotton as staples caused the firm establishment of plantations to utilize the fertile alluvial soil of the lowlands. The

* *Political Science Quarterly*, XXII (September, 1907), 416–39.

splendid harbor and the tongue of elevated and healthful land at Charleston caused the growth there of a genuine capital of the district. The regime thus promoted by the unchanging conditions of nature waxed strong and endured for generations, with far less change than is usual in American life. Lowland South Carolina began its successful career as a colony in the wilderness, producing staples by the use of negro labor under white control on plantations, with its center and soul at Charleston. Thus it stands today, decadent it is true, but not revolutionized. It stands thus far, indeed, as a monument to the power of soil and climate in shaping and preserving systems of human activity, and to the effectiveness of race distinctions in resisting even cataclysmal attempts at alteration.

The colony was founded in 1670, by settlers who came to seek their fortune. At first they had no staple industry. They labored to produce most of the things they needed, and exported only a small value in naval stores and peltry with which to buy a few European goods. About 1693 came the discovery of rice as a staple for export, and this gave an incentive for procuring a large labor supply and organizing it on the most effective system feasible. Negroes were found to be especially adapted to the climate, and the plantation system was borrowed from the West Indies, where it already flourished. A regime of plantation industrialism was instituted which was strong enough to dominate the situation. The Lords Proprietors, with their attempts at feudalism and arbitrary extraneous control, were brushed away; they were replaced after 1729 by a royal government, which was welcomed because it permitted a very large degree of self-government. The citizens worked out their own destiny, following the line of least resistance, which of course might or might not be the line of greatest permanent efficiency. There arose, then, a peculiar system of industry, commerce, and social life as the resultant of physiographic and ethnic influences. Its general features are too familiar to require description here. An important fact was the coordinate growth of the plantations to produce the staples and of the city of Charleston for commerce and incidental industry.

Indigo and long-staple cotton, as well as rice, were successively found to be producible with the profit in the Carolina lowlands. The great demand of the world for these staples caused the growth of a strong local demand for labor, and especially for negroes, who were known to be largely immune to malaria and unoppressed by the heat. Negro labor, of necessity unfree, furnished the chief supply in both country and city. Plantations were established wherever fertile land could be found in reach of navigation. These were scattered throughout the lowlands, mostly in isolation from one another, but all tending to have the same general features. It was found by experience that the best results in rice and indigo production were obtained from plantations with working forces of about thirty hands each, and the tendency was toward that size in the industrial unit.[1] The spread of a system like this, distributing one white family to every isolated group of from five to twenty or more negro families, in a malarial region, resulted in a situation not fully duplicated elsewhere on the continent. The Africans were too numerous in the early stages for the whites to succeed nearly so well as did the Virginians and the men of the upland cotton belt in taming them to the ways of civilization. The field work was always done in the crudest manner; and the necessity of the master's moving away from his estate in the warm months to escape the malaria, involved the adoption of some system of routine which would work with more or less automatic regularity without his own inspiring or impelling presence. Hence the system of "tasks," by which the white overseer or negro foreman (called a "driver") assigned a stated measure of land to be worked over by each laborer each day, varying in amount according to the laborer's classification as an able-bodied, prime or "full hand," a three-quarter hand, a half-hand, etc. When special work had to be done, like clearing land of its timber, the negroes might be worked in gangs under the master's direction; but as a rule the task system was followed, as being more nearly automatic and requiring less active and vigilant supervision. Aside from field labor, there was need of such work as cooperage, blacksmithing, boating, and domestic service, to

[1] B. R. Carrol, *Historical Collections of South Carolina*, II, 202, and American Historical Association *Report* for 1903, I, 445.

which chosen negroes were assigned. In general it was recognized as useless to expect a high degree of efficiency in any branch of plantation labor or service and there was a general contentment with moderate efficiency on the part of the negroes and moderate profits from their unstrenuous labor. Zeal and growth in skill were encouraged; but, in view of the great numerical preponderance of the negroes, to keep them docile was considered more important than to increase their labor-value.

In the first stage of plantation and city development, the unskilled labor supply was made up almost wholly of negro slaves, while the whites filled all other ranks, acting as artisans, foremen, farmers, planters, merchants, etc. A few of the whites were indentured servants, and a few white freemen were unskilled laborers, but only a few in either case, and the number was diminishing. It is safe to say that from about 1700 to 1720 there was fairly complete identity of racial, industrial and legal classes; the negroes were unskilled laborers and of slave status; the whites were skilled laborers and managers, and were freemen. The negroes were employed in routine work, the whites filled all the versatile and responsible occupations. There was well-nigh complete subordination of negroes to whites in every respect. Under this arrangement the economic and social needs, as the whites saw them, were harmonious.

But this simple relation could not long endure. Some of the negroes proved relatively intelligent, acquired moderate skill in handicrafts or proved their capacity for self-direction on a small scale in industry and commerce. These became foremen, boat captains (patroons), peddlers, custom blacksmiths, etc. The emergence of mulattoes, with far greater intelligence, hastened this development. Masters owning the labor of relatively high-grade workmen were naturally disposed to employ that labor to the best advantage—to encourage progress of their slaves in skill and thus to save themselves the expense of employing freemen for skilled tasks. The next step, following naturally, was for masters to secure instruction for their most capable youths through apprenticeship, and to set up some of the skilled slaves as craftsmen with shops for public patronage. The city, with its more rapidly growing complexity and specialization of industry, was of course the seat of the earliest and the fullest instances of this development.

The increasing competition of negro slave artisans with the whites was of the greatest importance as regarded the relations of the races, because the colony depended mainly upon the outside world for its supply of manufactures and the opportunities for craftsmen in the province were at the best very limited. Competition by the slaves tended to drive out a considerable proportion of the white freemen whose skilled labor would otherwise have been needed. Conditions were gradually becoming more complex: racial, legal and industrial classes were ceasing to be so nearly coterminous as in the earlier time. A number of negroes and mulattoes, indeed, were gradually coming to acquire legal status as freemen, exempt from slavery regulations, but in no wise recognized by the whites as their equals. The presence of these freedmen, of course, still further complicated the situation. The demand for labor was constantly growing, but mainly for unskilled labor. It was chiefly met by the slave trade and the natural increase of the negro population. Skilled trades were entered more and more largely by exceptional negroes and mulattoes. In times of depression, white mechanics were tempted to emigrate in search of better openings; but the persons of color, if slaves, could not migrate, and if legally free, had to stay in most cases because of the dearth of industrial opportunity for them in other quarters of America. Thus the proportion of negroes increased in the trades as well as in the total population, ctiy and country. This state of things aroused considerable apprehension.[2]

[2] An act of the Assembly, adopted as early as 1714, declared that "the number of negroes do extremely increase in this Province, and through the afflicting providence of God, the whites do not proportionably multiply, by reason whereof, the safety of the said province is greatly endangered." Thomas Cooper and D. J. McCord, *Statutes at Large of South Carolina*, VII, 367. The attitude of the public toward the labor and race problem in general is shown in the preamble to an act of 1712, "for the better ordering and governing of negroes and slaves." The preamble runs as follows: "Whereas, the plantations and estates of this Province cannot be well and sufficiently managed and brought into use without the labor and service of negroes and other slaves, and forasmuch as the said negroes and other slaves brought unto the people of this Province for that purpose, are of barbarous, wild, savage natures, and such as

The importation of negroes into America had been due, of course, to the economic motive of procuring a labor supply. The regulation of slavery had been instituted for their industrial control —to permit their "breaking in," their subjection to the rules of civilized labor. With the negroes once on hand in large numbers, however, the enormous contrast between them and the whites in intelligence, standards and institutions—in a word, in race character—brought up a social problem which over-shadowed all economic issues. Slavery, originating as a system of labor control, was maintained as still more valuable in safe-guarding the standards, institutions and social well-being of the few whites against possible demoralization and overthrow by the numerous blacks. The negroes were required by the system to abandon gradually the habits and points of view acquired in the African jungle, to accept and acquire as far as they could the ideas of the civilization into which they had been brought, and to abide by its rules of social conduct. Plantations and slavery made up a system of tutelage and police combined, providing education in civilized industry and life and at the same time preventing successful outbreaks of negro revolt against white control.

The system showed its kindly or its harsh features, other things being equal, according as the negroes in a given case were relatively docile or fractious. Other things were not always equal: in some cases the mingling of the races in daily life was free and abundant, so that the negroes had ample opportunity to use their imitative faculties and to acquire the white men's ways; in other cases the negroes were isolated, their masters absent for long periods, white neighbors few and models for imitation not within reach. Under conditions of the latter sort, subjection in full would be required of the negroes, little affection would be inspired, and little loyalty

---

renders them wholly unqualified to be governed by the laws, customs and practices of this Province, but that it is absolutely necessary that such other constitutions, laws and orders, should in this Province be made and enacted, for the good regulating and ordering of them, as may restrain the disorders, rapines and inhumanity to which they are naturally prone and inclined; and may also tend to the safety and security of the people of this Province and their estates; . . . Be it therefore enacted," etc. *Ibid.*, 352.

would be engendered to the system or to the society which it safeguarded.

The Carolina lowland plantations presented the less attractive of these sets of conditions. The acceptance of the situation was slow among the negroes, and their adaptation to it was imperfect. Strict police control was necessary. This firm regulation, in turn, making against the intimate personal associations common in Virginia and the uplands, tended to preserve the race alienation which had called it into being. The negroes of the South Carolina coast failed to acquire the English language in intelligible form; they clung to voodooism and other things African; and, in spite of their apparent and even oppressive sociability and friendliness, they remained largely foreign in spirit and in custom and subjects of mystery to their masters. The conditions in the Charleston district were always far more similar to those in the West Indies than to those in Virginia and the upland cotton belt.

Most of the South Carolina coast negroes were unambitious; but some few, as we have seen, and especially the mulattoes, were eager to learn and with their masters' aid became artisans or otherwise largely self-directing in industry. The situation grew complex and in some ways embarrassing. In the divergence of economic interests and social needs it became increasingly clear that the social needs were paramount. In frequent instances the financial interest of the master lay in giving his capable slaves as much industrial freedom as they could use; but it was a social necessity to keep under complete control every black who could possibly incite or take part in a servile insurrection or otherwise promote disorder. The situation was delicate, as all men knew; and the only sure safeguards against the outbreak of rapine and anarchy lay in watchfulness and masterfulness on the part of the whites.

It was recited in a legislative act as early as 1712 that

several owners of slaves [are] used to suffer their said slaves to do what and go whither they will and work where they please, upon condition that their said slaves do bring their aforesaid masters so much money as between the said master and slave is agreed upon, for every day the said slave shall be so permitted to employ himself, which practice hath been observed to occasion such slaves to spend their time aforesaid, in looking for opportunities to steal, in order to raise money to pay their masters, as well as to maintain themselves, and other slaves their companions, in drunkenness and other evil courses.[2]

The competitive phase of the race-labor problem was touched upon by the grand jury of the province in its presentments in 1742: "We present as a grievance the want of a law to prevent the hiring out of negro tradesmen, to the great discouragement of the white workmen coming into this province." [3]

There thus appeared two interests favoring the restriction of negro opportunity. The white laboring men wanted to keep the slaves out of the skilled trades as far as possible, and to that end opposed their being hired out under any circumstances for artisan's work. The men of the governing class opposed any broadening of negroes' range of personal freedom as increasing the danger of demoralization and revolt. The white artisans, it seems, had not enough political strength to get their will enacted into law[4]; and the statutes prohibiting the hiring of their time by slaves were not sufficiently supported by public opinion to secure their enforcement. Like most other provisions of the slave code, this rule was generally disregarded when the interest or inclination of master and slave agreed in favor of its violation. In many cases the law, if enforced, would have seriously hampered industry and commerce. In the city, for example, stevedores, boat hands, messengers, carpenters and day laborers in general were often needed for immediate service; and the employer could not submit to the delay and formality of seeking out and making contracts with the owners of the slaves whose labor he desired. For the sake of a flexible labor supply, some device like that of slaves hiring their own time was

[2] Cooper and McCord, *Statutes at Large of South Carolina*, VII, 363.

[3] Presentments of October 20, 1742, published in the *South Carolina Gazette*, November 8, 1742.

[4] An exception to this is noted by Sir Charles Lyell, *A Second Visit to the United States* (New York, 1849), II, 78–83, in the case of a Georgia enactment of 1845, prohibiting the competition of negroes as building contractors. Lyell gives a clear view of the conditions and the tendency which accompanied such legislation.

essential; and that being the case, the laws prohibiting this arrangement could not, of course, secure general observance. In quiet times, indeed, the citizens fell generally into easy-going practices, each following his own interest in managing his slaves (or letting them manage him) and thinking little of the provisions for public control. The discovery of negro conspiracies in 1720 [5] and 1740 [6] spread alarm in the province and for the time stimulated public sentiment in favor of efficient police and other safeguards; but relaxation of control was not long in following each spasm of police reform.

From about 1740 to the outbreak of the war for American independence was the heyday of prosperity for the Carolina lowlands. Rice and indigo prices were excellent; the laboring force was rapidly enlarged, the cultivated area was extended and the exports and imports increased. Merchants from many countries gathered at "Charles Town"; and many, acquiring wealth, adopted the Carolina standard of highest gentility and retired from commerce to enter planting careers. The city was beautified with handsome public buildings and private residences; the plantations were equipped with commodious mansions and substantial rice mills, smokehouses, negro quarters, etc., many of which endure in more or less dilapidation to the present day. Carolina merchants and planters were in close touch through newspapers and correspondence with the whole world of commerce and affairs. Carolina youths were often educated in the colleges of Old England. Planters of a fine

[5] Among the transcripts in the capitol at Columbia, S. C., from the British Public Record Office (B. P. R. O., S. C., B. T. 1, A2) is an official letter of 1720 from Charleston, unsigned, to Mr. Boone at London. It relates that a barbarous plot among the negroes has lately been discovered, by which they purposed to take the town in full body. Some of the negroes have been burnt, some banished. The leaders were slaves of Mr. Percival, who was absent in England. Percival is advised through Boone to sell his negroes singly or else to provide strict management for them, for otherwise "they will come to little profit."

[6] The revolt of 1740 is briefly described in an act of immunity which followed it. Cooper and McCord, Statutes at Large, VII, 416. Other conspiracies are listed and described in an anonymous pamphlet entitled, A Refutation of the Calumnies circulated against the Southern and Western States, respecting . . . Slavery. By a South Carolinian. (Charleston, 1820; 88 pp.).

type of manhood, culture, and ability set a high standard in the commonwealth; and sons strove to fall nothing short of their fathers' attainments. In consequence, there was efficiency and thorough honesty in government; honor, candor, and cordiality in private relations; and kindly consideration, as a very general rule, toward all persons not obviously undeserving. The native slaves were encouraged to progress as far as circumstances could be made to permit; the imported Africans were broken into service as mildly as possible; all were well fed, adequately clothed and sheltered, and subjected to as a mild a discipline as was compatible with public safety. On the whole, the province was as well ordered, prosperous, and happy in all its elements as could well be with such diverse racial components and so large a latent possibility for disorder and social revolution.

There were a few blemishes on the generally smooth surface of prosperity and contentment. The heavy volume of the slave trade caused a constant drain of capital to England and New England in payment to the traders; breaking in fresh and refractory Africans was, at the best, unpleasant business; the white mechanics disliked the competition of negroes and mulattoes in their trades, and though the wages of the whites were higher, their number was relatively decreasing; the great and ever-growing mass of half-savage negroes, many of them embittered by harsh treatment, was a constant cause for disquiet; and the increasingly strained relations with the mother country were distressing from many points of view. But on the whole, the people, flushed with their success in conquering the wilderness and their unchecked progress in wealth, were consciously happy and bravely optimistic.

When the war came, the situation was in several respects unique. South Carolina was the only colony that had to deal with large numbers of barbaric Africans. Among persons closely associated with these coast negroes there was little disposition to accept theories of human equality. The most influential citizens, whether "patriot" or "loyalist," were determined to preserve the existing industrial and social order as a necessary condition of life in the district, no matter what system of government and allegiance should prevail. The conservatism of the people, in fact, saved the state from such an upheaval as afflicted Virginia in the revolutionary period.

During the war, and for a while afterward, there was grave economic depression in the district. The closing of markets and the military depredations occasioned great though temporary damages, and the loss of the British bounty permanently killed indigo production. But the plantation system was not broken down. The planters in large number retained their lands and their slaves, and tided over the lean years with hopes for the return of better times.

About 1786 it was discovered that long-staple cotton, with its high-priced silky fibre, was available as a staple to replace indigo and to supplement rice. Within a few years the new industry was widespread through the Georgia–Carolina lowlands, and planters were becoming serenely prosperous again.

At the close of the century, however, a wholly new factor was introduced, and in the first decades of the following century the economic situation was seriously modified. As a result of Whitney's invention of the gin for short-staple cotton in 1793, the whole interior of the Carolinas, of Georgia and of the Southwest became capable of very profitable development by labor of any and every kind. In the relative scarcity of free labor for this vast region, an enormous demand was made by the upland and western cotton districts for slave labor, which after 1808 could be supplied, in the main, only from the old tobacco and rice districts. Slave prices rapidly mounted to unheard of figures; and with the planters of the Charleston district it became a serious question whether the lure of the golden West for their slaves and themselves could be permanently resisted. Many sold part of their negroes to inland settlers; many moved west carrying with them such slaves as they had or could buy. In some years, as in war times and in periods of low cotton prices, the slave trade and the migration slackened; again it would wax so great in volume that only the most conservative could preserve immunity from the Georgia, Alabama, or Texas fever. The migration fever and the interior slave trade carried off nearly or quite all the increase from births, importation, and immigration in the Charleston lowlands, as is shown by the returns of the successive censuses.[7] In some decades there was positive shrinkage in districts in which before the Revolution the doubling of numbers within a decade had not been unusual.

Charleston and all the surrounding country was seriously threatened with not only a relative but an actual decline of population, white and black, of crops and earnings and of political and social consequence. To save the situation, or even to mitigate the decline, it was necessary to improve the existing system of industry, so as to make every resource tell to the utmost. Labor must be made more productive. This result could be attained in part through improvement in administration. Some of the coast planters, for example, developed such fine varieties of cotton, and guarded their crops so well against careless picking, ginning and packing, that the output of their plantations commanded a heavy premium in the market.[8] But in its crux, the problem was, of course, to improve the quality and effectiveness of the labor itself. The system had to be made flexible by giving to every trustworthy slave, who was capable of self-direction, a personal incentive to increase his skill and assiduity. Under such conditions the laws which impeded industrial progress were increasingly disregarded and became dead letters. Slaves by hundreds hired their own time; whites and blacks, skilled and unskilled, worked side by side, with little notice of the color

---

[7] POPULATION STATISTICS FOR THE SOUTH CAROLINA LOWLANDS

Charleston District (i. e. *county*)	1790	1800	1810	1820	1830	1840	1850	1860
White	11,801	14,374	16,011	19,376	20,804	20,921	25,208	29,136
Slave	24,071	41,945	45,385	57,221	61,902	58,539	54,775	37,290
Free Colored	775	1,161	1,783	3,615	3,632	3,201	3,861	3,622
Colleton District								
White	3,601	4,394	4,290	4,341	5,354	5,874	6,775	9,255
Slave	16,562	20,471	21,858	21,770	21,484	19,246	21,372	32,307
Free Colored	175	38	211	293	418	428	319	354
Beaufort District								
White	4,364	4,199	4,792	4,679	5,664	5,650	5,947	6,714
Slave	14,236	16,031	20,914	27,339	30,861	29,692	32,279	32,530
Free Colored	153	198	181	181	507	462	579	809
Georgetown District								
White	......	......	1,710	1,830	1,931	2,093	2,193	3,013
Slave	......	......	13,867	15,546	17,798	15,993	18,253	18,109
Free Colored	......	......	102	227	214	188	201	183

Statistics for Georgetown prior to 1810 are omitted, because the district then had very different boundaries and area.

[8] W. B. Seabrook, *Memoir on Cotton* (Charleston, 1844), 35, 36.

line; trustworthy slaves were practically in a state of industrial freedom; and that *tertium quid,* the free person of color, always officially unwelcome, was now regarded in private life as a desirable
resident of a neighborhood, provided he were a good workman.
The liberalizing tendencies were fast relieving the hard-and-fast
character of the regime, so far at least as concerned all workmen
who were capable of better things than gang and task labor.[9]

The great mass of the common negroes, it is true, were regarded
as suited only for the gangs and unfit for any self-direction in
civilized industry; but even in this case a few thinking men saw

[9] That the white laboring class was disposed to obstruct the growth of industrial opportunity for slaves, and was acquiring strength for this as years
passed, is shown in a remarkable public letter written by L. W. Spratt, of
Charleston, early in 1861, to advocate the re-opening of the African slave trade.
The letter, nominally addressed to John Perkins, of Louisiana, was published
in the Charleston *Mercury,* Feb. 13, 1861. Its remarks upon free and slave
labor relations are as follows:

"Within ten years past, as many as ten thousand slaves have been drawn
away from Charleston by the attractive prices of the West, and laborers from
abroad have come to take their places. These laborers have every disposition to
work above the slave, and if there were opportunity would be glad to do so,
but without such opportunity they come into competition with him; they are
necessarily restive to the contact. Already there is disposition to exclude him
from the trades, from public works, from drays, and the tables of hotels; he is
even now excluded to a great extent. And . . . when . . . more laborers . . . shall
come in greater numbers to the South, they will still more increase the tendency to exclusion; they will question the right of masters to employ their
slaves in any works that they may wish for; they will invoke the aid of legislation; they will use the elective franchise to that end; they may acquire the
power to determine municipal elections; they will inexorably use it; and thus
the town of Charleston, at the very heart of slavery, may become a fortress of
democratic power against it. As it is in Charleston, so also is it to a less extent
in the interior towns. Nor is it only in the towns that the tendency appears.
The slaves from lighter lands within the State have been drawn away for years
by the higher prices in the West. They are now being drawn from rice culture.
Thousands are sold from rice fields every year. None are brought to them.
They have already been drawn from the culture of indigo and all manufacturing employments. They are as yet retained by cotton and the culture incident
to cotton; but as almost every negro offered in our markets is bid for by the
West, the drain is likely to continue; it is probable that more abundant pauper
labor may pour in, and it is to be feared that even this State, the purest in its
slave condition, democracy [*i.e.* industrial democracy or self-governing labor, as
opposed to slave labor] may gain a foothold, and that here also the contest for
existence may be waged between them."

vaguely from time to time that a less expensive method of control ought to be substituted for chattel slavery, involving as it did the heavy capitalization of lifetime labor as a commodity.[10] This period of economic liberalism produced that phenomenal generation of large-minded and powerful statesmen which included William Lowndes, Cheves, Calhoun, William Smith, and McDuffie, fitting successors to Rawlins Lowndes, Gadsden, Rutledge, Izard, Drayton, and the Pinckneys. No representatives of a perverse or reactionary commonwealth could have gained so decisive an influence upon American affairs as was exercised by these statesmen in the second decade of the century.

To this progress of liberalism a single event gave a violent check. In the early summer of 1822 there was discovered in Charleston a widespread and well-matured conspiracy among the slaves and free negroes for a servile revolt and the destruction of the whites. The leader was Denmark Vesey, and the headquarters of the conspiracy were in his blacksmith shop. Vesey was a native African of unusual ability, who had bought his freedom in 1800 with part of the proceeds of a prize drawn in a lottery and had made himself a dominating person among the negroes of the city. One of Vesey's right-hand men was Monday Gell, a negro slave of talent, in charge of a harness shop, able to write fluently and much indulged and trusted by his master. Monday, it was afterwards reported, professed to be in correspondence with men of power in Africa and San Domingo who would give aid in the Carolina revolt. The chief organizer among the half-savage, lowest-grade negroes was Gullah Jack, by inheritance a conjurer among the Angolas and reputed to lead a charmed life. Jack, himself little touched by civilization, was unable to plan, but was of great value in rousing the savage nature of his fellows to the desired pitch of frenzy. Another leader was Peter Poyas, who circulated the report that the whites had determined to thin out the negroes and would begin a great killing on July 4. He urged the blacks to rise quickly and forestall the blow. These ringleaders had selected the points at which the negroes in town and outside were to gather, upon a signal to be

---

[10] Cf. "The Economic Cost of Slaveholding," on page 117 of this volume.

given at midnight of June 16, and had laid out a program for seizing the guard-house and arsenal and sweeping the city with fire and sword.[11] An inkling of the conspiracy reached the police on May 30. The first negroes arrested denied all knowledge of a plot; but after a week's solitary confinement they were ready to talk. Their admissions then led to other arrests and, after another season of tongue-loosening confinement, to still more alarming admissions and in turn to still more arrests. Finally, the evidence brought out at the formal trial of the prisoners laid bare the whole machinery and extent of the plot. The public thus learned the disquieting details in cumulative installments. The general effect of alarm and horror may be better imagined than described. There was apparently, however, no popular hysteria. A special constabulary was appointed for public safety, and a special court to try the negroes under arrest. To its bench were appointed the most substantial, conservative, and respected citizens whom Charleston contained. Reputable attorneys were appointed for each side of every case; the trial of each slave was conducted in his owner's presence; and every other precaution was taken for fairness, justice, and security. During two months of unprecedented excitement in Charleston, while the trials were in progress, the Charleston corporation was "proud to say," in its official report, that "the laws, without even one violation, have ruled with uninterrupted sway—that no cruel, vindictive or barbarous modes of punishment have been resorted to—that justice has been blended with an enlightened humanity . . . to those who had meted out for us murder, rapine and conflagration in their most savage forms." As a result of the trials, thirty-five negroes were sentenced to death and hanged before August 10; twelve were sentenced to death but respited with a view to commutation of sentence; twenty-two were sentenced to transportation; nine were acquitted with a suggestion to their masters that they be transported; and fifty-two were acquitted and discharged. Denmark Vesey's plot had passed into his-

[11] *An Account of the late Intended Insurrection among a portion of the Blacks of this City.* Published by the Authority of the Corporation of Charleston. (Charleston, 1822; 48 pp.).

tory with little noise in the great world outside, but with lasting impress upon the lowland community.

The effect of Vesey's plot upon public sentiment in the Charleston district is eloquently shown in a memorial presented by the citizens of Charleston to the South Carolina legislature in the fall of 1822.[12] It begins with a description of the position of the negroes:

Under the influence of mild and generous feelings, the owners of slaves in our state were rearing up a system which extended many privileges to our negroes; afforded them greater protection; relieved them from numerous restraints; enabled them to assemble without the presence of a white person, for the purpose of social intercourse, or religious worship; yielding to them the facilities for securing most of the comforts and many of the luxuries of improved society; and what is of more importance, affording them means of enlarging their minds and extending their information; a system whose establishment many persons could not reflect on without concern and whose rapid extension the experienced among us could not observe but "with fear and trembling," nevertheless, a system which won the approbation of by far the greater number of our citizens, who exulted in what they termed the progress of liberal ideas upon the subject of slavery, while many good and pious persons fondly cherished the expectation that our negroes would be influenced in their conduct toward their owners by sentiments of affection and gratitude.

But, the document goes on to relate, a dreadful plot was forming which has now by providential means been discovered. It is the duty of the people and the state to provide preventives for such occurrences in force and hence this petition to the legislature. Constructive suggestions now follow:

[12] Memorial of the Citizens of Charleston to the Senate and House of Representatives of the State of South Carolina. Title-page wanting, and list of signers not printed. 12 pp. This pamphlet, like most others concerning South Carolina in the period, is of extreme rarity. Its text will be reprinted shortly, with kindred material, in a volume of documents on Plantation and Frontier Industrial Society, to be edited by the present writer and published by the American Bureau of Industrial Research, The Macmillan Company, New York. Cf., *American Historical Review*, XII, 207.

After a careful inquiry into the existing evils of our slave system, and after mature reflection on the remedies to be adopted, [we] humbly recommend that laws be passed to the following effects:

1st. To send out of our state, never again to return, all free persons of color . . . . They form a third class in our society, enjoying more privileges than the slaves, and yet possessing few of the rights of the master; a class of persons having and exercising the right of moving unrestrained over every part of the state; of acquiring property, of amassing wealth to an unlimited extent, of procuring information on every subject, and of uniting themselves in associations or societies— yet, still a class, deprived of all political rights, subjected equally with the slaves to the police regulations for persons of color, and sensible that by no peaceable and legal methods can they render themselves other than a degraded class in your society . . . Restraints are always irksome . . . . The free persons of color must be discontented with their situation. The hopes of the free negroes will increase with their numbers . . . .

The free persons of color will not emigrate, consequently the white people must; so that, as the free people of color are extending their lines, the whites are contracting theirs. This is not a mere speculation, but a fact sufficiently emphasized already. Every winter, considerable number of Germans, Swiss and Scotch arrive in Charleston, with the avowed intention of settling amongst us, but are soon induced to emigrate towards the West by perceiving most of the mechanical arts performed by free persons of color. Thus we learn, that the existence of this class among us is in the highest degree detrimental to our safety . . . .

The presence of free persons of color, the memorial continues, sets conditions before the eyes of the slaves which they cannot peaceably realize; it makes their labor irksome and offers many temptations; and the intimate association of these persons with the slaves permits at all times the dissemination of dangerous ideas and news items which the slaves would not otherwise learn. The memorialists admit that inconvenience would arise from the expulsion of the free persons of color, but urge that that must be tolerated for the general welfare. A stern policy, they assert, is necessary, "that we may extinguish at once every gleam of hope which the slaves may indulge of ever becoming free—and that we may proceed to govern them on the only principle that can maintain slavery, the 'principle of fear.' "

They recommend, further, that the number of slaves to be hired out should be limited by law, and no slave should be allowed to work as a mechanic unless under the immediate control of his master. Most of those who work out, they say, are largely released from control, to work or idle or attend meetings and conspire without hindrance.

But there is another consideration. The facility for obtaining work is not always the same . . . . Irregularity of habits is thus acquired; this irregularity produces restlessness of disposition, which delights in mischief and detests quiet. The same remarks will apply to the negro mechanics, who having a stated portion of labor to perform, are masters of the remainder of the day, when the work is ended.

The memorial closes with still other recommendations for the repression of free persons of color and a more strict police over negroes in general. On the whole, an authoritative expression of more reactionary sentiment would be hard to discover.

Two years prior to this excitement a pamphleteer had written: "We regard our negroes as the 'Jacobins' of the country, against whom we should always be upon our guard, and who, though we fear no permanent effects from any insurrectionary movement on their part, should be watched with an eye of steady and unremitted attention." [13] In 1820 little heed seems to have been given to this writer; but when the terrible discovery of the great plot had been made, his words were read as those of a prophet.

The fright of 1822 soon passed; no important changes in the general system were instituted; and the previous conditions of life and industry were in the main restored. That period of excitement, however, was epoch making, in that it checked the growth of liberalism and prepared the community for its sensitive hostility to the Garrisonian agitation for the overthrow of negro slavery.

[13] *A Refutation of the Calumnies, etc.* (cited above), p. 61.

During the remainder of the antebellum period the industrial and social conditions of the Charleston district underwent little change. The need for collective efficiency continued to be felt, and in most cases the actual restrictions on labor were no more severe. Racial, industrial, and legal classes were still by no means identical. That free persons of color had a really excellent industrial opportunity in Charleston, and that many of them used it to advantage, is proved by the tax lists of the city. The list for 1860, which is available in print,[14] gives the names of 360 persons of color whose property was assessed in that year. The real estate owned by them was valued for taxation at $724,570. Of these 360 taxpayers, there were 130 who owned slaves aggregating 390 in number. The largest number of slaves held by a person of color was fourteen; the average number was three. In this list of persons of color, thirteen were classed as Indians; their real estate aggregated $73,300, and nine of them owned thirty-three slaves. It is quite probable, however, that most of these so-called Indians had a large infusion of negro blood. This showing of the wealth and slaveholding of the free persons of color demonstrates that industrial opportunity was fairly free for them, and that a number of mulattoes, at least, made large use of their chance to earn money and save it.

By good fortune, we have a census of the city of Charleston for the year 1848,[15] which in its industrial tables gives complete data for a statistical view of the relation of racial, legal and industrial classes in the later antebellum period. In summary it is here presented. It shows how large was the intermingling of the races and legal classes in nearly all the important industrial occupations.[16]

[14] List of the Tax Payers of the City of Charleston for 1860. (Charleston, 1861; 335 pp.).

[15] J. L. Dawson and H. W. DeSaussure, Census of Charleston for 1848. (Charleston, 1849.) Industrial tables, pp. 31 to 36.

[16] Statistics of employments of the free persons of color in New Orleans and New York in 1850, valuable for comparison with that of Charleston, are printed in G. B. G. De Bow's Compendium of the Seventh Census of the United States, 1850, pp. 80, 81.

INDUSTRIAL CENSUS OF CHARLESTON FOR 1848

	WHITES		SLAVES		FREE COLORED	
	MEN	WOMEN	MEN	WOMEN	MEN	WOMEN
Artisans						
Carpenters and joiners	120	....	110	....	27	
Masons and stone cutters	67	....	68	....	10	
Painters and plasterers	18	....	16	....	4	
Plumbers and gas fitters	9					
Wharf builders	2	....	10			
Boot and shoe makers	30	....	6	....	17	
Tailors and cap makers	68	6	36	....	42	6
Bleachers and dyers	5					
Hair braiders and wig makers	3	2				
Barbers and hair dressers	....	6	4	14		
Bakers	35	1	39	....	1	
Butchers	10	....	5	....	1	
Blacksmiths	45	....	40	....	4	
Coopers	20	....	61	....	2	
Ship carpenters and joiners	52	....	51	....	6	
Riggers and sail makers	13					
Gun, copper and locksmiths	14	....	1	....	1	
Cigar makers	10	....	5	....	1	
Cabinet makers	26	....	8			
Carvers, gilders and upholsterers	16	....	1	....	1	
Tinners	10	....	3	....	1	
Millwrights	4	....	....	....	5	
Saddle and harness makers	29	....	2	....	1	
Wheelwrights	6	....	....	....	1	
Horseshoers	6	....				
Coach makers and trimmers	20	....	3			
Boiler makers	6					
Machinists	10					
Engineers	43					
Silversmiths and watch makers	38					
Bookbinders	10	....	3			
Printers	65	....	5			
Organ and piano builders	4					
Other mechanics and journeymen	27	....	45	....	2	
Miscellaneous						
Seamstresses and mantua makers	....	125	....	24	....	196
Milliners	....	44	....	....	....	7
Market women and milk venders	....	9				
Pastry cooks and cooks	....	1	3	12	....	16
Laundresses	....	....	....	33	....	45
Mid-wives and nurses	....	5	....	2	....	10
Coachmen	2	....	15	....	4	
Draymen	13	....	67	....	11	
Omnibus drivers	7					
Wharfingers, stevedores and porters	20	....	37	....	6	
Apprentices	56	5	43	8	14	7
Barkeepers	16					
Domestic servants	13	100	1888	3384	9	28
Laborers	192	....	838	378	19	2
Fishermen	10	....	11	....	14	
Superannuated	....	....	38	54	1	4

Neither the public dread of disorder nor the class dislike of negro competition could arrest the forces that urged the community toward the increase of its industrial efficiency.

The following table of slave prices is of value for study in many connections besides that in which it is here used. The prices quoted are the average prices, as well as can be ascertained, of prime field hands for the locality in the years stated. The averages for the Charleston district have been made from a great mass of manuscript bills of sale of slaves bought and sold in Charleston, recorded and now preserved among the archives in the state capitol at Columbia. The origin of the data for the Georgia cotton belt, and the method of handling the figures, have been explained in my article on the economic cost of slaveholding.[17]

Slave Prices in the Charleston District
Averages for Prime Field Hands

YEAR	PRICE	YEAR	PRICE	YEAR	PRICE	YEAR	PRICE
1800	$ 500	1814	$ 450	1830	$ 450	1844	$ 500
1801	550	1815	500	1831	475	1845	550
1802	550	1816	600	1832	500	1846	650
1803	575	1817	650	1833	525	1847	750
1804	600	1819	850	1834	650	1848	700
1805	550	1820	725	1835	750	1849	650
1806	550	1822	650	1836	1100	1850	700
1807	525	1823	600	1837	1200	1851	750
1808	550	1824	500	1838	1000	1852	800
1809	500	1825	500	1839	1000	1853	900
1810	500	1826	475	1840	800	1855	900
1811	550	1827	475	1841	650	1858	950
1812	500	1828	450	1842	600	1859	1100
1813	450	1829	475	1843	500	1860	1200

Slave Prices (for comparison) in Middle Georgia

YEAR	PRICE	YEAR	PRICE	YEAR	PRICE	YEAR	PRICE
1800	$ 450	1821	$ 700	1839	$1000	1853	$1200
1805	550	1826	800	1840	700	1859	1650
1808	650	1828	700	1844	600	1860	1800
1813	450	1835	900	1848	900		
1818	1000	1837	1300	1851	1050		

A comparison of these two local tables shows that slave prices at Charleston after about 1800 were practically never above those pre-

[17] See "The Economic Cost of Slaveholding in the Cotton Belt," on page 117 of this volume.

vailing in the upland cotton belt; but that the interior usually offered a premium which often ranged from one hundred to several hundred dollars per head for prime field hands. The fact that in the face of this premium the planting families of the coast retained such a multitude of slaves in their district throughout the whole period shows that the spirit of the planters was not wholly commercial. It shows that the typical slaveholder of the coast deliberately and constantly preferred the career of the useful captain of industry to the life of the idle rich. Otherwise, the temptation to sell his slaves west would have been irresistible. There is abundant unconscious evidence that the typical planter had a controlling distaste for selling slaves except in emergencies. The dominating consideration with masters and mistresses was not that of great profit, but that of comfortable living in pleasant surroundings, with a consciousness of important duties well performed. However radical they might by force of circumstances become in politics, the Carolina planters were beyond question careful, moderate and intelligently conservative in matters of industry and social policy. But invincible powers, through largely misinformed sentiment, were being arrayed against them; and their unending task of race discipline was destined to most serious disturbance, if not, as it may prove, to permanent arrest.

With the great Civil War and its aftermath we are not now concerned. The killing off of the flower of Carolina manhood in the war time, the heartbreaking sorrow of the women and the old men who stayed at home, the black despair of the oncoming generation, the great upheaval and demoralization in the so-called Reconstruction period and the gradual return thereafter to moderately healthful conditions do not lie within the scope of this paper. It remains only to attempt a general résumé of the situation in the later antebellum period.

In the slaveholding districts there was fully as much particularism and competition among the industrial units as anywhere else in America. A condition of the life of the system, in such a region as the Carolina lowlands, was efficiency; and the increasing competition of the West called for an increase of efficiency if the relative standards of prosperity and of comfort were to be maintained. This affected both city and country and was the direct concern of every member of the industrial and commercial community. The struggle for increased efficiency tended to make every laborer who was capable of self-direction free to direct his own industrial efforts and to promote his full equipment by education for his work. It tended to cause negroes, mulattoes, and whites to be put upon the same industrial footing, and to cause the capable slave to be given industrial freedom, under the system of hiring him to himself or otherwise securing to him rewards in some measure proportional to the value of the work done by him. This was the economic requirement of the times.

But the social requirement was largely in direct conflict with this. The community had always in contemplation the possibility of social death from negro upheaval and control, as illustrated in San Domingo, and the milder fate of industrial stagnation and decay from premature emancipation, as illustrated in Jamaica.[18] To save their commonwealth from approaching either fate, the Carolinians contended with might and main against any abolition to be imposed from without, and in their local regulations they introduced every possible safeguard against successful conspiracy. Through laws enacted, reenacted and fortified, they provided for strict patrol and general police, forbade the teaching of negroes to read, forbade masters to hire to slaves their time, forbade negroes to assemble without white persons being present, and restricted private emancipation. These laws were more or less observed or more or less disregarded according to the course of events and the play of public sentiment between the social and economic points of view.

[18] Still another conceivable alternative would have been the fusion of the two races by interbreeding, the attempted blending of moral codes and the consequent degradation of standards, which occurred in several of the Latin American states. That this development was impossible and little thought of in South Carolina was largely due to the English origin of the citizens. They were sturdy, proud, masterful, staunch. To recognize negroid morality and institutions as in any way entitled to equal footing with their own in the community was for them impossible. The tendency of the Garrisonian agitation in that direction was perhaps its most irritating feature.

From the social point of view, all persons of color were of one class and regarded as all very possibly dangerous; from the economic point of view all capable negroes and mulattoes were looked upon as the equals of the whites in their industrial class, and therefore meriting and requiring the same industrial freedom and incentive that the whites enjoyed. Public opinion oscillated between these two positions; but inclined more generally to the restrictive point of view after Vesey's plot and during the Garrisonian agitation. Official policy in general inclined toward safeguarding society; but private policy was more controlled by economic needs, and in that highly individualistic community private policy largely dominated. Society and industry in fact confronted an *impasse*, and politics were at a loss to find a way out of it unless by the policy of drifting.

In 1860, failing to solve its part of the world's problem of equity in human relationships, the commonwealth clashed with the dominant idea of the period. In the championship of their system the planters and their neighbors were defeated, and their system was shattered as far as it could be by its victorious enemies encamped upon the field. But the pendulum swings again. Facts of human nature and the law of civilized social welfare are too stubborn for the theories of negrophiles as well as of negrophobes. The slave labor problem has disappeared, but the negro problem remains.

PART FOUR

A Glance at the
British West Indies

16

An Antigua Plantation, 1769-1818

DETAILED records of West India sugar plantations are so rare and significant that a newly available one invites prompt analysis.* The present study is a digest of thirty thin manuscript account books bequeathed to the Massachusetts Historical Society in 1924 by David S. Greenough.[1]

Shute Shrimpton Yeamans, Esq., a man of affairs in London and a stockholder and official of the South Sea Company, died in 1769, possessed of a handsomely furnished home on Richmond Green, sundry securities, many tracts of land in Massachusetts and New Hampshire, a five-hundreth share (specified as being "1/5th of 1/90th of 90/100ths") of the province of West New Jersey, and a sugar plantation in Antigua with its complement of slaves. The first of the volumes at hand records the administration of Yeamans' property by the executors of his will, from 1769 to 1775. Certain of its entries note that William Hyslop of London was among the beneficiaries of the testament;[2] that Thomas Greenough of Boston was Yeamans' agent for the North Ameri-

---

* *North Carolina Historical Review*, III (July, 1926), 439–45.

[1] I am indebted to Dr. Worthington C. Ford for calling my attention to these materials and facilitating my use of them. The present paper is in a sense complementary to "A Jamaica Slave Plantation," printed in the *American Historical Review*, XIX, 543-558, in which I digested the record of the Worthy Park plantation for the years 1792–1796. Mary Gaunt, *Where the Twain Meet* (London, 1922), has more briefly analyzed the record book of the same plantation for 1787–1792 which she examined while on a visit to the estate in 1920.

[2] The chief beneficiary was Shute Yeamans, then a minor, who received an allowance of £600 sterling a year by order of the Lord Chancellor, and for whose tutoring and incidental expenses John Redman was one year paid £120.

can properties; and that Yeamans had some business relations with one Charles Chauncey.[3] The remaining volumes are yearly financial reports of the Antigua plantation in ledger form, from 1779 to 1817, with an extra report for the first three months of 1818,[4] but with the volumes for 1790 to 1795 missing.

By 1779 the plantation had become the property of William Hyslop, Charles Chauncey, and Thomas Greenough as partners in equal interest.[5] This condition continued until Chauncey died and his share fell to sundry heirs in one-sixth parts. In 1797 Samuel Athill of Antigua, who had previously held a contract for medical services on the plantation, acquired the interests of all the Chauncey heirs. Thereafter Athill held a one-third interest in the property, while two-thirds were held by Hyslop and Greenough jointly. Meanwhile, in 1788, David Greenough had replaced Thomas Greenough among the proprietors.

The acreage of the plantation was continually reported at two hundred and nine, of which thirty acres were taxed by Saint Paul's Parish and the rest by Saint Peter's. This suggests that it lay near the center of the island; but, even so, it could not have been more than ten or twelve miles from the sea in any direction. The slaves as returned for taxation in 1779 numbered 121. This number declined to 109 in 1784 when eleven "new negroes," which means fresh importations from Africa, were bought in two parcels at £36 and £37 sterling per head. Thereafter the corps increased to 122 in 1787, where it remained stationary until 1801. It then declined to 104 in 1806, with mentions of vaccination suggesting an epidemic

[3] The fact that this Charles Chauncey died before 1797 demonstrates that he was not the Connecticut jurist of that name. He may possibly have been Charles Chauncy, the Boston clergyman.

[4] This special accounting on March 31, 1818, suggests that a change was then made in the proprietorship; and absence of further records in the Greenough file suggests that Greenough's interest was then extinguished.

[5] In some of the later records the plantation is designated as belonging to the heirs of Shute Shrimpton Yeamans, deceased. Shute Yeamans (see note 2) may have died between 1775 and 1779; or possibly a suit in chancery, which is mentioned in the executors' accounts, may have dispossessed young Yeamans in favor of Hyslop, Chauncey and Greenough. It is noteworthy that Greenough, who presumably still dwelt in Boston, was not disturbed as an owner of property elsewhere in the British Empire during the war for American independence.

of smallpox. Through the rest of the period the number was virtually unchanged. No sales of slaves are recorded. The draft animals comprised both mules and oxen, the numbers of which are never stated. The cylinders for pressing the cane were turned by a windmill, with canvas-covered sails, the repairs and replacements of which were quite expensive; and the boiling house had two sets

The Yeamans Plantation in Antigua
Crops, Earnings and Expenditures

(Money items are given in local currency, depreciated to about 4 per cent of the value of sterling. Shillings and pence are omitted.)

Years	Production		Income from		Expenditures	Net earnings	Net losses
	Sugar in cwts.	Rum, in gallons	Sugar (partly at appraised values)	Rum (actual proceeds of sales)			
1779	503	3102			£ 1123		
1780	303	1669			577		
1781	666	2704			989		
1782	1402	5296			1591		
1783	341	1894			1228		
1784	1784	5225			2284		
1785	1348	5158			2046		
1786	823	3468			1684		
1787	2162	6375			1643		
1788	1380	5263			1772		
1789	1247	4760			1646		
1790 to 1795, records missing.							
1796	769	2814	£ 3075	£ 1210	2289	£ 1997	
1797	702	2565	3048	968	1822	2199	
1798	267	1069	1120	432	1721		£ 165
1799	1779	2625	7260	718	4430	3764	
1800	1065	2926	3980	679	3742	936	
1801	1380*	2592	3905	842	3550	1507	
1802	1650	4427	4634	1109	2490	3258	
1803	1239	3853	3338	896	2229	2214	
1804	1313	5232	3547	1325	2253	2671	
1805	745	2176	2194	549	2500	293	
1806	942	3773	2524	954	3082	431	
1807	1050	4254	2123	965	2631	886	
1808	797	4296	1634	877	2376	235	
1809	1426	5612	3774	1506	2686	2628	
1810	2087	6356	5055	1665	2916	4241	
1811	1555	2828	2373	813	2326	1089	
1812	962	3660	2424	1010	2558	1145	
1813	671	2330	2428	682	2090	1129	
1814	406	918	1865	249	3559		1222
1815	1479	4698	5229	1329	3443	3476	
1816	1514	5070	4189	1267	4180	1995	
1817	956	2615	2952	609	2428	1304	

* The record for 1801 does not give the sugar crop in pounds, as usual, but states it only as 84 hogsheads and 12 tierces. The standard West India hogshead contained sixteen hundredweight of muscovado sugar, but those of this plantation averaged only 15 hundredweight conjecturing a content of 1000 pounds for each tierce, the estimate of 1380 hundredweight results.

of four copper cauldrons each. The rum still also was on a considerable scale.[6] The tools bought for coopers, carpenters, and masons were in full assortment; but for tillage the purchase of hoes by dozens compares with allusion to but a single plough and a single ploughman in the whole record. The ratio of less than two acres of land per slave indicates little use of the plough; and an occasional item of expenditure for the "holing" of fields[7] by jobbing gangs at £7 to £12 currency per acre confirms this indication.

The crops and the net earnings, nevertheless, compare favorably with the common West India experience in the period, for the general practice was to use the plough very little. The sugar and rum outputs are recorded through the years of the ledger statements;[8] but the gross, and therefore the net, incomes are available only from 1796.[9] The money items here tabulated are in the local currency, which had about four-sevenths the value of sterling.

The plantation had factors in London and elsewhere to handle its overseas purchases and sales on commission; a local agent (usually styled "attorney" in West Indian parlance), residing in one of the towns of Antigua, to represent the absentee proprietors and hire and fire the other employed personnel; a manager in charge of operations; and an overseer, sometimes styled in these records under-overseer (the etymology invites attention), subordinate to

[6] Illustrative items of replacement are: in 1779 a still-head weighing 789 pounds, costing £39 9s., and a pewter still-neck, 186 pounds, costing £11 12s. 6d. sterling; in 1801 a windmill spindle of hardwood, at £165 currency; and in 1814 a cogwheel for the mill, at £200 currency. In 1799 and 1800 the boiling house and its apparatus were renovated at a cost of several thousand pounds.

[7] Furrowing preparatory to planting with cane.

[8] For the years in which the Yeamans executors were in charge the sugar sales were: in 1770, 82 hogsheads at a total price of £1826 5s. 8d. sterling; in 1771, 83 hhds.; in 1772, 64 hhds.; in 1773, 65 hhds.; in 1774, 105 hhds., yielding £1650.

[9] The available statements of income are in some part results of appraising the sugar as it left Antigua rather than of actual sales at London, Liverpool, Dublin, Greenock, Boston, etc., whither it was shipped for sale. The accounts as kept on the plantation were merely tentative as to final results. Definitive accounts were doubtless made by the London factors, who distributed the net returns among the proprietors. The London factors were the firm styled in 1779 Robert, Robert and Ebenezer Maitland. Its name underwent many changes: e.g. Ebenezer and John Maitland and John Ede; Maitlands, Ede and Bond; and finally Ede and Bond.

the manager. The agent, who was Samuel Eliot from Yeamans' time until 1799 and Samuel Athill thereafter, received in compensation a commission of twenty shillings sterling per hogshead of sugar produced. The manager drew a salary of £90 currency in 1799, which advanced by stages to £150 in 1817. There were five changes of personnel in this office during the thirty-three years of record. The overseer, paid £60 currency in 1779 and £90 in 1817, was changed twenty-eight times in the same period. Several of the overseers were re-engaged after intervals; and two of them were promoted to the managership, though neither of these was long retained in that office. The manager was entitled to forty pounds of fresh beef every Christmas or a commutation of £4 currency, and the overseer to half as much. There were also on the payroll a bookkeeper at £20, later £30 a year, and a town agent to attend to wharfage, cooperage, etc., at £20, later £35 a year. For a time these two functions were combined in the one person of John Smith.

Among fixed charges, there were taxes paid to the government of Antigua and to the parishes of Saint Peter and Saint Paul, and an imperial tax of 4½ per cent on sugar exported.[10] A special tax was paid to the island government in most years at a somewhat heavy rate, for the deficiency of white servants, i.e., the failure to maintain a ratio of one white man on the plantation for every thirty slaves.[11] Wharf rental at the Port of Parham was also a fixed charge of £16 a year; and medical services on contact at six shillings, increased to nine shillings after 1804, per head of slaves and £5 per head of white employees each year. Medicines were included in

[10] This export tax was not included in the account of expenses. It was paid in sugar at the island port and omitted from all further reckoning. Somewhat likewise, marine insurance on sugar was deducted from the account of sugar sales, and not included in the account of plantation expense. In 1805, the year of Trafalgar, the cost of marine insurance ran as high as 15 per cent but commonly it was very much lower.

[11] There was usually also a tax paid for "deficiency of cisterns." This may be explained by an item written by Lord Adam Gordon while on a visit to the island in 1764: "As much of Antigua as I saw is pleasant. The want of Springs and Rivers is in some degree compensated by the pains they have taken in making for each house one or more large Cisterns (or tancks) which are Terrassed over and catch all the rain Water that falls on the Houses, by Conduits and Pipes well adapted for that end. But the want of Water to cool the stills used in the making of Rum is much felt by the poor Negroes, who carry it on their heads in large vessels and sometimes from a considerable distance."

these flat rates; but vaccinations, the setting of broken bones, and obstetrical services were charged extra. There were expenditures nearly every year also for coppersmith, blacksmith, millwright, and other artisan work; for certain food supplies; for cloth, at from one to three shillings per yard for osnaburgs or other sorts of "negro cloth"; for hogsheads and puncheons, or staves, heading, and hoops with which to make them; and for freight. From time to time there were outlays for lumber and mules from North America,[12] for oxen from unspecified sources, and for nails, rivets, apparatus, and miscellaneous goods, including hogsheads of beans, from England. The total of expenditures fluctuated widely from year to year, with a strong upward tendency as time passed.

Revenues came chiefly from sugar, most of which was marketed in England. The by-product, molasses, was sometimes sold as such in small quantities; but as a rule it was converted into rum and sold locally, with five shillings a gallon the most common price. Income from other sources, for example from the sale of yams, old oxen and scrap metal, was generally small. The sugar output varied from a maximum of 216,216 pounds in 1787 to a minimum but one-eighth as large in 1798. The fluctuations in the volume of rum did not correspond closely with those of sugar, presumably because in poor crop years part of the cane did not yield juice good enough for boiling. Net returns distributed accruing to the proprietors were at a maximum of £4241 5s. 6d. in 1810, while in two years there were net losses instead. The average net returns in the twenty-two years of the record available in these premises were about £1638, local currency, or perhaps £936 sterling. This may have been as much as eight or ten per cent upon the current value of the investment.

[12] Staves usually cost about £25 per thousand for red oak, and £30 for white oak; and pine lumber from £20 to £30 per thousand feet. Hoops were of either ash, hickory or iron. Hardwood was bought locally for mill cylinders, cogs and spokes at high prices. Mules cost £40 to £45 each, and oxen, curiously, about as much. All prices, where not specified as sterling, were in the depreciated currency. It is remarkable that the "new negroes" bought in 1784 cost less than twice as much per head as did mules or oxen at that time. Seasoned slaves, of course, were considered much more valuable than those freshly imported, and slaves born and reared in America were still more valuable.

Various items of expenditure cast sidelights upon the regime. For some years five slave men were hired, some of them partly skilled. The usual rate was £16 per head; but in 1801 it was at 14 per cent on their valuation of £730 as a lot. Slave artisans were hired at sixty-six to seventy-two shillings per month, and white carpenters and a free negro at similar rates. In addition to the wages paid their masters, the slave artisans were themselves paid "allowances," which may have been commutation of board, or payment for overtime work, or possibly a reward for good service. The slaves belonging to the plantation were sometimes paid for Sunday work, at four or six shillings for artisans and two shillings for common laborers. In 1815 a slave owned by Samuel Athill was hired as a sugar maker, and was given £2 5s. for improving the quality of the sugar. Once in a while Cudjoe was paid by the job for veterinary services. Whether he was a slave or a free negro is not indicated.

That slaves ran away, even in that small island, is shown by payments nearly every year for recaptures, usually at a standard rate of 8s. 3d. In one instance the fee was paid to a slave for the recapture of another. In several cases the fugitive was jailed by the public authorities, which entailed considerable expense. Thus Andrew cost £3 13s. 9d. in January, 1784, and £2 1s. 6d. again in the following June. In the winter of 1812–1813 Hamand was sick in the public jail and afterward on the plantation, with expenses including four bottles of Madeira (£1 16s.) prescribed by a physician. Sundry other expenditures for "sick house," or hospital supplies on the plantation, year after year, specify wine, beef, mutton, lamb, chickens, cassava, rice, flour, ship's bread and candles. Purchases for the general food supply included corn and corn meal at widely fluctuating prices, beans, peas, yams, and occasional flour or "navy bread" when other breadstuffs were unavailable; and barreled shad, herrings, alewives and mackerel. In each December there were bought several, usually four, barrels of salt pork or beef and a similar quantity of flour "for the negroes' Xmas"; and in one year there was an additional outlay of £13 for Christmas allowance to the slaves. On the whole the plantation was conducted with severe frugality. How severe the management was in other respects does not appear in the record.

17

A Jamaica Slave Plantation

WHEN Lord Chesterfield endeavored in 1767 to buy his son a seat in Parliament, he learned "that there was no such thing as a borough to be had now, for that the rich East and West Indians had secured them all at the rate of three thousand pounds at least." * The nabobs from the Antilles were rivalling those from India in their display. The sugar islands were the most cherished of the imperial possessions, and the sugar estates were the greatest and most famous industrial enterprises in the world. Bulky descriptions of the West Indian regime, of an excellence never attained by the accounts of the continental colonies, found sale in large editions, and few were the moneyed men of England who felt no stir at the rumors of Jamaica planters' profits. But Jamaica's heyday was already waning, for her soils were becoming depleted and sugar prices had fallen. Of the three chief writers on Jamaica in the later eighteenth century, Long, Edwards, and Beckford, the two last illustrated in their own lives the extremes of planters' fortunes. Edwards was one of the nabobs who sat in the British House of Commons, but Beckford wrote his *Descriptive Account of Jamaica* in the Fleet prison where he lay in 1790, an insolvent debtor at the end of a planting career. These general works have left little to be desired except the intimate details which might be drawn only from the routine working of individual plantations. Records of this kind are of course exceedingly few; but we are not wholly bereft.

* *American Historical Review*, XIX (April, 1914), 543–58

Rose Price, Esquire, was the manager of Worthy Park plantation and its outlying properties in St. John's Parish, Jamaica, belonging to "Robert Price of Penzance in the Kingdom of Great Britain Esquire"; and Rose Price had an eye to the edification of posterity. Seeing that "the Books of Estates are the only Records by which future Generations can inform themselves of the management of Plantations," he set down directions in detail for the making and preservation of elaborate accounts of current operations. The special books for the sugar mill, the rum distillery, the commissary, and the field-labor routine, which he ordered kept, have apparently been lost; but the "great plantation book" for the years from 1792 to 1796 inclusive has survived and come to my hands. This comprises yearly inventories, records of the increase and decrease of slaves and draught animals, vestry returns, salary lists, vouchers, crop summaries, and accounts of the receipt and distribution of implements, clothing, foodstuffs, and other supplies.[1]

This plantation, which in its organization and experience appears to have been fully typical of the estates of the largest scale, lay near the centre of the island, perhaps twenty miles from the sea, on the rugged southern slope of the mountain chain. One of its dependencies was Spring Garden "cattle pen," lying higher on a nearby mountainside and serving as a place of recuperation for slaves and cattle as well as yielding a few oxen and some foodstuffs for the plantation. The other was Mickleton, presumably a farmstead used as a relay station for the teams hauling sugar and rum to Port Henderson, where they were embarked for Kingston on the way to market at London. The plantation itself probably contained several thousand acres, of which about 560 were in sugar cane, several score in guinea-grass for grazing, and a few in plantain and cocoa groves, while the rest was in woodland with occasional

---

[1] I am not acquainted with the history of this document beyond the fact that it came into my possession through an auction sale in New York a few years ago. The book, which measures twelve by eight inches, contains about five hundred pages of brittle paper, similar in texture to the modern product of wood-pulp, though with a somewhat oily quality. The accounts which fill the volume were made in excellent form. A few of the pages which were ruled into columns are now completely split into strips, however, and a number of others are more or less broken.

clearings where the negro families cultivated their own food crops in their hours of release from gang labor.

A cane field was not ripe for its first harvest (the "plant cane") until the second winter after its planting. When the stalks were then cut, new shoots ("rattoons") would spring up from the old roots and yield a diminished second crop the next winter, and so on for several years more, the output steadily growing smaller. After the fourth crop, according to the routine on Worthy Park, the field was planted anew. Thus in any year, while 560 acres were in constant cultivation, about one-fifth of the fields were freshly planted and four-fifths were harvested.

The slaves on the estate at the beginning of 1792 numbered 355, of whom 150 constituted the main field gangs; thirty-four were artificers and gang foremen; forty were watchmen, gardeners, and cattle tenders; thirteen were in the hospital corps; twenty-two were on the domestic staff: twenty-four girls and boys made up the "grass gang"; thirty-nine were young children; and thirty-three were invalids and superannuated. From the absence of indications that any of these were freshly imported Africans it may be assumed that all were seasoned negroes. The draught animals comprised eighty mules and one hundred and forty oxen. The stock of slaves was not adequate for the full routine of the plantation, for in this year "jobbing gangs" from the outside were employed at a cost of £1,832, reckoned probably in Jamaica currency which stood at thirty per cent discount. The jobbing contracts were recorded at rates from 2s.6d. to 3s. per laborer per day.

During the year the proprietor began to make great additions to his working force, with a view apparently to dispensing with the services of jobbing gangs. In March he bought ten new Africans, five men and five women; and in October ninety more, comprising twenty-five men, twenty-seven women, sixteen boys, sixteen girls, and six children, all new Congoes. In 1793 he added eighty-one more, fifty-one males and thirty females, part Congoes and part Coromantees, and nearly all of them about eighteen to twenty years old.

The advice of experienced planters was entirely opposed to such a proceeding as this. Edward Long, for example, had written:

The introduction of too many recruits at once has sometimes proved fatal to them. It is very evident that a small number can be much easier and better provided for, lodged, fed, and taken care of, than a multitude. The planter therefore, who buys only eight or ten at a time, will in the end derive more advantage from them, than the planter who buys thirty; for, by the greater leisure and attention in his power to bestow upon them, he will greatly lessen the ordinary chances against their life, and the sooner prepare them for an effectual course of labour. The comparison, indeed, founded upon fact and observation, is, that, at the end of three years, the former may possibly have lost one fifth, but the other will most probably have lost one half, of their respective numbers.[2]

All of the island authorities who wrote on the subject endorsed these precepts, but the Worthy Park administration was nothing daunted thereby. Thirty new huts were built; special cooks and nurses were detailed for the service of the new negroes; and quantities of special food-stuffs were bought—yams, plantains, flour, fresh and salt fish, and fresh beef heads, tongues, hearts, and bellies; but it is not surprising to find that the next outlay for equipment was for a large new hospital in 1794, costing £341 for building its brick walls alone. The emergency became pressing. Some of the newcomers, as was common in such case, developed yaws, a chronic and contagious African disease of the blood and skin closely akin to syphilis. These had to be lodged in an isolation hospital tended by a special nurse and cook, and worked, when worked at all, in a separate gang under a separate foreman. But yaws was a trifle as compared with dysentery—the "bloody flux" as it was then called. Pleurisy, pneumonia, fever, and dropsy had also to be reckoned with. About fifty of the new negroes were quartered for several years in a sort of hospital camp at Spring Garden, where the work for even the able-bodied was much lighter than on Worthy Park.

One of the new negroes died in 1792, and another the next year. With the spring of 1794 the period of heavy mortality began. Two pages of the record for this year are broken and partly missing. From the pages and fragments remaining it may be gathered that

[2] Long, *The History of Jamaica* (London, 1744), II, 435.

the total of the year's deaths was fifty-two (thirty-seven males and fifteen females) of which at least thirty-one were new negroes. One of the new women died in child-bed, one of the men died of a brain disorder, one of a paralytic stroke, and two were thought to have killed themselves. Virtually all the other deaths of new-comers were due to dysentery. By 1795 this disease was no longer epidemic. In that year the total of deaths was twenty-three, including at least five new negroes, two of these dying from dirt-eating,[3] one from yaws, and two from ulcers. The three years of the seasoning period were now ended, with about three-fourths of the number imported still alive. This loss was perhaps less than was usual in such cases; but it demonstrates the strength of shock involved in the transplantation from Africa, even after the severities of the "middle passage" had been survived, and after the most debilitated negroes had been culled out at the ports. In 1796 the new negroes were no longer discriminated in the mortality record. The total of deaths for the year was twenty-three, of which eight were from old age and decline, seven from dropsy, two each from fever, dysentery, and poison, one from consumption, and one from yaws. The outlay for jobbing gangs declined to £1,374 in 1793 and

[3] Of the "fatal habit of eating dirt," Thomas Roughley, who on his title-page described himself as "nearly twenty years a sugar planter in Jamaica," wrote in his *Planter's Guide* (London, 1823, pp. 118-120): "Nothing is more horribly disgusting, nothing more to be dreaded, nothing exhibiting a more heart-rending, ghastly spectacle, than a negro child possessed of this malady. Such is the craving appetite for this abominable custom that few, either children or adults, can be broken of it when once they begin to taste and swallow its insidious, slow poison. For if by incessant care, watchfulness, or keeping them about the dwelling house, giving them abundance of the best nourishing food, stomachic medicines, and kind treatment, it is possible to counteract the effects and habit of it for some time, the creature will be found wistfully and irresistibly to steal an opportunity of procuring and swallowing the deadly substance. The symptoms arising from it are a shortness of breathing, almost perpetual languor, irregular throbbing, weak pulse, a horrid cadaverous aspect, the lips and whites of the eyes a deadly pale (the sure signs of malady in the negro), the tongue thickly covered with scurf, violent palpitation of the heart, inordinate swelled belly, the legs and arms reduced in size and muscle, the whole appearance of the body becomes a dirty yellow, the flesh a quivering, pellucid jelly. The creature sinks into total indifference, insensible to everything around it, till death at last declares his victory in its dissolution."

to £506 in 1794. It rose to £632 in 1795, but disappeared in the final year of the record.

The list of slaves made at the beginning of 1794 is the only one in which full data are preserved as to ages, colors, health, and occupations. The ages given were of course in many cases mere approximations. The "great house negroes" head the list, fourteen in number. Four of these were "housekeepers," of whom two were forty-year-old women of "sambo" color, i.e., between mulatto and black, and the other two were mulatto girls of nineteen and eight years. There were three waiting boys, twenty, nineteen, and ten years old, one of them black and two mulatto. Susannah, black, fifty-five years old, and Joanny, sambo, twenty-six, were washerwomen, Penzance, black, fifty, was the cook; Spain, forty-five but not able-bodied, and Old Lucy, sixty, both black, were gardeners; and Old Tom, black, fifty, had the task of carrying grass. Quadroon Lizette, who had been hired out for several years to Peter Douglas, the owner of a jobbing gang, was manumitted during this year.

The slaves listed at the overseer's house, forty-two in number, included domestic servants, the hospital corps, and a group in industrial pursuits. Fanny, twenty-seven, mulatto, Harodine, twenty-four, sambo, and Sychie, black, sixty, who was troubled with the bone ache, were housekeepers; Peggy and Sally, mulatto girls of thirteen and fourteen, were "simstresses"; Jenny, forty-one, black, and Nancy, nineteen, mulatto, were washerwomen; Esther, thirty-five, black, was cook; and Harry, twenty-one, John, fifteen, and Richmond, fourteen, all black, were waiting boys. In the nursing and industrial groups all were black except one mulatto boy of ten years, a hog tender. Will Morris, the "black doctor," headed the hospital corps; Henrietta, sixty, was midwife; Dolly, thirty-six, and Sally, twenty-eight, were hospital nurses; Douglas, sixty, Grace, sixty, Emma, forty-five, and Blind Olive, thirty, tended the new negroes; Cimbrie, sixty-five, Old Molly, sixty, and Old Beneba were in charge of young children; and Old Sylvia, sixty, was field nurse for the suckling children of the women in the gangs. Abba, forty, who had lost a hand, and Flora were cooks to the "big gang," and Bessey, forty, cook to the second gang. Prince, thirty-five who had elephantiasis, was a groom; Yellow's Cuba and Peg's Nancy, both sixty, had charge of the poultry house; Dontcare, forty, and Solomon, twenty-three, the one ruptured and the other "distempered," were hog tenders, along with Robert the mulatto boy above mentioned; Quashy Prapra and Abba's Moll, sixty-five and sixty, mended pads; and Quamina, forty, and six others, sixty to sixty-five, gathered grass and hog feed.

Next are listed the watchmen, thirty-one in number, ranging from twenty-seven to seventy-five years in age, and all black but the mulatto foreman. Only six were described as able-bodied. Among the disabilities mentioned were a bad sore leg, a broken back, lameness, partial blindness, distemper, weakliness, and cocobees. The number in this night-watch was apparently not unusual. When the cane crop was green it might be severely damaged by the invasion of hungry cattle, and when it approached maturity a spark might set the fields into conflagration. A law of Barbados, in precaution against fire, prohibited the smoking of tobacco on paths bordering cane-fields.

A considerable number of the negroes already mentioned were in such condition that little work could be required of them. Those completely laid off were nine superannuated, two men and seven women ranging from seventy to eighty-five years old; four invalids, fourteen to thirty-five years old; and three women relieved of work, as by law required, for having reared six children each.

Among the tradesmen, virtually all the blacks were stated to be fit for field work, but the five mulattoes and the one quadroon, though mostly youthful and healthy, were described as not fit for the field. There were eleven carpenters, eight coopers, four sawyers, two blacksmiths, three masons, and twelve cattlemen, each squad with a foreman; and there were two ratcatchers. The tradesmen were all in early manhood or middle age except Old Quashy, the head carpenter, Old England, a sawyer, and Poole, Teckford, and Boot Cudjoe, cattlemen, who were from sixty to sixty-five, and Reeves and Little Sam, cattle boys, of fifteen and fourteen years.

The two ratcatchers followed an essential trade. Beckford wrote in his account of sugar-cane culture:

The rats are very great enemies to this plant, but particularly in proportion to its advance to ripeness. It will hardly be credited how very numerous these reptiles are in the Island of Jamaica, and what destruction, especially if the canes be lodged [*i.e.*, fallen to the ground], they annually commit upon a plantation: in a not less proportion do they injure the crops than a diminution of five hogsheads of sugar in every hundred, without adding much in proportion, by those that are tainted, to the increase of rum. Many and unremitting endeavours are daily put in practice for their extirpation. . . . Great numbers are taken off by poison immediately after the crop, and when their natural food is apparently exhausted; many are killed by dogs; and prodigious quantities destroyed by the negroes in the fields, when the canes are cut; and such innumerable proportions by the watchmen who are dispersed over the different parts of the plantation, to protect them from general trespass, and the particular destruction of these animals, that I was informed by a man of observation and veracity, that upon the estate of which, as overseer, he had charge, not less than nine and thirty thousand were caught by the latter, and, if I remember right, in the short space of five or six months.[4]

In the "weeding gang," a sort of industrial kindergarten in which most of the children from five to eight years old were kept, as much for control as for achievement, there were twenty pickaninnies, all black, under Mirtilla as "driveress," who had borne and lost seven children of her own. Thirty-nine children were too young for the weeding gang, at least six of whom were quadroons. Two of these children, Joanney's Henry Richards, quadroon, and Joanney's Valentina, whose color is not stated, were manumitted in 1795.

Fifty-five, all new negroes except Darby the foreman, and including Blossom, the infant daughter of one of the women, comprised the Spring Garden squad. Nearly all of these were twenty or twenty-one years old. The men included Washington, Franklin, Hamilton, Burke, Fox, Milton, Spencer, Hume, and Sheridan; the women, Spring, Summer, July, Bashfull, Virtue, Frolic, Game-

[4] Beckford, A *Descriptive Account of the Island of Jamaica* (London, 1790).

some, Lady, Madame, Dutchess, Mirtle, and Cowslip. Seventeen of the number died within the year.

The "big gang" on Worthy Park numbered 137, comprising sixty-four men from nineteen to sixty years old and seventy-three women of from nineteen to fifty years, though but four of the women and nine of the men, including Quashy, sixty, the "head driver" or foreman, were past forty years. The gang included Douglas Cuffee, forty, "head home wainman," May, twenty-three, "head road wainman" and ploughman, McGregor, forty, head muleman, McPherson, forty, McAllister, forty, and France, twenty-five, distillers, Tim's Cubena, forty, boiler, McDonald and McKein, each forty-five, sugar potters, and Raphael and Forest, each twenty-five, "sugar guards" for the wagons carrying the crop to port. All members of the gang were described as healthy, able-bodied, and black. It was this battalion of the stalwart, armed with hoes and "bills" (sugar knives), whose work would "make or break" the proprietor. A considerable number in the gang were new negroes, but only seven of the whole died in this year of heaviest mortality.

The "second gang," employed in a somewhat lighter routine under Sharper, fifty, as foreman, comprised forty women and twenty-seven men ranging from fifteen to sixty years old, all black. While most of them were healthy, five were consumptive, four were ulcerated, one was "inclined to be bloated," one was "very weak," and Pheba was "healthy but worthless." Eleven of this gang died within the year.

Finally, in the third or "small gang," for yet lighter work under Baddy as driveress with Old Robin, sixty, as assistant, were listed sixty-eight boys and girls, all black, mostly between twelve and fifteen years old, but including Mutton, eighteen, and Cyrus, six. Cyrus and the few others below the normal age may have been allowed to join this gang for the companionship of brothers or sisters, or some of them may have been among Baddy's own four children. Five of the gang died within the year.

Among the 528 slaves all told—284 males and 244 females— seventy-four, equally divided between the sexes, were fifty years old and upwards. If the number of the new negroes, virtually all of whom were doubtless in early life, be subtracted from the gross, it appears that one-fifth of the seasoned stock had reached the half century, and one-eighth were sixty years old and over. This is a good showing of longevity.

About eighty of the seasoned women were within the age limits of childbearing. The births entered in the chronological record averaged nine per year for the five years covered. This was hardly half as many as might have been expected under favorable conditions. Rose Price entered special note in 1795 of the number of children each woman had borne during her life, the number of these living at the time this record was made, and the number of miscarriages each woman had had. The total of births thus recorded was 345; of children then living 159; of miscarriages seventy-five. Old Quasheba and Betty Madge each had borne fifteen children; and sixteen other women had borne from six to eleven each. On the other hand, seventeen women of thirty years and upwards had had no children and no miscarriages. It cannot be said whether or not these barren women had husbands, for matings were listed in the record only in connection with the births of children.

The childbearing records of the women past middle age ran higher than those of the younger ones, to a somewhat surprising degree. Perhaps conditions on Worthy Park had been more favorable at an earlier period, when the owner and his family may possibly have been resident there. The fact that more than half of the children whom these women had borne were dead at the time of the record comports with the reputation of the sugar colonies for heavy infant mortality.[5] With births so infrequent and infant deaths so many it may well appear that the notorious failure of the island-bred stock to maintain its own numbers was not due to the working of the slaves to death.

[5] Sir Warner Bryan, attorney-general of Grenada, said, "It is generally remarked that ½ the children die under 2 years, and most of that ½ the first 9 days, from the jaw-fall." *Abridgment of the Minutes of Evidence taken before a Committee of the Whole House* [on] *the Slave Trade, No. 2.* (London, 1790), p. 48. Mr. John Castle, long a surgeon in Grenada, testified before the same committee that generally one-third of the negro children died in the first month of their lives, and that few of the imported women bore children. *Ibid.*, 80.

The poor care of the young children may be attributed largely to the absence of a white mistress, an absence characteristic of the Jamaica plantations. The only white woman mentioned in the parish returns of this estate was Susannah Phelps, doubtless the wife of Edward Phelps who drew no salary but received a yearly food allowance "for saving deficiency," and who probably lived not on Worthy Park but at Mickleton.

In addition to Rose Price, who was not salaried but who may have received a manager's commission of six per cent upon gross crop sales as contemplated in the laws of the colony, the administrative staff of white men on Worthy Park comprised an overseer at £200, later £300 a year, and four bookkeepers at £50 to £60. There was also a white carpenter at £120, and a white ploughman at £56. The overseer was changed three times during the time of the record, and the bookkeepers were generally replaced annually. The bachelor staff were most probably responsible for the mulatto and quadroon offspring and were doubtless responsible also for the occasional manumission of women and children. In 1795 and perhaps in other years the plantation had a contract for medical attendance by "J. Quier and G. Clark" at the rate of £140 per year.

There is no true summer and winter in Jamaica, but a wet and a dry season instead—the former extending generally from May to November, the latter from December to April. The sugar-cane got its growth during the rains; it ripened and was harvested during the drought. If things went well the harvest, or "grinding," began in January. All available hands were provided with bills and sent to the fields to cut the stalks and trim off their leaves and tops. The tainted canes were laid aside for the distillery; the sound ones were sent at once to the mill. On the steepest hillsides the crop had oftentimes to be carried on the heads of the negroes or on the backs of mules to points which the carts could reach.

The mill consisted merely of three cylinders, two of them set against the third, turned by wind, water, or cattle. The canes, tied into small bundles for better compression, were given a double squeezing while passing through the mill. The juice expressed found its way through a trough into the "boiling house" while the "mill trash" or "megass" [6] was carted off to sheds and left to dry for later use as fuel under the coppers and stills.

In the boiling house the cane-juice flowed first into a large receptacle, the clarifier, where by treatment with lime and moderate heat it was separated from its grosser impurities. The juice then passed into the first copper, where evaporation by boiling began. This vessel on Worthy Park was of such a size that in 1795 one of the negroes fell in while it was full of boiling liquor and died ten days after his scalding. After further evaporation in smaller coppers the juice, now reduced to a syrup, was ladled into a final copper, the teache, for a last boiling and concentration; and when the product of the teache was ready for crystallization it was carried to the "curing house."

The mill, unless it were a most exceptional one for the time, expressed barely two-thirds of the juice from the canes; the clarifier was not supplemented by filters; the coppers were wasteful of labor and fuel. But if the apparatus and processes thus far were crude by comparison with modern standards, the curing process was primitive by any standard whatever. The curing house was merely a roof above, a timber framework on the main level, and a great shallow sloping vat at the bottom. The syrup from the teache was potted directly into hogsheads resting on the timbers, and was allowed to cool with too great rapidity and with occasional stirrings which are said by modern critics to have hindered more than they helped the crystallization. Most of the sugar stayed in the hogsheads, while the mother liquor, molasses, still carrying some of the sugar, trickled through perforations in the hogshead bottoms into the vat below. When the hogsheads were full of the crudely cured, moist, and impure "muscovado" sugar they were headed up and sent to port. The molasses was carried to vats in the distillery where with yeast and water added it fermented and when passed twice through the distilling process yielded rum.[7]

[6] In Louisiana this is called "bagasse."

[7] This description of mill equipment and methods is drawn from eighteenth-century writings. Slightly improved apparatus introduced in the early nineteenth century was described in Thomas Roughley, *The Jamaica Planter's Guide*. As to sugar-cane cultivation and labor control, the general works already mentioned were supplemented by Clement Caines in his *Letters on the Culti-*

The grinding season, extending from January to spring or summer according to the speed of harvesting, was the time of heaviest labor on the plantations. If the rains came before the reaping was ended the work became increasingly severe, particularly for the draught animals, which must haul their loads over the muddy fields and roads. On Worthy Park the grinding was ended in May in some years; in others it extended to July.

As soon as the harvest was ended preparations were begun for replanting the fields from which the crop of third rattoons had just been taken. The chief operation in this was the opening of broad furrows or "cane holes" about six feet apart. Five ploughs were mentioned in the Worthy Park inventories, but only three ploughmen were listed, one hired white and two negro slaves. Some of the hillside fields were doubtless too rough for convenient ploughing, and the heat of the climate prevented the use of teams for such heavy work for more than a few hours daily; but the lack of thrift and enterprise was doubtless even more influential. The smallness of the area planted each year demonstrates that the hoe was by far the main reliance. After the cane holes were made and manure spread, four canes were laid side by side continuously in each furrow, and a shallow covering of earth was drawn over them. This completed the planting process.

The holing and the planting occupied the major part of the "big gang" for most of the summer and fall. Meanwhile the wagons were hauling the sugar and rum to port, and the second and third gangs, with occasional assistance from the first, were cleaning the grass and weeds from the fields of growing cane and stripping the dry leaves from the stalks and drawing earth to the roots. With the return of the dry season cordwood must be cut in the mountains and brought to the boiling house to supplement the megass, and the roads and the works must be put in order for the stress of the coming harvest. Then came Christmas when oxen were slaughtered for the negroes and a feast was made and rules relaxed for a week of celebration by Christians and pagans alike.

---

vation of the Otahiete Cane (London, 1801), and by an anonymous "Professional Planter" in his Rules for the Management and Medical Treatment of Negro Slaves in the Sugar Colonies (London, 1803).

Rewards for zeal in service were given chiefly to the "drivers" or gang foremen. Each of these had for example a "double milled cloth coloured great coat" costing 11s.6d. and a "fine bound hat with girdle and buckle" costing 10s.6d. As a more direct and frequent stimulus a quart of rum was served weekly to each of three drivers, three carpenters, four boilers, two head cattlemen, two head mulemen, the "stoke-hole boatswain," and the black doctor, and to the foremen respectively of the sawyers, coopers, blacksmiths, watchmen, and road wainmen, and a pint weekly to the head home wainman, the potter, the midwife, and the young children's field nurse. The allowances totalled about three hundred gallons yearly. But a considerably greater quantity than this was distributed, mostly at Christmas perhaps, for in 1796 for example 922 gallons were recorded of "rum used for the negroes on the estate." Upon the birth of each child the mother was given a Scotch rug and a silver dollar.

No records of whippings appear to have been kept, nor of crimes or misdemeanors except absconding. In the list of deaths for 1793, however, it was noted that Roman was shot and killed by a watchman on a neighboring estate while stealing provisions from the negro grounds.

The runaway slaves who were in hiding at the end of each quarter were usually listed in a quarterly report to the parish authorities. In 1792 none were reported until the end of the year when it was stated that two were out, a man and a woman, the names not given. In March, 1793, these had returned, but Greenwich, May, and Beneba's Cuffee, men, and the woman called Strumpet had run off. The June report for this year is missing. In September, Greenwich, May, and Strumpet had returned, and Boot Cudjoe, Nero, Spring Garden Quaw, Toney, and Abba's Moll had taken flight. In December Toney and Quaw had returned. London and Rumbold, a twelve-year-old boy, had now fled, but they came back within the next quarter. In the early months of 1794 Sam, October, Pilot, and Christian Grace had brief outings, and in the second quarter Ann and Prince; and Cesar and Rhino now added their names to the list of the long-term runaways. In the third quarter Pulteney and Rippon, and in the fourth Dickie, made brief escapes, while Ann made a second and longer flight. Early in 1795 three runaways, veterans in a double sense for each was sixty years old, came back whether willingly or as captives. They were Sam, a field hand; Boot Cudjoe, a cattleman; and Abba's Moll, whose task was the mending of pads. Fletcher, Billy Scott, and Spring Garden Roger now took flight, and Quaw for a second time. In February Billy Scott, along with Moses and Hester who were attempting escape, were taken up and lodged in a public workhouse and sent back to the estate when claimed, at an expense of £4 11s.4¾d. In May £2 6s.2½d. was paid to the supervisor of the workhouse at Spanish Town as jail fees for Beneba's Cuffee; but his name continued to appear in the plantation list of runaways. Perhaps he promptly departed again. In the second quarter the long-absconding Cesar was also returned, and Spring Garden Tom took flight.

The recaptured absconders were now put into a special "vagabond gang" for better surveillance. This comprised Billy Scott, reduced from the capacity of mason and sugar guard; Oxford who as head cooper had enjoyed a weekly quart of rum but had apparently betrayed a special trust; Cesar who had followed the sawyer's trade; and Moll and Rumbold, and the following whose names had not appeared in the quarterly lists: McLean, Green, Bob, Damsel, Polly, and the young boys Little Sam and Mulatto Robert. The gang was so wretchedly assorted for industrial purposes that it was probably not long before it was disbanded and its members distributed to more proper tasks.

In the runaway list for the third quarter of 1795 three new names appear—Frank, Reilly, and Rennals. In November Appea fled, and Toney went upon a second truancy. Toney returned in January, 1796, and left for the third time the next month. About this time Sam, Strumpet, and Prince began second outings, but returned in the spring along with Beneba's Cuffee. Rightwell and Rosey now took short flights, and in November Sam took a third leave which again proved a brief one. In February, 1797, Quadroon Charles ran off, and Rumbold for the second time. At the end of the next month, when the last of the runaway lists in this record was made, these two were still out, along with Nero who had fled in 1793, Fletcher and Appea in 1795, and Toney in 1796. Of these

Fletcher was a distempered watchman forty-five years old, and the others were members of the big gang, forty-five, thirty, and sixty years old respectively. Obviously the impulse to run away was not confined to either sex nor to any age or class. The fugitives were utterly miscellaneous and their flights were apparently not organized but sporadic.

These conclusions if extended into a generalization to cover the whole island would appear to be borne out by an analysis of the notices of runaway slaves published by the workhouse officials in the newspapers. Throughout the year 1803, for which I have procured these statistics from a file of the *Royal Gazette* of Kingston,[8] the number of runaways taken into custody each week was fairly constant; and no group of slaves appears over-represented. Of the grand total of 1,721 runaways advertised as in custody, 187 were merely stated to be negroes without further classification, 426 were "creoles," i. e., native Jamaicans; and the neighboring islands had scattering representations. Sixty per cent (1046) were of African birth. Of these 101 were Mandingoes from Senegambia and the upper Niger; sixty were Chambas from the region since known as Liberia; seventy were Coromantees from the Gold Coast; thirty-three were Nagoes and twenty-four Pawpaws from the Slave Coast (Dahomey); and one hundred and eighty-five were Eboes and ninety-seven Mocoes from the Bight of Benin. All of the foregoing were from regions north of the equator. From the southern tropic there were one hundred and eighty-five Congoes, one hundred and sixty-five Mungolas, and ninety-four Angolas. The remaining thirty were scattering and mostly from places which I have not been able to identify in maps old or new. Only one, a Gaza, was positively from the east coast of Africa.

The Congoes and Coromantees, the tribal stocks with which Worthy Park was chiefly concerned, were as wide apart in their characteristics as negro nature permitted. The former were noted

[8] A file for 1803 is preserved in the Charleston Library, Charleston, South Carolina. The tabulation here used was generously made for me by Dr. Charles S. Boucher of the University of Michigan.

for lightness of heart, mildness of temper, and dullness of intellect. Of the latter Christopher Codrington, governor of the Leeward Islands, wrote in 1701 to the British Board of Trade:

> The Corramantes . . . are not only the best and most faithful of our slaves, but are really all born Heroes. There is a difference between them and all other negroes beyond what 'tis possible for your Lordships to conceive. There never was a raskal or coward of that nation, intrepid to the last degree, not a man of them but will stand to be cut to pieces without a sigh or groan, grateful and obedient to a kind master, but implacably revengeful when ill-treated. My Father, who had studied the genius and temper of all kinds of negroes 45 years with a very nice observation, would say, Noe man deserved a Corramante that would not treat him like a Friend rather than a Slave.[9]

Bryan Edwards endorsed the staunchness and industry of the Coromantees, but attributed to them the plotting of the serious Jamaica revolt of 1760.

A large proportion of the fugitive slaves in custody were described as bearing brands on their breasts or shoulders. It is not surprising to find in a Worthy Park inventory "1 silver mark LP for negroes." Edwards wrote that a friend of his who had bought a parcel of young Ebo and Coromantee boys told him that at the branding,

> when the first boy, who happened to be one of the Eboes, and the stoutest of the whole, was led forward to receive the mark, he screamed dreadfully, while his companions of the same nation manifested strong emotions of sympathetic terror. The gentleman stopt his hand; but the Koromantyn boys, laughing aloud, and, immediately coming forward of their own accord, offered their bosoms undauntedly to the brand, and receiving its impression without flinching in the least, snapt their fingers in exultation over the poor Eboes.[10]

[9] *Calendar of State Papers, Colonial Series, America and West Indies,* 1701, pp. 720-721.
[10] Edwards, *The History, Civil and Commercial, of the British Colonies in the West Indies* (Philadelphia, 1806), II, 275, 276.

The prevalence of unusually cruel customs among the tribes of the Gold Coast [11] may account in part for the fortitude of the Coromantees.

Worthy Park bought nearly all of its hardware, dry goods, drugs, and sundries in London, and its herrings for the negroes and salt pork and beef for the white staff in Cork. Staves and heading were procured locally, but hoops were imported. Corn was cultivated between the rows in some of the cane fields on the plantation, and some guinea-corn was bought from neighbors. The negroes raised their own yams and other vegetables, and doubtless pigs and poultry as well. Plantains were likely to be plentiful, and the island abounded in edible land crabs.

Every October cloth was issued, at the rate of seven yards of osnaburgs, three of checks, and three of baize for each adult, and proportionately for children. The first was to be made into coats, trousers, and frocks, the second into shirts and waists, the third into bedclothes. The cutting and sewing were done in the cabins. A hat and a cap were also issued to each slave old enough to go to the field, and a clasp-knife to each one above the age of the third gang. The slaves' feet were not pinched by shoes.

The Irish provisions cost annually about £300, and the English supplies about £1,000, not including such extra outlays as that of £1,355 in 1793 for new stills, worms, and coppers. Local expenditures were probably reckoned in currency. Converted into sterling, the salary list amounted to about £500, and the local outlay for medical services, wharfage, and petty supplies came to a like amount. Taxes, manager's commissions, and the depreciation of apparatus must have amounted collectively to £800. The net death-loss of slaves, not including that from the breaking-in of new negroes, averaged about two and a quarter per cent; that of the mules and oxen ten per cent. When reckoned upon the numbers on hand in 1796 when the plantation, with 470 slaves, was operating with no outside help, these losses, which must be replaced by new purchases if the scale of output was to be maintained, amounted

[11] *Cf.* A. B. Ellis, *The Tshi-Speaking Peoples of the Gold Coast of West Africa* (London, 1887), chapter XI.

to about £900. Thus a total of £3,000 sterling is reached as the average current expense in years when no mishaps occurred.

The corps during the years of the record averaged 311 hogsheads of sugar, sixteen hundredweight each, worth in the island about £15 sterling per hogshead,[12] and 133 puncheons of rum, 110 gallons each, worth about £10 per puncheon. The value of the average crop was thus about £6,000, and the net earnings of the establishment not above £3,000. The investment in slaves, mules, and oxen was about £28,000, and that in land, buildings, and equipment, according to the general reckoning of the island authorities, reached a similar sum.[13] The net earnings in good years were thus barely more than five per cent on the investment; but the liability to hurricanes, earthquakes, fires, epidemics, and mutinies would lead conservative investors to reckon the safe expectations considerably lower. A mere pestilence which carried off about sixty mules and two hundred oxen on Worthy Park in 1793–1794 wiped out more than a year's earnings.

Bryan Edwards[14] gave statistics showing that between 1772 and 1791 more than one-third of the 767 sugar plantations in Jamaica had gone through bankruptcy, fifty-five had been abandoned, and forty-seven new ones established. It was generally agreed that, within the limits of efficient operation, the larger a plantation was, the better its prospect for net earnings. But though Worthy Park had more than twice the number of slaves that the average plantation employed, it was barely paying its way.

[12] Owing to bad seasons, the crop on Worthy Park in 1796 fell to 268 hogsheads; but the shortness of the crop at large caused an exceptional rise in sugar prices, which kept plantation earnings that year at least as high as the normal.

[13] In the dearth of original data on Jamaica prices of land, slaves, and produce, I have depended mainly on Bryan Edwards (vol. III., book V., chapter 3), after checking up his figures as far as has been practicable.

[14] Edwards, vol. I., book II., appendix 2.

PART FIVE

The Legacy

18

The Decadence of the
Plantation System

THE sinister prominence of slavery and negro controversies has long obscured the historical importance of the plantation system.* That system was as essential a correlative to the institution of slavery as the southern white man has been to the southern negro. It, indeed, was less dependent upon slavery than slavery was upon it; and the plantation regime has persisted on a considerable scale to the present day in spite of the destruction of slavery a half century since. The plantation system formed, so to speak, the industrial and social frame of government in the black-belt communities, while slavery was a code of written laws enacted for the furtherance of that system's purposes. Since the overthrow of slavery the present or former plantation communities have had to provide new laws and customs for the adjustment of employers and employees. In some localities these new codes have centered about the historic plantation system; in others the old regime has been almost completely discarded and the present adjustments have grown up *de novo*. Its concentration of labor under skilled management made the plantation system, with its overseers, foremen, blacksmiths, carpenters, hostlers, cooks, nurses, plow hands and hoe hands, practically the factory system applied to agriculture. Since the replacement of domestic manufacturing by the factory has become established in history as the industrial revolu-

* *Annals of the American Academy of Political and Social Science,* XXXV (January, 1910), 37–41.

tion, the counter replacement of the plantation system by peasant farming or other decentralized types of rural industry seems to require description as an industrial counter-revolution. That this counter-revolution has not wrought such havoc in the South as it did in Jamaica and Hayti is at the same time a cause for warm congratulation and an evidence of the greater vigor, adaptability and resourcefulness of both the white and negro elements of our continental population.

To enumerate its achievements, whether good or bad: the plantation system furnished an early means of large-scale prosperity, and made America attractive to high-grade captains of industry; in colonial Virginia and Maryland it imported under indentures great numbers of white servants, who soon worked out their terms of service and became independent yeomen; it imported great numbers of negroes in slavery into all the Southern colonies, gave them discipline and instruction, and spread them through all the districts where the soil, climate and facilities for transportation were good for producing and marketing tobacco, rice, indigo, sugar, or cotton; it thereby crowded many of the yeomen whites out of the staple districts and drove them away to the mountains or the pine-barrens, or to the great non-slaveholding Northwest; it kept, on the other hand, a large element of the Southern whites in fairly close and fairly friendly association with the negroes, and in considerable degree welded the two races into one community; it certainly shaped the views and tradition of nearly all elements of the Southern population; and it controlled the public policy of numerous states and in large measure that of the United States government. It was so thoroughly dominant in all the districts where staple production prevailed that few there questioned its thorough and lasting efficacy and expediency.

The plantation system provided for the steady employment of labor, mainly in gangs and in routine tasks, for the large-scale production of the staple crops. It utilized crude labor, and it depended upon fairly cheap and abundant labor for its maintenance. The economic strength of the system depended in large degree upon the ability of the planters to direct the energies of the laborers on hand to better effect than each laborer could direct his own energies in isolation. Now, when steam power and machinery are not in question, large units of industry are more efficient than small ones only in cases where the work may be reduced to a steady routine. In truck farming, dairying, cereal production, when there are long lay-by intervals to be filled economically with odd jobs, and in most sorts of frontier industry, there are positive requirements of versatility and reliability on the part of the laborers; and in these cases no amount of knowledge and will-power on the part of a large-scale employer can make up for a deficiency in the necessary qualities on the part of his employees. Therefore the plantation system, with its crude type of labor, was clearly debarred from these enterprises. The five great Southern staples became plantation staples because each of them permitted long-continued routine work in their production. The nature of their system and their labor supply, in fact, made the planters depend upon their respective staples to a degree which proved a positive vice in the long run and eventually created a need for economic reform if not of actual revolution.

The plantation system was highly excellent for its primary and principal purpose of employing the available low-grade labor supply to serviceable ends; and also in giving industrial education to the laboring population, in promoting certain moral virtues, and in spreading the amenities. On the other hand, like other capitalistic systems, it sadly restricted the opportunity of such men as were of better industrial quality than was required for the field gangs, yet could not control the capital required to make themselves captains of industry. The prevalence of the plantation regime stratified industrial society, and society in general, to a greater degree than was expedient for developing the greatest resources and power from the population on hand. In particular, while it utilized the productive strength of the negro population to excellent effect, it substantially discouraged the non-planter whites and thereby reduced their service to the world and to themselves. Furthermore, to say the least, it did not check the American disposition, born of the wilderness environment, to skim the fields and waste the natural fertility. Worst of all, perhaps, the predominance of the system hindered all diversification in southern industry, and kept the whole community in a state of commercial dependence upon the North and Europe like that of any normal colony upon its mother country. The antebellum South achieved no industrial complexity, and its several interests were deprived of any advantage from economic interdependence and mutual gain from mutual satisfaction of wants. Whereas the settlement of Ohio proved of great benefit to New York and Pennsylvania by extending the demand for their manufactures and swelling the volume of their commerce, the settlement of Alabama yielded no economic benefit to Virginia, and was of actual detriment to South Carolina, because of its flooding the world's market with the same fleecy staple upon which that older community, with its partially exhausted lands, continued to depend for prosperity.

In the antebellum regime in the black belts, unfortunately, the plantation system was in most cases not only the beginning of the development, but its end as well. The system led normally to nothing else. If a large number of planters had customarily educated a large proportion of their laborers into fitness for better things than gang work, the skilled occupations on the plantations would have been glutted and the superior ability of the laborers in large degree wasted. This was the fault of slavery as well as of the plantation system. Slavery, or in other words, the capitalization of labor control, was also responsible for the calamitous fact that the antebellum planters were involved in a cut-throat competition in buying labor and in selling produce. These shortcomings impaired the industrial efficiency of the Southern community, and, at the same time, prevented that community from securing the full normal earnings from such productive efficiency as it did achieve.

If no cataclysm of war and false reconstruction had accompanied the displacement of slavery, the plantation system might well have experienced something of a happy further progress with free wage-earning labor. The increase of its service to the community would have required some provision whereby such laborers as the system had schooled into superior efficiency might easily withdraw from the gangs and set themselves up as independent artisans, merchants, or farmers. The gangs must graduate at least the ablest of their laborers into the industrial democracy, and the regime must permit small farms, factories, and cities to flourish in the same districts as the plantations. In a word, for the best economic results, industrial resources and the industrial mechanism of society must be made varied, complex, and elastic, and every distinctly capable member of the community must be permitted to find his own suitable employment. On the other hand, wherever there is a large element of the population deficient in industrial talents and economic motives, as a great number of the Southern negroes still are, it is desirable for the sake of order and general prosperity that the inefficient and unstable element be provided with firm control and skilled management. The historic Southern system met this particular need more successfully than any other device yet brought to the world's knowledge. The remodeling and partial replacement of that system was necessary in the progress of industrial society. The extent of its decadence can hardly be measured at the present day, since the United States census figures are entirely misleading in the premises and the character and tendencies of the numerous rural industrial adjustments which have arisen in the latter-day South can hardly be estimated without more elaborate study than has yet been made in the field. But it seems fairly safe to conclude that retention of the plantation system in some form or other, in suitable districts and for the proper elements of the population, is fortunate at the present day and both expedient and inevitable for a long period in the future, as one among the bases of adjustment in Southern industrial society.

19

Plantations with Slave Labor
and Free

IT has been my fortune within recent months to visit an establishment comprising nine thousand acres of delta land in cultivation.* The great levees which guard it from flood border not the Mississippi but the Sacramento and Mokelumne rivers. A hoe gang in which I counted thirty-nine laborers, working straight abreast, each upon a furrow a measured mile in length, comprised not negroes, but Hindus, Sicilians, Mexicans, and men of yet other stocks. The crop was not sugar cane, rice, or cotton, but sugar beets. The place is called a ranch, not a plantation—but that is the fashion in California.

The laborers whether at hoe or plough included no women or children (this was not a Japanese enterprise!). There were no cottages, except those of the foremen, whether clustered at ranch headquarters or scattered about the fields, but bunkhouses instead. Until two years ago many of the laborers had families on the place; but the management, finding that women made for strife, changed the regime to the present stag basis. Wages of ploughmen are $3.50 per day and board, which is reckoned to cost $1.50 additional. The hoeing and harvest are not financed directly by the ranch management but are let to Italian contractors at $50 per acre for the season; and the contractors employ, feed, and bunk their own hands, paying them such wages as the market may require. Harvest comprises merely the pulling, topping, and loading of the beets, since the ranch does not convert its crop into sugar. The hoe

* *American Historical Review*, XXX (July, 1925), 738–53.

hands depart at the season's end; some of the ploughmen remain.[1]

Apart from the families of the manager and foremen, and except for the cooks and "matrons" of the bunkhouses, the ranch is a womanless world. As such it would seem to be fairly representative of California large-scale farming, if the hundreds of migratory laborers whom the tourist encounters are an index—weather-beaten men with bedding-rolls over their shoulders, trudging the highways or the railroad tracks, shifting from fields to vineyards, from orange and lemon groves to walnuts and olives, from plums and peaches to prunes and pears, almost literally from figs to thistles, since burr artichokes are but the unblown blossoms of highly educated thistle plants!

In the region of Kansas and Colorado, likewise, there are huge tracts devoted to sugar beets and other crops, owned by corporations and cultivated in large part by a shifting personnel. Along both flanks of the Rocky Mountains, furthermore, every "dirt farmer" seeds many more acres in small grain than he can hope to harvest alone. The migratory laborers move from the San Joaquin to the Kootenay or from the Red River of the South to its namesake of the North on a schedule of the ripening wheat. Widely in the West, and considerably indeed in more easterly regions, the farmers and their families do by no means all the work of their farm, but depend essentially upon employees in considerable volume.

In all the foregoing there are suggestions of the plantation system. Sugar beets among Western crops invite the closest approach to the classic plantation type, essentially because they require continuous cultivation through a fairly long growing season, and they must be worked with hoe as well as plough. The cultivation, indeed, is much like that of cotton, for the seed are drilled thickly in the furrow, the seedlings are thinned by chopping, and the plants which remain are set too closely to permit of cross-ploughing. In other respects the Western regime is in sharp contrast to that of

[1] Alfalfa, asparagus (eight hundred acres in this), and fruits are minor crops on the ranch. Virtually nothing consumed by the personnel on the place is produced upon it. Even the butter is brought each week from San Francisco.

the South, whether past or present—most notably in its heavy turnover of labor and its lack of domesticity.

The slave-plantation regime owed its origins, curiously, to conditions in which negroes figured little. In the Spanish West Indies, on the one hand, the first agglomerations of labor were of conscripted aborigines; and in early Virginia they were of white indentured servants. In either case the degree of domesticity was presumably small, and the turnover was rather large; for the coerced Indians died with disconcerting speed, and the indentured whites went their several ways when their terms expired—if haply they did not die or escape in advance. It was in large part to diminish this turnover that recourse was had to Guinea, a country discovered half a century before America, whose deported natives had promptly been adjudged in Europe "very loyal and obedient servants, without malice," who "never more tried to fly, but rather in time forgot all about their own country." [2] Their sturdiness of physique and their amiability of temper led eventually to the replacement of virtually all other sorts of massed labor by negroes wherever the work was of simple routine character, and to the development of slavery as a scheme for their industrial and social control. Thus in the production of tobacco, rice, cotton, and cane-sugar, negro slave labor came to have no rival except that of white yeomen upon their own small farms.

By this recourse to negroes in slavery, the turnover was almost wholly eliminated except as involved in the flight, the sale, or the death of slaves, and the death or bankruptcy of masters. From year to year overseers, where there were such, constituted as a rule the only changing personnel on the plantations. Now this absence of turnover, this lifetime adjustment, this permanent proprietorship of labor created problems, conditions, and an atmosphere of its own. In the first place it made labor inelastic. The same force must be fed, clothed, and sheltered the year round, and must be kept from unproductive idleness. Even when slaves were hired, the standard unit was a year's service. This meant an inescapable problem of flattening the peaks and filling the troughs in the curve of

[2] Azurara, in Hakluyt Society *Publications*, XCV, 85.

the labor demand. A planter's maxim was: "The ways of industry are constant and regular, not to be in a hurry at one time and do nothing at another, but to be always usefully and steadily employed." [3] The solution was easy in the West Indies, where the tropical climate gave leeway at all seasons. In continental crops, peaks were inevitable, particularly in the sugar cane harvest to escape frost, in the transplanting of tobacco, and in the picking of cotton.[4] The contemplation of these peaks controlled the planning for the year. Just so much land was assigned to the staple as it was reckoned the force could cover at peak tasks. The troughs were slight in cotton and sugar cane, for the planters' adage that these crops required thirteen months in the year had considerable

[3] Ulrich B. Phillips (ed.), *Plantation and Frontier*, Vol. I and II of *A Documentary History of American Industrial Society* (Cleveland: A. H. Clark Co., 1910), I, 109.

[4] In the eight or ten weeks of the "grinding season" in Louisiana the peak was so pronounced that overtime work, on Sundays in the field and both at night and on Sundays in the mill, was of common recourse. In the other staples overtime was quite unusual. The following illustrative items are from the diary of William Bolling of Bolling Hall, Goochland County, Virginia, the manuscript of which for 1827 and 1828 is on deposit with the Virginia Historical Society. The special occasion in each instance was the occurrence of rain—for wet ground was required for transplanting the tobacco seedlings and moist air was essential for striking and prizing [i.e., packing] the cured crop.

1828, Apr. 5. "Striking tob'o finished about 1 o'clock this morning. Rain commenced last ev'g, which bro't it rapidly in order. I had a supper cook'd for my people, sent them whiskey and a lanthorn with candles to the prize house, —and thus we have struck our whole crop in the last three days from one season [i.e., rain], which was very favourable."

1828, June 9, a rainy Sunday. "My people all engaged in planting tob'o, a thing I rarely do [i.e., Sunday work], but compelled on this occasion by the scarcity of plants, not to miss an opportunity so late in the season."

1828, July 5, Saturday. "Gave my people here a holiday in compensation for their work in planting tob'o on Sunday last."

For the wheat harvest in Virginia, extra hands were procured on hire. Examples of this are in Bolling's diary under dates of June 13, June 15, and July 7, 1828, and in "The Westover Journal of John A. Selden" (printed in the *Smith College Studies in History*, vol. VI., no. 4) under dates of July 21, Aug. 11, and Aug. 19, 1858, June 30 and July 22, 1859, and July 20, 1861. After his wheat harvest of 1859 Selden gave his slaves a holiday; but needing some work done, he hired five of them, at seventy-five cents each, to glean and plough that day (entries of July 2 and 3, 1859). Westover was typical of Tidewater Virginia plantations in this period in producing no tobacco, but using wheat as its chief crop.

substance. It meant, of course, that preparation for a new crop ought to begin before the old harvest was done and that the work when once begun was fairly continuous. Periods "out of crop" as regards the staple were filled in part by auxiliary crops, notably Indian corn, and in part by the clearing of new grounds, the cutting and hauling of fuel, and varied jobs of renovation.

Furthermore every parcel of slaves comprised some who at some periods or at all times were not fit for field work or were too valuable to be employed therein. Blacksmithing, shoemaking, spinning, weaving, nursing, as well as domestic service, were available for these, in furtherance of the policy of making each plantation self-sufficient in every expedient regard.

Segregation was accepted as necessary, and self-containment was promoted as highly desirable. Matings among the slaves were encouraged within the plantation group, though not strictly confined within its limits. The planter expected his future laborers in the main to be born, reared, and trained on the place. His obvious method was to promote family life among the slaves, and to insure the care of children. Here his wife had special functions. The master's household gave lessons to the slaves, whether by precept or example, and the play-time intermingling of white and black children contributed a positive link of domestic interrelation. The plantation was not merely a seat of industry, but was permanently and potently a homestead.

There was perpetual need of adjustment and readjustment, conciliation, stimulus, and control. Negro slave labor tended to be slothful, because the negroes were slaves, and also because the slaves were negroes, imperfectly habituated to a civilized regime. Various devices by way of appeal, reward, or other inducement were utilized in efforts to increase the zeal, energy, and initiative of the laborers; but achievement by the planter was always limited by the quality of the children whom his women chanced to bear, by the inertia implied in slave status, and by any deficit in the vigor and finesse of the management. The greater the scale of a plantation and the greater the variety of its undertakings, the greater was the task of administration. The sagacious overseer of a great plantation reported to his employer in 1827: "I killed twenty-eight head of beef for the people's Christmas dinner. I can do more with them in this way than if all the hides of the cattle were made into lashes." And again in the following year: "You justly observe that if punishment is in one hand, reward should be in the other." [5] The ideal in slave control may perhaps be symbolized by an iron hand in a velvet glove. Sometimes the velvet was lacking, but sometimes the iron. Failure was not far to seek in either case.

Upon prosperous plantations there was wide variety in the details of regulation, with definite system the tendency on large units but with blurred schedules on the small. This may be illustrated from a parcel of six affidavits made by as many Georgia planters in 1853, whose slaves ranged in number from as many as 450 to as few as 16.[6] The six coincided as regards hours of work by the slaves (from dawn to sunset, with some two hours of rest at noon). They substantially agreed also as to the issue of clothing (two outfits each year) and as to the age (ten or twelve years) at which young slaves began field work. The five largest plantations allowed child-bearing women a month as a minimum of leisure after confinement: upon this the sixth did not report. The four largest had schedules for mothers to leave the field to suckle their children; but the owner of forty gave his women full discretion and "free permission to leave their work for this purpose." Here again the owner of sixteen was silent. The largest proprietor had a yearly contract with a physician providing for twice-a-week visits at a minimum. The owner of 150 also reported a contract with a physician, but did not specify any visiting schedule. As to children he wrote: "I think we have lost one child in every four during sickness— caused generally by carelessness of the mothers. Since the adoption of my plan of a nursery, few die after being weaned, compared to

[5] Frances Butler Leigh, *Ten Years on a Georgia Plantation* (London, 1883), 233.

[6] These affidavits, which were made in response to a questionnaire issued by Judge Ebenezer Starnes of the Georgia superior court, in pursuit of an inquiry which was mainly concerned with questions of criminality, are printed in *The Slaveholder Abroad . . . A series of letters from Dr. Pleasant Jones to Major Joseph Jones, of Georgia* (Philadelphia, 1860), 492–504. Mr. Leonard L. Mackall of Savannah has ascertained that Judge Starnes was himself the author of this book.

what died formerly, probably not more than one a year on the average—one or two." All reported, with statistics, very large proportions of children in the number of their slaves; and the owner of sixty-five said as to births: "In connection with this subject, I may remark that eleven years after the death of my father, the slaves that I inherited from him had more than doubled."

The fifth one of these documents is perhaps the most interesting of the group. It reads in part:

I have sixteen negro slaves—five males that are field-hands, and three women—two of them child-bearing, the other aged; and there are eight children, under ten years old. We give them as much food as they want and can eat, treating them as the white family in this respect— their food being prepared for them by the same cook which prepares the meals for the family. . . . I cannot give the quantity in pounds, for we don't allowance.

This was in contrast with the practice of the other five planters, each of whom had a fairly definite schedule of rations. The owner of sixteen continued, as to children: "When they are not under the care of the mother, they are taken to the yard, and cared for by the cook." And as to medical service: "I have never needed a physician for my negroes—indeed, I have never needed a physician for my whites until last fall. I would send for a physician for my slaves under the same circumstances as for my white family."

It is regrettable that data descriptive of small plantations and farms are very scant. Such documents as exist point unmistakably to informality of control and intimacy of white and black personnel on such units. This is highly important in its bearing upon race relations, for according to the census of 1860, for example, one-fourth of all the slaves in the United States were held in parcels of less than ten slaves each, and nearly another fourth in parcels of ten to twenty slaves.[7] This means that about one-half of the slaves had a distinct facilitation in obtaining an appreciable share

[7] *Eighth Census*, III. 247. The statistics for Arkansas in this table are obviously wrong; the true numbers for that commonwealth may be found on p. 224. On p. 248 of the same volume is a table of slaveholdings in 1850.

in the social heritage of their masters. *Per contra*, it should be observed that the small proprietors were not generally of the most cultured class of society. The larger planters were as a rule the better educated, nicer in speech, more polished in manner, more urbane and refined. While their domestic servants in many cases possessed and notably improved an opportunity for procuring gentle breeding, the crowds of field negroes were left very much to their own crude devices in a cultural sense. Nevertheless, the very fact that the negroes were slaves linked them as a whole more closely to the whites than any scheme of wage-labor could well have done.

Lifelong adjustment and the prospect of it brought habituation and accommodation. John Randolph, it is true, wrote in 1814: "My plantation affairs, always irksome, are now revolting," [8] and Thomas Ruffin wrote of his wife: "she has been unable to reconcile herself to the particular place we are at or to vocations that unavoidably engage the attention of the master and mistress of slaves on a large plantation." [9] The careers and predilections of these two had made them devoid of the traits necessary and standard in plantation life: the faculty of unruffled response to the multitudinous calls of slaves upon the attention, and the tolerance of slack service. The roses, real or fancied, in the planter's bed made most folk ignore the thorns. A keen observer said with little exaggeration: "A plantation well stocked with hands is the *ne plus ultra* of every man's ambition who resides at the south." [10] The planters themselves, as a rule, relished and even exalted their calling. As one of them put it, with a bit of bombast: "Planting . . . in this country is the only independent and really honorable occupation. . . . The planters here are essentially what the nobility are in other countries." [11] Now this exaltation was greatly to the advan-

[8] H. A. Garland, *Life of John Randolph*, II, 42, quoted in Gamaliel Bradford, *Damaged Souls*, 140. The sentence which follows in Randolph's letter, which Bradford fails to quote, blunts the point of this indictment: "I have lost three-fourths of the finest and largest crop I ever had."

[9] *Papers of Thomas Ruffin*, ed. Hamilton (North Carolina Historical Commission), II, 153.

[10] [J. H. Ingraham], *The South-west* (New York, 1835), II, 84.

[11] James H. Hammond, quoted by Elizabeth Merritt, in John Hopkins University *Studies*, XLI, 377.

tage of the slaves. The grandiloquence was based upon genuine self-respect, of which an essential ingredient is respect for others. Severity, even brutality, was not absent from the regime; but the "lords of the lash," while depending upon the lash in last resort, were certainly among "the mildest mannered men that ever scuttled ship or cut a throat."

To speak more soberly, the consciousness of power, together with a sense of gentility, promoted toleration and self-restraint. This was well discussed by the writer of an essay packed with sagacious analysis in the *American Quarterly Review*, in 1827, who is regretably anonymous. He said:

The high sense of personal dignity with which the habit of authority and command inspires him [the slaveholder], makes him courteous in his manners, liberal in his sentiments, generous in his actions. But, with his disdain of all that is coarse, and little, and mean, there often mingle the failings of a too sensitive pride; jealousy of all superiority; impatience of contradiction; quick and violent resentment. His liability to these vices is so obvious, that it is often an especial purpose of early instruction to guard against them; and thus is formed in happy natures, such a habit of self-command and virtuous discipline, as to make them remarkable for their mildness and moderation. . . . Mr. Jefferson, who has given so lively a description of the effects of slavery on the temper of the slaveholder, and whose views are so just in the general, was himself a remarkable exception to the unamiable picture which he has drawn.[12]

Plantation industry was the "big business" of colonial and antebellum times. It had a certain rigidity of regimentation due to the racial factor and to the slave status of the laborers. But as a rule it was free from the absenteeism of proprietorship and the consequent impersonality which regrettably prevail in the modern factory regime. The plantation system was not essentially static. Surely not in a territorial sense. Small-scale pioneers made the first clearings in the wilderness, but the planters followed close on their heels and consolidated the gains. A proof of their quickness and thoroughness in exploiting their opportunity lies in the population

[12] *American Quarterly Review*, II, 251–52.

map of the United States, of even the present time. Everywhere east of Texas the best cotton districts are peopled by a majority of negroes today, because within the space of threescore years and seven from the invention of the gin, planters had carried slaves in predominant numbers to all these districts and had maintained market inducements causing slave traders to supplement the effects of their own migration. In the same period they placed the American cotton belt in an unchallenged primacy in the world's production of the staple. Texas was marked as the one remaining province of prospective conquest. A planter migrating thither in 1846 remarked to a fellow traveller "that he had been eaten out of Alabama by his negroes." [18] Competition was very keen among the planters, and the very scale of their concerns made them the more sensitive to the need of moving. And yet a multitude avoided the necessity.

It has been charged repeatedly by writers whose opinions are in general worthy of respect that the plantation system devoured the soil, while the farming system did not. This may frankly be challenged. The lands of the South, which of course were nowhere glaciated, fall into three main classes: that of virtually no soil, that of shallow soil, and that of deep soil. The first comprises large tracts in the coastal plain so sandy as to support no indigenous vegetation but pine trees and wire-grass. The second consists mainly of the Piedmont, where the clay, though lean in plant food, supported hardwood forests, which in turn overlaid the land with a thin stratum of leafmold. The third comprised alluvial strips (notably the "Mississippi bottoms") and scattered limestone tracts and loess areas. Now no one who could pay any price for farmland would dally with the pine-barrens before the introduction of commercial fertilizers. Certainly the planters avoided them with one accord. At the other extreme, the alluvial tracts were occupied by planters from the beginning, with little participation by farmers —partly because the problem of flood-control put a premium upon large-scale undertakings. It was only in the region of shallow soil

[18] Sir Charles Lyell, *Second Visit to the United States* (London, 1850), II, 109.

that sharp competition between the types occurred. This was entered upon by planters and farmers alike, eager to exploit such resources as it offered. Its limited supply of plant food might possibly be husbanded for a time by rotation of crops; but where the surface was sloping, as nearly everywhere it was, the runoff of the heavy Southern rains quickly washed the surface away except where the rush of water was checked by special devices—horizontal furrows, hillside ditches, and grass-balks which by catching the flow gradually terraced the hills. When once the leaf mold was gone, which was but a question of time, there was a deficit of humus to hold moisture against times of drought. The absence of deep frost in winter meant a lack of loosening by thaw in spring. In short, while the climate was good for cotton, the soil was not long very good for anything.

Now, so long as population was sparse and inconsequence land was "dirt cheap," shallow soil was regarded, though regretfully, as a consumable commodity. Under economic circumstances but one remove from frontier conditions, the sacrifice of the forests was little less inevitable than the exhaustion of the soil which the forests had made. In earning a livelihood planters and farmers were in competition, each growing cotton to the top of his bent and each tempted to sell his soil in the form of lint and then move on whither fresh forests might be felled.[14] Statistical evidence is available that the planters resisted this temptation distinctly more than did the farmers. In Oglethorpe County, for example, which is typical of the Georgia Piedmont, the white population was nearly stationary from 1800 to 1820 at something less than 7,000 souls. Thereafter it steadily declined to 4,000 in 1860. The slaves, however, increased from 3,000 in 1800 to 7,000 in 1820, and slightly increased thereafter—or, in the course of sixty years 4,000 slaves replaced 3,000 whites. The slaveholding families increased from 520 in 1800 to 760 in 1810, maintained their number for the following

[14] The same conditions prevailed, of course, in the tobacco zone. A citizen of Halifax County, Virginia, wrote in 1835: "The spirit of emigration here is entirely at war with the spirit of improvement. Men constantly say, 'Why improve? I am going in a short time to the West.' Others again, 'My land will support me as long as I live, and my children will, as soon as they are of age, go out.'" *Farmers' Register* (III), 508.

decade, then declined to 540 in 1860, while the scale of average slaveholding was more than doubling in size and the scale of the largest unit in slaveholding was quadrupling. The number of non-slaveholding white families declined continuously from some 800 in the year 1800 to little more than 200 in 1860.[15] That is to say, when the land was fresh at the beginning of the century, and the cotton industry was an infant, the farmers were in fairly full possession; but the planters were already coming in with a rush which continued for two decades and filled the county to its fullest for the whole antebellum period. Prodded by planters from the eastward who offered to buy their farms, and lured by the free, fresh lands of the West, the farmers, in homely phrase, cleared, cropped, and cleared out. After 1820 an occasional planter also sold and moved, but the bulk of them stayed and enlarged their holdings of both land and slaves.

In the stress of competition every man in such a region of shallow soil faced an alternative of moving or improving. The farmers most copiously moved;[16] the planters more commonly improved. Among them were the first to resort to horizontal ploughing, the first also to buy guano and other fertilizers to replenish the plant food in their soil, and the most active in seed selection and in experimenting with new crops.[17] All this was no more than was to have been expected; for the planters had leisure, which the farmers

[15] For fuller data and discussion, see "The Origin and Growth of the Southern Black Belts," on page 95 of this volume.

[16] This process was not without contemporary comment. In 1838, for example, R. B. Buckner wrote concerning his neighborhood in Fauquier County, Va.: "The farms . . . are generally rather large, with a strong, but very natural tendency to accumulation in the hands of the few, to the exclusion of the many. 'The rich are becoming richer', but the poor, not being willing to become poorer, are going where they can 'get richer' too—they are going to 'the great West'." *Farmers' Register* (VI), 458.

[17] A Virginian who signed himself "Conservator" did not exaggerate greatly when he wrote in 1836: "Wealth is not always (nor indeed often) accompanied by education, intelligence and public spirit—nor does poverty always banish these qualities and their valuable effects. But yet no one can deny that every benefit from these sources that has served to improve the state of agriculture, has been owing to the occupiers of large farms." *Farmers' Register* (IV), 566.

had not, and by reason of their scale the planters had prospect of richer profits from any successful innovation. What was not to be expected is that latter-day students should fail to see the probabilities and actualities in the case.

When the small remainder of the suitable climatic zone had come to be occupied—dealing now with the prospect in 1860—opportunity for enhancing fortune by migration must have dwindled, and pressure to improve methods must have increased upon all the population. This need not have brought a decline of the plantation system, though it would impinge upon the regime of slavery. Already in the fifties planters far and wide were employing Irish gangs to dig their ditches, build their levees, and perform other tasks involving exposure or strain.[18] They were embracing a new means to cherish the lives, health, strength, and good will of their precious slaves. In addition they were seeking increasingly to raise the level and broaden the scope of slave capacity and to find special openings for such of their slaves as developed special aptitudes. The economic problem as regards personnel put emphasis of course upon rewards as well as upon opportunities for skilled work by slaves, and this suggested the relaxation of the restraints of slavery. That more was not accomplished in this line was due in part to the abolition agitation, the repercussion of which in the South put reactionary emphasis upon the race problem and police.

The interesting and not wholly hideous career of the slave-plantation system was cut short by revolution imposed by force from without. Abolition was followed by reconstruction—not merely the radical rule known to political historians, but simultaneously a home-grown industrial reorganization, achieved painfully and piecemeal.

Many folk of the old regime were destroyed by the war—not merely soldiers on the battlefield, but civilians white and black, driven or lured from shelter, sustenance, and sanitation. Slaves died by uncounted thousands, and many of their masters were utterly broken. The case of Thomas Hamilton Cooper of "Hope-

[18] *Cf.* U. B. Phillips, *American Negro Slavery* (New York, 1918), pp. 301-302.

ton" on the Altamaha River is an example. Sir Charles Lyell, recognizing him as a distinguished fellow naturalist, paid him a long visit in 1846 and made laudatory notes upon the library, the household, and the plantation with its five hundred slaves.[19] Another pen has left an account of his burial in 1866, after his death in poverty and despair:

The steps of the church were broken down, so we had to walk up a plank to get in; the roof was fallen in, so that the sun streamed down on our heads; while the seats were all cut up and marked with the names of Northern soldiers, who had been quartered there during the war. . . . The funeral party arrived. The coffin was in a cart drawn by one miserable horse, and was followed by the Cooper family on foot, having come this way from the landing, two miles off. From the cart to the grave the coffin was carried by four old family negroes, faithful to the end.[20]

The survivors of the cataclysm had to solve the problem of economic life afresh under conditions of general derangement and almost universal poverty. The landholders possessed land and managerial experience—and worthless Confederate currency. The freedmen had liberty, and little else but a residual acquiescence in the necessity of working for a living.

Crop-sharing was adopted in some quarters of the cotton belt as early as 1865, and crop liens came quickly after—the one to relink labor with land and management in the absence of money, the other to link all these to banks or merchants when credit was imperative but land so cheap that mortgageable values were inadequate. The lien laid fresh emphasis upon the staple crop; and crop-sharing tended to stereotype schedules in order to diminish the points of possible friction between the two parties to each contract. Tenancy at fixed rentals also attained considerable vogue; but this promoted soil exhaustion by divorcing the temporary interest of the tenant from the permanent interest of the proprie-

[19] Sir Charles Lyell, *Second Visit to the United States*, I, 328–63.
[20] Frances B. Leigh, *Ten Years on a Georgia Plantation*, 46–47.

tor.[21] In any case the cluster of cabins near the landowner's dwelling was generally abandoned, and isolated houses instead were scattered over the land.[22] The freedmen had fairly copious opportunity to procure farms of their own, as may be gathered from the fact, for example, that as late as the census of 1900 the average value of farmland throughout the state of Mississippi was reckoned at $6.30 per acre, as compared with sevenfold that sum in Illinois. But improvidence was so ingrained in the field negroes that the development along this line was far less than might otherwise have been expected.

As an example of plantations operated on the crop-sharing basis, the system and experience on "Dunleith," which lies in the Yazoo-Mississippi delta, have been so clearly and cogently set forth by its owner, Mr. Alfred H. Stone, in a book so widely known,[23] that I need not discuss this type in detail. Suffice it to say that under the most effective management crop-sharing implies nearly as full supervision as does wage-labor.[24]

Among wage-labor plantations in the cotton belt the most notable has been that of James M. Smith in Oglethorpe County, Georgia, where the land, as has been noted above, was considerably depleted before his day. Mr. Smith began as a youth in 1866 with a one-horse farm. Undaunted by crop failure from drought in his first year, he persevered so thriftily and prospered so largely that by 1904 he had accumulated some 23,000 acres of land, from which he was deriving an income of about $100,000 a year.[25] At this time he had scores of convicts on lease from the state of Georgia and hundreds of laborers on wages, many of them bound by voluntary indenture for terms as long as five years. His contracts with these provided, on locally printed forms, that he was to furnish board, lodging, clothes and washing, to pay wages of stip-

---

[21] E. M. Banks, "The Economics of Land Tenure in Georgia", in Columbia University *Studies*, XXIII, no. 1; R. P. Brooks, "The Agrarian Revolution in Georgia", in University of Wisconsin *Bulletin*, History Series, III, no. 3.

[22] D. C. Barrow, "A Georgia Plantation," *Scribner's Monthly* (XXI), 830-36 (April, 1881).

[23] A. H. Stone, *Studies in the American Race Problem* (New York, 1908).

[24] Carl Kelsey, *The Negro Farmer* (Chicago, 1903).

[25] Harry Hodgson, in *World's Work*, IX (January, 1905), 5723-33.

ulated amount on a specified day of each year, and to teach the apprentice a specified trade, usually that of farming. The laborer, on his part, bound himself to work faithfully, to "respect and obey all orders and commands with respect to the business" and "demean" himself "orderly and soberly" for the full term of the contract, and to account for all loss of time except in case of temporary sickness continuing not longer than six days at any one time. This contemplated a bunkhouse basis for a stag personnel. Doubtless there were contracts of other sorts for the numerous laborers who had families. As to the specifications of these I failed to take note when on a visit to the plantation twenty years ago, perhaps because I was diverted by the phenomena of a convict camp, the huge barns, the stalwart mules, the many handicrafts, the model dairy, the plantation railroad, the cottonseed oil mill, the corps of boy messengers on the planter's piazza steps at Smithsonia, and the crops which were far more flourishing than was common in that quarter of the state. The Smithsonia establishment had so many peculiar features as to make it rather a demonstration of what might conceivably be done than an example of what was at all commonly accomplished in the Piedmont cotton zone. In cotton culture, and in tobacco likewise, tenancy in some form was by far the most common recourse.

In Carolina rice and Louisiana sugar, on the other hand, large-scale industry under unit control was well-nigh imperative; and this led to wage-labor as almost the sole reliance from immediately after the abolition of slavery. Plantations were reorganized intact, and the negro cabins remained clustered. Payrolls were instituted, overseers were styled managers, and drivers were rechristened captains for greater dignity. Strikes were not unknown; but gang or task work was the normal order of the day, and efficient routine the key to success. The financial risk was concentrated upon the planters, whom vicissitudes or ineptitude occasionally bankrupted; but new entrepreneurs generally appeared to replace those who failed, except in the rice industry, which, by force of competition from Louisiana and Texas, has dwindled almost to the vanishing point in its old habitat.

The sugar regime may be illustrated from the diary of work on Corinne Plantation, lying just below New Orleans, for the year 1876.[26] The milling of the crop of the preceding year continued to the middle of January. Then, while for a short time a gang of Irishmen were levelling certain fields on special contract, negroes began ploughing, with two men and four mules to each of eight ploughs for the heavy work, which was first the deep stirring of the soil alongside the dormant "rattoons" and then, beginning in late February, the fresh planting of fields in which the three-year cycle of sugar cane was to begin anew. For the planting and cultivating season additional negroes were engaged in February; and early in March the force was recruited with twenty Portuguese laborers. For March 18 the record runs: "Hoe hands left the field, because they said the task was too large." Five days later the management reduced the daily hoeing stint by one-third, and work was resumed. From the beginning of May to the middle of July the fields were cultivated with lighter ploughs, drawn by one or two mules; and the hoeing continued till the first of August. With the crop now "laid by," miscellaneous work filled the time of a reduced corps in the late summer and early fall. Harvest began October 26, with an enlarged force, paid a dollar a day.

For November 7 the diary reads: "Today being the election day, no field work was done, only 12 white men cording cane at sugar house." This was at the climax of radical rule in Louisiana—the famous Hayes-Tilden contest, which eventually required an electoral commission at Washington to determine for whom the electoral vote of the state should be counted. On election days in subsequent years there were doubtless not so many negroes absent from the plantation. On November 8 the mill began to grind the cane. The diary reports: "We had but a small force; but considering today being after election day, everything went off well enough."

With the harvest now at its crest, and every hour precious for getting the crop out of danger from frost, Sundays were included in the work schedule, though about half the field force usually took half of each Sunday off. The normal distribution of the per-

[26] Manuscript in private possession.

sonnel on the payroll at the height of the grinding was about 50 cutting cane, 16 loading the carts, 8 hauling, and 36 operating the mill. The mill doubtless ran night and day; but this was so much a matter of course that the diarist did not note it. From the 280 acres in cane the yield, which was heavily diminished by severe frost and subsequent souring of cane, was 534,000 pounds of sugar and 820 barrels of molasses. There were also gathered as auxiliary products 1,640 bushels of corn and 117 loads of peavine and other hay.

As later decades have passed, the role of the immigrants has lessened in the South; and nowadays many of the negroes are seeking the higher wages at Northern industrial centers. What will come of this remains to be seen; but the blacks who stay in the Southern fields do not appear to be experiencing any drastic change. A newcomer in Georgia, Frances Butler Leigh, the daughter of Fanny Kemble—whose book is an implicit commentary upon her mother's *Journal*—wrote in 1866:

I generally found that if I wanted a thing done I first had to tell the negroes to do it, then show them how, and finally do it myself. Their way of managing not to do it was very ingenious, for they always were perfectly good-tempered, and received my orders with, "Dat's so, missus; just as missus says," and then always somehow or other left the thing undone.[27]

A migrant to Mississippi, having chafed for ten years at similar experiences, wrote in 1919: "A field negro lives in a kind of perpetual doze, a dreamy haze. . . . Nothing disturbs for any length of time the uniform and listless torpor of his existence. . . . Life moves at a low pressure; at times the wheels can barely be seen to turn." [28]

The tether binding the two races in a single system has been broken by many individuals—negroes have set up for themselves, and whites have dispensed altogether with negro labor. But with

[27] Leigh, *Ten Years on a Georgia Plantation*, 57.
[28] Howard Snyder, "Plantation Pictures," *Atlantic Monthly* (CXXVII), 171, 175.

most the tether has merely been lengthened, to the mingled grati-
fication and regret of nearly all concerned. The rural negroes in
bulk remain primitive and slack. Poverty has been a clog upon the
whole Southern community; and negro slackness, along with poor
soil, has been a chief cause of poverty.

The most common tether continues to be the plantation system,
with tenancy the most widely prevalent basis. But whether the
scheme be that of wages or crop-sharing, there is not much turnover except perhaps at the year-end; habitations are fixed for the
year; life is lived in family units; and white folk, often of high
grade, are tolerantly and affably, if patronizingly, concerned close
at hand with the improvement not only of negro work but of
negro life.

But we have not come to praise the plantation, and certainly not
to bury it. That system now flourishes in California and Colorado,
in the West Indies and the East Indies; and its introduction even
into England is advocated as a means of improvement.[29] It is idle
to expect its early demise in the "black belt" of the United States,
where the census takers in a confessedly incomplete survey in 1910
found 39,073 plantations operating on a tenant basis with as many
as five tenant families each, to say nothing of the many estates
cultivated by wage labor.[30]

[29] Sir A. Daniel Hall has just written, concerning English agriculture: "For
obvious reasons the small farm is less efficient, less economic of human labor
than the large one. It is handicapped physically in that the size of its fields does
not permit of the effective use of machinery or the orderly disposition of
labor. Overhead charges are high; the capitalization of the small farm is excessive. . . . Intellectually the small farming community tends to become hide-
bound and unprogressive." The road to future improvement, he continues, is
toward large corporation farms, in which profit-sharing may well be a feature.
"The unit of farming should be something between two and ten thousand
acres of mixed farming, and the management should be a hierarchy of director
and assistants such as prevails in any great business." *Atlantic Monthly*,
CXXXV (May, 1925), 684, 685.

[30] *Thirteenth Census of the United States*, V, 877-89.

20

The Plantation Product of Men

THE plantation is largely a thing of the past, and yet it is of the present.* We do not live in the past, but the past in us. Every man and woman is the product of his or her environment and of the environment of his or her forbears, for we are controlled by tradition. Our minds are the resultant of the experiences of those who gave us birth and rearing; and this plantation regime of which we speak was a powerful influence in the lives of millions of men and women.

We think of the plantations as producing staples, tobacco, rice, cotton, indigo, but they had a product of equally staple character and personality. The plantations were large farms or industrial establishments, but, more than that, they were homesteads. They were equipped with negro laborers, but that was incidental, because they originated with other than negro labor. For example, in Jamaica aboriginal or Indian labor was used; in Virginia the laborers were white men brought over seas as indented servants. In that colony the plantation reached its full type with British labor. Then with the continent of Africa available as a source of lusty and cheap labor, it was found advisable to supplement the failing supply of indented servants; and the institution of slavery was revived for the negroes' adjustment and control.

The plantation system was confined in its habitat to that part of North America which we speak of as the South, for only under certain conditions could it flourish. The most important of these

* *Proceedings of the Second Annual Session of the Georgia Historical Association* (Atlanta, 1918), 14–15.

was climate as determining crops. The essential requirement was that the crops under cultivation should be such as to require labor virtually the year round. The plantation system was the factory system applied to agriculture, employing considerable groups laboring under supervision. Whereas in wheat production, labor is seasonal only at seed-time and harvest, in the raising of the Southern staples, work was needed for many months of the year. It was an adage among cotton planters that it took thirteen months in the year to raise a crop. It was only in the regions where work was long continued in simple routine that plantation industry could flourish. Accordingly, that system was distinctive of the South, and it has left an imprint upon the South. It left to us a philosophy which we must pass on in our turn. That philosophy is expressed in many ways. For example, I learned only yesterday that when a newly fledged officer in the National Army was recently assigned to a negro regiment he expressed utter dismay at the prospect; but the Major said very simply, "Just bear down hard on the non-commissioned officers and don't believe anything the negro soldiers may say." At Camp Gordon it is a pleasure to be with the negroes, for they are, for the most part, plantation negroes, and it is easy to manage them. Those who know the type, know when and where to count on it, and when otherwise.

The plantation was a homestead, one of considerable scale, and isolated. The planter and his household served in a sense as the settlement workers do in metropolitan betterment now. They served as patterns of life as well as preceptors in the training of a backward people. The spirit of the plantation was that of neighborliness, and that again is a thing to be cherished—a thing which is now coming into high esteem among social students.

The planters were quite distinctively magistrates as well as administrators. The laborers were in their custody and under their care for twenty-four hours of every day and three hundred and sixty-five days of every year. It is the curse of modern industrialism that the laborer is the thought and care of the employer only during the hours of labor. Employers have no knowledge of or concern with the wives and children or other dependents of the employees. This impersonality of modern industrialism is a thing which has a menace in it that was utterly alien to the plantation regime, for the manager of the establishment was not merely the owner of the land and apparatus, but the owner of the laborers and of their dependents. And the master was thoroughly concerned with the food, clothing, training, and the health and happiness of the children of his establishment, the offspring of his laborers, for they were his future prospects. The mistress was on her own score head-seamstress, nurse, and housekeeper for the whole establishment. These twain were the over-father and the over-mother of all; and the children, white and black, were reared in large measure in common. A spirit of camaraderie was common among the youngsters; and between adults and children alike there was a quite general intimacy and cordiality. This was not universal, but was general enough to be characteristic. We find the fruits of it at Camp Gordon, where white and black enlisted men from the same county meet in warm friendliness. The cordiality between the two elements dates from plantation times. Men who view the old Southern regime from afar off and with a theorist's eye are likely to think it was an agency of race alienation. So far as my understanding goes this is fundamentally erroneous. The grouping of persons of the two races in the intimate relationship of possession tended strongly to counteract that antipathy which all races feel toward each other. The possession was not wholly of the slave by the master, but also of the master by the slave.

The typical plantation was fairly large, though not as large as tradition has it in some cases. One often hears of planters who owned a thousand or more slaves, but the census does not bear out the claim. Most commonly, their working squads comprised but a dozen slaves or so. Nevertheless, as compared with ordinary farms, plantations were large establishments, and the management of them came within the scope of large affairs. The necessity of administering them in great detail required on the part of the proprietors ability of a high order, both in the control of routine and in the making of constructive plans for future operations. This habitual experience was in itself somewhat a training for military service and for statecraft. The plantation regime, accordingly, produced types of men and women, white and black, that are distinctive in the world; and as a student of the history of the South I consider that I am not a student of local history but of things significant in the history of the world.

Of course, the plantation system did not occupy everybody in the South. Millions were outside of plantation boundaries. But it gave an impress to the thought of large, if not all, elements of the Southern people. It made for strength of character and readiness to meet emergencies, for patience and tact, for large-mindedness, gentility, and self-control. Now we are in some danger of losing the tradition of these things in the whirl of modern life; but I think that the impress of the old regime is strong enough to endure long—and if those who cherish its memory will zealously propagate the qualities it fostered, I think that the South may remain in long future times as wholesome, constructive, and strong as she has been in the past.

21

The Central Theme of
Southern History

A N Ohio River ferryman has a stock remark when approaching the right bank: "We are nearing the American shore." *
A thousand times has he said it with a gratifying repercussion from among his passengers; for its implications are a little startling. The northern shore is American without question; the southern is American with a difference. Kentucky had by slender pretense a star in the Confederate flag; for a time she was officially neutral; for all time her citizens have been self-consciously Kentuckians, a distinctive people. They are Southerners in main sentiment, and so are Marylanders and Missourians.

Southernism did not arise from any selectiveness of migration, for the sort of people who went to Virginia, Maryland, or Carolina, were not as a group different from those who went to Pennsylvania or the West Indies. It does not lie in religion or language. It was not created by one-crop tillage, nor did agriculture in the large tend to produce a Southern scheme of life and thought. The Mohawk valley was for decades as rural as that of the Roanoke; wheat is as dominant in Dakota as cotton has ever been in Alabama; tobacco is as much a staple along the Ontario shore of Lake Erie as in the Kentucky pennyroyal; and the growing of rice and cotton in California has not prevented Los Angeles from being in a sense the capital of Iowa. On the other hand the rise of mill towns in the Carolina Piedmont and the growth of manufacturing at Richmond and Birmingham have not made these Northern. It may be

* *American Historical Review*, XXIV (October, 1928), 30–43.

admitted, however, that Miami, Palm Beach, and Coral Gables are Southern only in latitude. They were vacant wastes until Flagler, Fifth Avenue, and the realtors discovered and subdivided them.

The South has never had a focus. New York has plied as much of its trade as Baltimore or New Orleans; and White Sulphur Springs did not quite eclipse all other mountain and coast resorts for vacation patronage. The lack of a metropolis was lamented in 1857 by an advocate of Southern independence,[1] as an essential for shaping and radiating a coherent philosophy to fit the prevailing conditions of life. But without a consolidating press or pulpit or other definite apparatus the South has maintained a considerable solidarity through thick and thin, through peace and war and peace again. What is its essence? Not state rights—Calhoun himself was for years a nationalist, and some advocates of independence hoped for a complete merging of the several states into a unitary Southern republic; not free trade—sugar and hemp growers have ever been protectionists; not slavery—in the eighteenth century this was of continental legality, and in the twentieth it is legal nowhere; not Democracy—there were many Federalists in Washington's day and many Whigs in Clay's; not party predominance by any name, for Virginia, Georgia, and Mississippi were "doubtful states" from Jackson's time to Buchanan's. It is not the land of cotton alone or of plantations alone; and it has not always been the land of "Dixie," for before its ecstatic adoption in 1861 that spine-tingling tune was a mere "walk around" of Christie's minstrels. Yet it is a land with a unity despite its diversity, with a people having common joys and common sorrows, and, above all, as to the white folk a people with a common resolve indomitably maintained—that it shall be and remain a white man's country. The consciousness of a function in these premises, whether expressed with the frenzy of a demagogue or maintained with a patrician's quietude, is the cardinal test of a Southerner and the central theme of Southern history.

It arose as soon as the negroes became numerous enough to create a problem of race control in the interest of orderly govern-

[1] *Russell's Magazine* (I), 106.

ment and the maintenance of Caucasian civilization. Slavery was instituted not merely to provide control of labor but also as a system of racial adjustment and social order. And when in the course of time slavery was attacked, it was defended not only as a vested interest, but with vigor and vehemence as a guarantee of white supremacy and civilization. Its defenders did not always take pains to say that this was what they chiefly meant, but it may nearly always be read between their lines, and their hearers and readers understood it without overt expression.[2] Otherwise it would be impossible to account for the fervid secessionism of many non-slaveholders and eager service of thousands in the Confederate army.

The non-slaveholders of course were diverse in their conditions and sentiments. Those in the mountains and the deep pine woods were insulated to such degree that public opinion hardly existed, and they chose between alternatives only when issues created in other quarters were forced upon them. Those in the black belt on the other hand, had their lives conditioned by the presence of the negroes; and they had apparatus of court days, militia musters, and political barbecues as well as neighborhood conversation to keep them abreast of affairs. A mechanic of Iuka, Mississippi, wrote in the summer of 1861: "I am a Georgian Raised I am Forty years Old A tinner By Trade I Raised the First Confederate Flag that I Ever Heard Of that was in 1851 in the Town of Macon Miss. Notwithstanding the Many Radicules I Encounter'd I Told the Citizens that they would All Be Glad to Rally under Such a Flag Some Day which is at present true."[3] This personal tale was told to prove his title to a voice in Confederate policy. His main theme

[2] Many expressions were explicit, for example, the remarks of Mr. Standard at Richmond in 1829: "The property we seek to protect . . . is not mere brute matter . . . but it consists of intelligent, sentient, responsible beings, that have passions to be inflamed, hearts to feel, understandings to be enlightened, and who are capable of catching the flame of enthusiasm from the eloquent effusions of agitators . . . ; and who may not only be lost to their masters as property, but may change conditions and become masters themselves, so far at least as the ravages of a servile war shall have [error for leave] any subject to be ruled over." *Proceedings and Debates of the Virginia State Convention of 1829–30* (Richmond, 1830), 306.

[3] Manuscript letter in private possession.

was a demand that the permanent Confederate constitution exclude negroes from all employment except agricultural labor and
domestic service in order that the handicrafts be reserved for white
artisans like himself.

The overseer of a sugar estate forty miles below New Orleans
inscribed a prayer on the plantation journal:

Thursday 13 June 1861

This Day is set a part By presedent Jefferson Davis for fasting and
praying owing to the Deplorable condition ower southern country is In
My Prayer Sincerely to God is that every Black Republican in the Hole
combined whorl either man woman o chile that is opposed to negro
slavery as it existed in the Southern confederacy shal be trubled with
pestilents and calamitys of all Kinds and Drag out the Balance of there
existance in Misray and Degradation with scarsely food and rayment
enughf to keep sole and Body to gather and o God I pray the to Direct
a bullet or a bayonet to pirce The Hart of every northern soldier that
invades southern soile and after the Body has rendered up its traterish
sole gave it a trators reward a Birth In the Lake of Fires and Brimstone
my honest convicksion is that every man wome and chile that has gave
aide to the abolishionist are fit subjects for Hell I all so ask the to aide
the southern Confederacy in maintaining ower rites and establishing
the confederate Government Believing this case the prares from the
wicked will prevaileth much Amen[4]

This overseer's pencilled prayer is the most rampant fire-eating
expression which I have encountered in any quarter. He and the
tinner had an economic interest in the maintenance of slavery, the
one to assure the presence of laborers for him to boss, the other to
restrain competition in his trade. But both of them, and a million
of their non-slaveholding like, had a still stronger social prompt-
ing: the white men's ways must prevail; the negroes must be kept
innocuous.

In the forties when most of the planters were Whig, some of the
Democratic politicians thought it strange that their own party

[4] When I made this transcript twenty years ago the manuscript journal was
on Magnolia plantation in Plaquemines Parish, Louisiana. The item is in the
handwriting of J. A. Randall, overseer.

should be the more energetic in defense of slavery; and in 1860 they were perhaps puzzled again that the Bell and Everett Constitutional Union ticket drew its main support from among the slaveholders. The reason for this apparent anomaly lay doubtless in the two facts, that men of wealth had more to lose in any cataclysm, and that masters had less antipathy to negroes than non-slaveholders did. In daily contact with blacks from birth, and often on a friendly basis of patron and retainer, the planters were in a sort of partnership with their slaves, reckoning upon their good-will or at least possessing a sense of security as a fruit of long habituation to fairly serene conditions. But the white toilers lived outside this partnership and suffered somewhat from its competition. H. R. Helper in his *Impending Crisis* (1857) urged them to wreck the system by destroying slavery; and when this had been accomplished without their aid he vented in his fantastic *Nojoque* (1867) a spleen against the negroes, advocating their expulsion from the United States as a preliminary to their universal extermination. Thus he called for class war upon a double front, to humble the "lords of the lash" and then to destroy the "black and bi-colored caitiffs" who cumbered the white man's world. By his alliterative rhetoric and shrewdly selected statistics Helper captured some Northern propagandists and the historians whom they begat, but if he made any converts among Southern yeomen they are not of record. His notions had come to him during residence in California and the North; they were therefore to be taken skeptically. His programmes repudiated humane tradition, disregarded vital actualities, and evoked Northern aid to make over the South in its own image. These things, and perhaps the last especially, were not to be sanctioned. In fact, for reasons common in the world at large, the Southern whites were not to be divided into sharply antagonistic classes. Robert J. Walker said quite soundly in 1856:

In all the slave States there is a large majority of voters who are non-slaveholders; but they are devoted to the institutions of the South—they would defend them with their lives—and on this question the South are [sic] a united people. The class, composed of many small farmers, of merchants, professional men, mechanics, overseers, and other industrial classes, constitute mainly the patrol of the South, and cheerfully unite in carrying out those laws essential to preserve the institution. Against a powerful minority and constant agitation slavery could not exist in any State.[5]

He wrote this to explain the poor prospect of slavery in Kansas; he might have used the same phrasing to explain its persistence in Delaware or Missouri. Habitat grouping, it is clear, had a cementing force great enough to overcome the cleaving tendency of economic stratification. So strong was it, indeed, that sundry free negroes gave warm endorsement to the project of Southern independence.[6]

It is perhaps less fruitful to seek the social classes at large which were warm and those which were cool toward independence than to inquire why the citizens of certain areas were prevailingly ardent while those in another zone were indifferent or opposed, why for example the whole tier from South Carolina to Texas seceded spontaneously but no other states joined them until after Lincoln's call for troops. The reason lay in preceding history as well as in current conditions. The economic factor of the cotton belt's interest in free trade and its recurrent chagrin at protective tariff enactments is by no means negligible. The rancor produced by nullification and the "force bill" had been revived in South Carolina by the repeal of the compromise tariff in 1842, and it did not then die. The quarrels of Georgia with the federal authorities over Indian lands, with Alabama and Mississippi looking on in interested sympathy, were contributing episodes to make the Lower South alert; and the heavy negro proportions in their black belts, together with immaturity in the social order, made their people more sensitive than those of Virginia to the menace of disturbance from outside.

Slavery questions, which had never been quite negligible since the framing of the Constitution, gained a febrile activity from the abolition agitation; and the study of congressional mathematics

[5] *De Bow's Review* (XXI), 591–92.
[6] Phillips, *American Negro Slavery*, 436; R. H. Williams, *With the Border Ruffians* (London, 1908), 441.

focussed the main attention upon the rivalry of the sections in territorial enlargement. The North had control of the lower house, as recurrent votes on the Wilmot Proviso showed; and California's admission upset the sectional equilibrium in the Senate. For Yancey, Rhett, and Quitman and for the pamphleteers Longstreet, Bryan, and Trescot, this was enough. The North now had the strength of a giant; the South should strike for independence before that strength should grow yet greater and be consolidated for crushing purposes. But the gestures of Cass, Webster, and Fillmore gave ground for hope that the giant would not use his power against Southern home rule, and the crisis was deferred. Southern friends and foes of the Compromise of 1850 were alert thenceforward for tokens of Northern will. Events through the ensuing decade, somewhat assisted by the fire-eaters and culminating in a Republican's election to the Presidency, converted a new multitude to the shibboleth: "The alternative: a separate nationality or the Africanization of the South." [7]

Walter Lippmann has analyzed political process in general as if he had our present study specifically in mind:

Since the general opinions of large numbers of persons are almost certain to be a vague and confusing medley, action cannot be taken until those opinions have been factored down, canalized, compressed and made uniform. The making of one general will out of a multitude of general wishes . . . consists essentially in the use of symbols which assemble emotions after they have been detached from their ideas. . . . The process, therefore, by which general opinions are brought to cooperation consists in an intensification of feeling and a degradation of significance. [8]

The tension of 1850 had brought much achievement in this direction. "Southern rights" had come to mean racial security, self-determination by the whites whether in or out of the Union, and all things ancillary to the assured possession of these. Furthermore

[7] The title of a pamphlet by William H. Holcombe, M.D. (New Orleans, 1860).
[8] Walter Lippmann, *The Phantom Public* (New York, 1925), 47.

a programme had been framed to utilize state sovereignty whether to safeguard the South as a minority within the Union or to legitimate its exit into national independence.

The resurgence of these notions and emotions after their abeyance in 1851 need not be traced in detail. Suffice it to say that legal sanction for the spread of slaveholding, regardless of geographical potentialities, became the touchstone of Southern rights; and the rapid rise of the Republican Party which denied this sanction, equally regardless of geographical potentialities, tipped the balance in lower Southern policy. Many were primed in 1856 for a stroke in case Frémont should be elected that year; and though he fell short of an electoral majority, the strength shown by his ticket increased the zeal of South-savers through the next quadrennium. The so-called Southern commercial conventions became a forum and *De Bow's Review*, an organ for the airing of projects, mad or sane, for annexing Cuba, promoting direct trade with Europe, boycotting Northern manufactures and Northern colleges, procuring Southern textbooks for Southern schools, reopening the African slave trade—anything and everything which might agitate and perhaps consolidate the South in a sense of bafflement within the Union and a feeling of separate destiny. Many clergymen gave their aid, particularly by praising slavery as a biblical and benevolent institution.

Pierre Soulé tried in 1857, as Calhoun had done eight years before, to create a Southern party separate from the Democrats;[9] and next year Yancey launched his League of United Southerners. Ere long a rural editor blurted what many must have been thinking:

That the North sectionalized will acquire possession of this Government at no distant day we look upon as no longer a matter of doubt. . . . It is inevitable. The South—the whole South even—cannot avert it. We may determine to fight the battle with our foes within the Union, . . . but we will fight only to be defeated. The Union of the South is indeed of great moment—not however for successful resistance in this Union, but for going out of it under circumstances the

[9] New Orleans *Crescent*, June 17, 1857.

most favorable to the speedy formation of a separate and independent government.[10]

Various expressions in Northern papers, debates in Congress, and events in Kansas and elsewhere had fanned these flames when the stroke of John Brown fell upon Harper's Ferry. This event was taken as a demonstration that abolitionists had lied in saying they were concerned with moral suasion only, and it stimulated suspicion that Republicans were abolitionists in disguise. In December the South Carolina legislature when expressing sympathy with Virginia intimated that she was ripe for secession and invited all Southern states to meet in convention at once to concert measures for united action. In February the Alabama legislature asserted that under no circumstances would the commonwealth submit to "the foul domination of a sectional Northern party," and it instructed the governor in the event of a Republican's election to the Presidency to order the election of delegates to a convention of the state to consider and do whatever in its judgment her rights, interests, and honor might require.

There was little to do in the interim but discuss principles and portents and to jockey the situation slightly to prepare for the crisis or try to prevent it according to what individuals might think best. In an editorial of January 9, 1860, on "The true position of the South: Not aggrandisement but safety," the New Orleans *Crescent*, which was long an advocate of moderation, said:

The South does not claim the right of controlling the North in the choice of a President; she admits fully and explicitly that the Northern people possess the prerogative of voting as they please. But at the same time the South asserts that while the North holds the legal rights of casting her voice as to her may seem best, she has no *moral* right to so cast it as to effect the ruin of the South; and if she does so cast it, in full view of its injurious effects upon us, . . . she, in effect, commits an act of covert hostility upon us that will render it impossible for us to live longer in intimate relations.

[10] The *Southron* (Orangeburg, S.C.), quoted in the *Southern Guardian* (Columbia, S.C.), May 20, 1859.

On April 15, the *Delta*, replying to a recent lecture at New Orleans by George D. Prentice of Louisville, denied that Clay and Webster, "those demiurgic heroes of his political faith," could have sufficed for the present occasion:

The period of mere political formation is past, and the period for the solution of great social and industrial problems is at hand. Mere constitutional lore here can do nothing; mere skill in adjusting balances of political power can do nothing. Is it just to hold the negro in bondage? Is negro slavery inimical to the rights of white men? Is it best for both the white and black man—best for the interests of agriculture, best for the needs of commerce and useful arts, and best for social stability and civilization? These and kindred questions imperiously demand to be answered, and they are precisely the questions which the old school of statesmen strenuously refused to look in the face. . . . The truth is, we are in the midst of facts having a philosophy of their own which we must master for ourselves, leaving dead men to take care of the dead past. The Sphinx which is now propounding its riddles to us the dead knew nothing about; consequently no voice from the grave can tell us how to get rid of the monster.

After the nominating conventions had put four tickets in the field the newspapers began a running debate upon the relative merits of Douglas, Breckinridge, and Bell for Southern purposes and the degree of menace in the Lincoln candidacy. The Natchez *Free Trader*, which until June 27 mastheaded the names of Albert G. Brown and Fernando Wood, accepted next day the Richmond nominations:

We hoist today the flag of the Union-saving National Democratic nominees, Breckinridge and Lane, *sans peur et sans reproche*. With records so fair that none can attack them, they will win the hearts of all the people of the land, be elected by a vote so flattering as to cause the hearts of the noblest and best to beat with honest exaltation and pride, and so administer the Government as to have the blessings of the people showered on them and elicit the unrestrained admiration of an enlightened world.

Such bombast as this might survive the summer; but when the October elections brought a virtual certainty of Lincoln's election the discussion took another phase. The friends of each minor ticket demanded that the other two be withdrawn or forsaken. Douglas and Bell men agreed at least that Breckinridge ought to be abandoned. The Nashville *Union and American,* in reply on October 16 to such a demand from the Nashville *Patriot,* said that Breckinridge might still be elected by Southern concentration upon him, "in as much as it will prove to the North that we are determined to have our rights." And as a last appeal, November 6, the New Orleans *Delta* said, urging votes for Breckinridge as against Bell or Douglas:

Is this the time to indorse the representatives of a half-way, compromising, submissive policy? When the whole North is sectional shall the South be national, when nationality can mean nothing but an acquiescence in the employment of national means to accomplish sectional purposes? Never before in the history of any free and brave people was so bold a challenge as that which the North now throws at us received in any other way than the stern and proud defiance of a united and determined community.

Among the Bell organs the New Orleans *Bee* gave a remarkably sound analysis in an editorial of July 27: "The restlessness of the South touching the agitation of the slavery question arises rather from the apprehension of what the aggressive policy of the North may hereafter effect, than from what it has already accomplished. For . . . we may safely affirm that thus far no practical injury has resulted." The Southern failure in colonizing Kansas, it continued, was not a grievance, for: "prudent and far-seeing men predicted the utter impracticability of carrying the design into execution. . . . Slavery will go where it will pay. No slaveholder for the sake of an abstraction will amuse himself by earning five per cent in Kansas on the labor of his chattels, when with absolutely less toil it will give him fifteen per cent in the cotton or sugar fields of Louisiana." On its own score the *Bee* concluded: "We apprehend that the Black Republicans are dogs whose bark is more dangerous than their bite. The South is too precious to the North to be driven out of the Union." Its colleague the *Crescent* expressed a belief as late as October 20 that, if the Republican party should win the contest, its "unnatural and feverish vitality" would reach exhaustion within a year or two. In the United States thus far, the *Crescent* argued, parties had arisen and fallen in rapid succession.

But all of these parties were national. The principles they advocated were of common application to the whole country, and their members and adherents were found in every quarter and every State of the Union. If these parties were temporary and short-lived in their character and constitution, still more so must the Black Republican party be, sectional as it is in its organization and principles, and obnoxious to a deeper hatred and more bitter opposition than any other organization that has yet made its appearance in the political arena. It is impossible that such a party can long exist.

Just before election day George Fitzhugh of Virginia wrote to the Charleston *Mercury* a long letter concluding: "In the Union there is no hope for us. Let us gather courage from despair, and quit the Union." The editor when printing this, November 9, remarked: "Mr. Fitzhugh is a little excitable. We intend to 'quit the Union', but without any 'despair' whatever. We'll quit it with a round hip! hip! hurrah! !'"

But now that the partizans of Breckinridge, Bell, and Douglas had met a common defeat, their lines were broken with regard to the Southern recourse. Some of the Breckinridge men opposed secession unless and until the Lincoln government should commit an "overt act" of injury, but many supporters of Bell and Douglas turned to the policy of prompt strokes.[11] The New Orleans *Crescent* and *Bee* are again clear exponents. On November 8 the *Crescent* said: "We read the result in the face of every citizen upon the street. There is an universal feeling that an insult has

[11] Unionism among many of the Bell supporters had been conditioned from the first, almost explicitly, upon constitutionalism as interpreted in favor of Southern rights. For example the convention in Georgia which responded to the call for organizing the party and sent delegates to Baltimore adopted a platform asserting that slavery was established in the Constitution, that the territories were the property of the states jointly, that Congress and the territorial legislatures were alike incapable of impairing the right of slave property, and that it was the duty of Congress to protect the rights of slaveholders in the territories. *Southern Recorder* (Milledgeville, Ga.), May 8, 1860.

been deliberately tendered our people, which is responded to not by noisy threats or passionate objurgations, but a settled determination that the South shall never be oppressed under Mr. Lincoln's administration." But it cherished a shadowy hope that electors chosen on the Republican ticket might yet refrain from putting "a sectional President in the chair of Washington!" On December 17 the *Bee* admitted that it had yielded to the prodigious tide of public sentiment, and said in explanation: "It was evident indeed, that amid all the lip service professed for the Union there had dwelt in the hearts of Southerners a tacit determination to regard the election of Lincoln as proof of a settled and immutable policy of aggression by the North toward the South, and to refuse further political affiliation with those who by that act should declare themselves our enemies." On the following January 3 the *Crescent* said:

It is by secession alone that we [Louisiana] can be placed in close affinity with all of our sisters of the Gulf and South Atlantic seaboard, who have given guarantees . . . that they will be out of the Union long in advance of our action and ready to receive us in the Government that shall have been established.[12] South Carolina, Georgia, Mississippi, Florida, Alabama, Louisiana and Texas are knit by God and their own hearts indissolubly together. . . .

Believe not that any State has the right to expect another to await her action in an emergency like this. *We have as much right to complain of the tardiness of the border States as they have of our haste.* . . . A people who wait for others to aid them in vindicating their rights are already enslaved, for now, as in every other period of history—

"In native swords and native ranks
The only hope of freedom dwells."

The Upper South had votaries of independence no less outspoken than those of the cotton belt, but they were too few to

[12] These pledges had been conveyed by commissioners appointed by the governors of sundry commonwealths to convey to the governors, legislatures, and conventions of other states assurances of secession as soon as the procedure could be completed and invitations for union in a new nation or confederacy. A study of these commissioners as agents of coördination has been made by Mr. Dwight L. Dumond of the University of Michigan, but has not yet been published.

carry their states prior to a Northern "overt act." Arguments and eloquence by visiting commissioners might sway the minds and thrill the hearts of delegates, but none of these conventions took a decisive step until Lincoln's call for troops. Indeed there was a project of organizing the border states for a course of their own, even to the extreme of a central confederacy separate alike from the "Black Republican" North and the "hotspur" South. When this was pinched out, the sequel showed that the boundary of predominant Southern loyalty was not Mason and Dixon's Line but a curving zone seldom touching that landmark.

Many Virginians, perhaps most of them, sanctioned the change of allegiance reluctantly; and some, chiefly in the Wheeling panhandle, revolted sharply against it. On the other hand the course of the Federal government during the war and after its close alienated so many borderers that in a sense Kentucky joined the Confederacy after the war was over.

While the war dragged its disheartening length and the hopes of independence faded, queries were raised in some Southern quarters as to whether yielding might not be the wiser course. Lincoln in his plan of reconstruction had shown unexpected magnanimity; the Republican party, discarding that obnoxious name, had officially styled itself merely Unionist; and the Northern Democrats, although outvoted, were still a friendly force to be reckoned upon. Die-hard statesmen and loyal soldiers carried on till the collapse. The governors in the "late so-called Confederate States" were now ready with soft speeches, but the Federal soldiery clapped them into prison until Andrew Johnson relaxed from his brief punitive phase.

With Johnson then on Lincoln's path "back to normalcy," Southern hearts were lightened only to sink again when radicals in Congress, calling themselves Republicans once more, overslaughed the presidential programme and set events in train which seemed to make "the Africanization of the South" inescapable. To most of the whites, doubtless, the prospect showed no gleam of hope.

But Edward A. Pollard, a Virginian critic of Davis, chronicler of the war and bewailer of the "lost cause," took courage in 1868 to write his most significant book, *The Lost Cause Regained.* The folly of politicians, he said, had made the South defend slavery seemingly "as a property tenure, or as a peculiar institution of labour; when the true ground of defence was as of a barrier against a contention and war of races." [13] The pro-slavery claims on the basis of constitutional right he denounced in retrospect as flimsily technical and utterly futile in the face of a steadily encroaching moral sentiment; and the stroke for independence in the name of liberty he thought as fallacious as the later expectation of generosity which had brought the Confederate collapse.[14]

It has been curiously reserved for the South to obtain *after* the war the actual experience of oppression, and of that measure of despotism which would have amply justified the commencement of hostilities. If it fought, in 1860, for principles too abstract, it has superabundant causes for rebellion now, which although they may not, and need not produce another war, yet have the effect to justify, in a remarkable way, the first appeal to arms.[15]

In elaboration of this: "The black thread of the Negro has been spun throughout the scheme of Reconstruction. A design is betrayed to give to him the political control of the South, not so much as a benefit to him, . . . as to secure power to the Republican party." [16]

But in the defeats of proposals for negro suffrage in seven states from Connecticut to Colorado, and particularly in the ovation with which the Philadelphia convention of 1866 had received a resolution urging the Southern whites not to submit to negro rule, he saw promise of effective support and eventual success in undoing Reconstruction. [17] Therefore:

Let us come back to the true hope of the South. It is to enter bravely with new allies and new auspices the contest for the supremacy of the white man, and with it the preservation of the dearest political tradi-

[13] E. A. Pollard, *The Lost Cause Regained* (New York, 1868), 13.
[14] *Ibid.*, 20, 50, 116.
[15] *Ibid.*, 51–52.
[16] *Ibid.*, 129.
[17] *Ibid.*, 133, 162.

tions of the country. "WHITE" is the winning word, says a North Carolina paper, and let us never be done repeating it. . . . It is the irresistible sympathy of races, which will not, cannot fail. . . . It is this instinct which the South will at last summon to her aid, when her extremity demands it.[18]

Before the farther bank of the slough of despond was fully attained, the question was raised as to the path beyond. In a remarkable address in 1875 Wiley P. Harris of Mississippi lamented the political exploitation of the negroes: "The mass of them don't vote, but are literally voted. They are ridden and driven by a little nest of men who are alien to the state in feeling. . . . The result is a government at once imperious and contemptible, a tyranny at once loathsome and deadly." He bade the carpet-baggers farewell in advance of their going: "I assure these men that their last card has been played, and it has not won. This trumpery no longer deceives anybody, and it matters not which party prevails in 1876, no national administration will again incur the odium of propping them up." But with merely restoring white local domination he would not be content. Appealing specifically for a renewed and permanent union of Democrats with liberal Republicans throughout the country, he said:

To reconcile and nationalize the South, to lead it out of the cul de sac of sectionalism into the broad stream of national life, . . . to restore peace, good will and confidence between the members of this great family of States, will lay the solid and durable foundation of a party which will surely win and long retain the hearts of the American people. . . . For one, I long to see a government at Washington, and a government here, toward which I can feel a genuine sentiment of reverence and respect. It is a dreary life we lead here, with a national government ever suspicious and ever frowning, and a home government feeble, furtive, false and fraudulent. Under such influences the feeling of patriotism must die out amongst us, and this will accomplish the ruin of a noble population. . . . We are in a new world. We are moving on a new plane. It is better that we hang a millstone about our

[18] *Ibid.*, 165.

necks than cling to these old issues. To cling to them is to perpetuate sectional seclusion.[19]

Lamar's eulogy of Sumner and the speeches and editorials of Grady were much to the same effect, and likewise were the efforts of other broad-minded men. But a certain sense of bafflement and of defensive self-containment persists to our own day, because the negro population remains as at least a symbolic potentiality. Virtually all respectable whites had entered the Democratic ranks in the later sixties to combat à *outrance* the Republican programme of negro incitement. A dozen years sufficed to restore white control, whereupon they began to differ among themselves upon various issues. Many joined the People's Party; and in some quarters a fusion was arranged of Populists and Republicans to carry elections. In the stress of campaigning this threatened to bring from within the South a stimulus to negroes as political auxiliaries.

But by Southern hypothesis, exalted into a creed, negroes in the mass were incompetent for any good political purpose and by reason of their inexperience and racial unwisdom were likely to prove subversive. To remove the temptation to white politicians to lead negroes to the polls again, "white primaries" were instituted to control nominations, educational requirements for the suffrage were inserted in the state constitutions, and the Bryanizing of the Democratic party was accepted as a means of healing a white rift. Even these devices did not wholly lay the spectre of "negro domination"; for the fifteenth amendment stood in the Constitution and the calendar of Congress was not yet free of "force bills." For every Lodge and Foraker there arose a Tillman and a Vardaman, with a Watson and a Blease to spare.

The sentiments and symbols have not been wholly divorced from reason. When California whites made extravagant demands in fear that her three per cent of Japanese might increase to four and capture the business of "The Coast," Congress responded as if it were an appendage of the state legislature. But white South-

[19] Speech of W. P. Harris at a Democratic campaign meeting, Jackson, Mississippi, Aug. 23, 1875. Lowry and McCardle, *History of Mississippi*, 396–400.

erners when facing problems real or fancied concerning the ten million negroes in their midst can look to the federal authorities for no more at best than a tacit acquiescence in what their state governments may do. Acquiescence does not evoke enthusiasm; and until an issue shall arise predominant over the lingering one of race, political solidarity at the price of provincial status is maintained to keep assurance doubly, trebly sure that the South shall remain "a white man's country."

A Bibliography of the Printed Writings of Ulrich Bonnell Phillips[1]

Compiled by David M. Potter [*]

A. Editorial and Bibliographical Works

1. books

The Correspondence of Robert Toombs, Alexander H. Stephens, and Howell Cobb, in American Historical Association *Report*, 1911, II, 759 pp. Washington: Government Printing Office, 1913.

(In collaboration with James David Glunt), *Florida Plantation Records from the Papers of George Noble Jones*, 596 pp., plates, map. St. Louis: Missouri Historical Society, 1927. (in *Publications* of the Missouri Historical Society).

Containing an extensive introduction, written by Professor Phillips.

Plantation and Frontier, 1649–1863, Vols. I and II in A *Documentary History of American Industrial Society*, pp. 67-375, 9–379, facsimiles. Cleveland, Ohio: A. H. Clark Co., 1910.

Printed separately as *Plantation and Frontier Documents: 1649–1863, illustrative of industrial history in the Colonial and Antebellum South; collected from MSS and other rare sources.* Cleveland, Ohio: A. H. Clark Co., 1909.

[*] The publisher acknowledges permission to reprint the bibliography of the printed writings of Ulrich Bonnell Phillips which appeared in the *Georgia Historical Quarterly*, XVIII (September, 1934), 270-82.

[1] The compiler is indebted to D. Appleton and Co., MacMillan Co., and Little, Brown, and Co. for information as to editions; to Dr. Dumas Malone and Dr. Alvin Johnson for lists of items in the *Dictionary of American Biography* and the *Encyclopaedia of the Social Sciences* respectively; to Prof. R. H. McLean for helpful suggestions; and the late U. B. Phillips, Jr., for suggestions that led to the discovery of two or three items which might otherwise have been overlooked.

2. CONTRIBUTIONS TO PERIODICALS

Some documents from the Draper MSS. [No title], in *Gulf States Historical Magazine*, II, 58-60.

"Some Letters of Joseph Habersham," in *Georgia Historical Quarterly*, X, 144–63.

"South Carolina Federalist Correspondence, 1789–1797," in *American Historical Review*, XIV, 776–90.
> Reprinted with "The South Carolina Federalists," in *The South Carolina Federalists, with Accompanying Documents* [Listed below].

3. SURVEYS OF HISTORICAL SOURCES

"The Public Archives of Georgia," in American Historical Association *Report*, 1903, I, 439–74. Washington: Government Printing Office, 1904.
> Printed separately, same place and time, under title, "The Archives of Georgia."

"Georgia Local Archives," in American Historical Association *Report*, 1904, 555–96. Washington: Government Printing Office, 1905.
> Printed separately, same place and time. Many of the archives listed in this and the preceding paper have been moved or destroyed.

"Documentary Collections and Publications in the Older States of the South," in American Historical Association *Report*, 1905, I, 200–204. Washington: Government Printing Office, 1906.

B. ORIGINAL WORKS

1. BOOKS

Georgia and State Rights. A Study of the Political History of Georgia from the Revolution to the Civil War, with Particular Regard to Federal Relations, in American Historical Association, *Report*, 1901, II, 3-224 pp., maps. Washington: Government Printing Office, 1902.
> Printed separately, same place and time.
> Also printed separately, same place and time with imprint as Columbia University Ph.D. Thesis. The Justin Winsor Prize of the American Historical Association was awarded for this monograph.

A History of Transportation in the Eastern Cotton Belt to 1860, xvii and 405 pp., illus., maps, tables. New York: Columbia University Press, 1908.

The Life of Robert Toombs, ix and 281 pp., portrait. New York: Macmillan 1913.

American Negro Slavery; a Survey of the Supply, Employment, and Control of Negro Labor, as Determined by the Plantation Régime, xi and 529 pp. New York and London: D. Appleton, 1918.
  Subsequent editions in 1927, 1928, 1929, and 1933.
  Paperback edition, Louisiana State University Press, 1966.

Life and Labor in the Old South, xix and 375 pp., illus., maps, diagram. Boston: Little, Brown, and Co., 1929.
  The prize offered in 1928 by Little, Brown, and Company for the best unpublished work in American history was awarded for this study.
  Subsequent editions in 1929 (second), 1930 (third. Trade and Students' edition), and 1931 (fourth).
  Paperback edition, Little, Brown and Company, 1963.

2. ESSAYS AND ADDRESSES

(a) In Books

"The Southern Whigs, 1834-1854," in *Essays in American History dedicated to Frederick Jackson Turner,* 203–29. New York: Henry Holt, 1910.
  Also printed separately, same place and time.

"The Literary Movement for Secession," in *Studies in Southern History and Politics; inscribed to William Archibald Dunning . . . by his former pupils, the authors,* 33–60. New York: Columbia University Press, 1914.
  Also printed separately, same place and time.

(b) Separate

The South Carolina Federalists, with Accompanying Documents, 529–43, 731–43, 776–90. New York: Macmillan and Company, 1909.
  Reprinted from the *American Historical Review,* XIV, where pages 529–43 and 731–43 were entitled "The South Carolina Federalists," and pages 776–90 were entitled "South Carolina Federalist Correspondence."

(c) In *The South in the Building of the Nation,*
(Richmond: Southern Publication Society, 1909). (Twelve volume edition)

"The Economic and Political Essays of the Antebellum South," VII, 173–99.
Also printed separately, same place and time.

"The Economics of Slave Labor in the South," V, 121–24.

"The Economics of the Slave Trade, foreign and domestic," V, 124–29.

"Financial Crises in the Antebellum South," V, 435–41.

"Georgia in the Federal Union, 1776–1861," II, 146–71.

"Racial Problems, Adjustments, and Disturbances" IV, pp. 194–241.
Also printed separately, same time and place.

"Railroads in the South," V, 358–67.

"Railway Transportation in the South," VI, 305–16.

"The Slavery Issue in Federal Politics," IV, 382–422.
Also printed separately, same time and place.

"State and Local Public Regulation of Industry in the South," V, 475–78.

(d) In the *American Historical Reivew*

"The Central Theme of Southern History," XXXIV, 30–43.
Also printed separately, Lancaster, Pennsylvania: Lancaster Press, 1928.
Presents the race issue as the dominant theme of Southern history.

"A Jamaica Slave Plantation," XIX, 543–58.
Also printed separately Washington, 1914.
Summary of data in "plantation book" for years 1792–96, for Worthy Park Plantation, Saint John's Parish, Jamaica.

"The Origin and Growth of the Southern Black Belts," XI, 798–816.
Also printed separately, New York, 1906.
Deals with the tendency of slavery to concentrate wealth.

"Plantations with Slave Labor and Free," XXX, 738–53.
Comparison of plantations of the antebellum South and of the present day West.

"Slave Crime in Virginia," XX, 336–40.
Memoranda from documents in Virginia State Library containing

some 1,300 vouchers, recording the conviction of slaves for capital crime.

"The South Carolina Federalists," XIV, 529–43, 731–43.
    Reprinted, with "South Carolina Federalist Correspondence," in *The South Carolina Federalists with Accompanying Documents* [listed above].

(e) In the *South Atlantic Quarterly*

"Conservatism and Progress in the Cotton Belt," III, 1–10.
    Also printed separately, Durham, North Carolina, 1904.

"The Economics of the Plantation," II, 231–36.

"The Overproduction of Cotton, and a Possible Remedy," IV, 148–58.

(f) In the *Yale Review*

"An American State-owned Railroad: The Western and Atlantic," XV, 259–82, (Old Series).
    Also printed separately [New Haven?] 1906.

"Azandeland," XX, 293–313 (New Series).
    Dealing with the author's observations in Central Africa.

(g) In *Political Science Quarterly*

"The Economic Cost of Slave-holding in the Cotton Belt," XX, 257–75.
    Also printed separately, Boston: Ginn & Company, 1905.

"The Slave Labor Problem in the Charleston District," XXII, 416–39.
    Also printed separately, Boston: Ginn & Company, 1907.

(h) In Various Publications

"Plantations East and South of Suez," in *Agricultural History*, V, 93–109.
    Read before the Agricultural History Society and the American Historical Association at Boston, December 29, 1930.
    Also printed separately.

"The Decadence of the Plantation System," in *Annals of the American Academy of Political and Social Science*, XXXV, 37–41.
    Also printed separately, Philadelphia, 1910, in American Academy of Political and Social Science, *Publications*, No. 589.
    This paper was read before the Tulane Society of Economics, at New Orleans, Jan. 12, 1909.

"On the Economics of Slavery, 1815–1860," in American Historical Association *Report* 1912, pp. 150–51. Washington: Government Printing Office, 1914.

"The Plantation Product of Men," in Georgia Historical Association, *Proceedings for 1918*, pp. 12–15.

An informal address delivered April 6, 1918, at Atlanta, before the Georgia Historical Association.

"New Light Upon the Founding of Georgia," in *Georgia Historical Quarterly*, VI, 277–84.

Also printed separately [Savannah?, 1922].

Resume of items relating to the beginnings of Georgia, in the Diary of the Earl of Egmont, published in 1920.

"Historical Notes of Milledgeville, Georgia," in *Gulf States Historical Magazine*, II, 161–71.

Also printed separately, Montgomery, Alabama, 1903.

"Nilotics and Azande. Report to the Trustees of the Albert Kahn Foundation for the Foreign Travel of American Teachers," in *Reports* of the Kahn Foundation for the Foreign Travel of American Teachers, IX, 11–47. New York, 1930.

Prof. Phillips was Albert Kahn Fellow in 1929–30. During his travels, he penetrated Central Africa, and this report deals with his observations there.

"An Antigua Plantation, 1769–1818," in *North Carolina Historical Review*, III, 439–45.

"In a sense complementary to 'A Jamaica Slave Plantation'," [listed above].

"Transportation in the Antebellum South; An Economic Analysis," in *Quarterly Journal of Economics*, XIX, 434–51.

Also printed separately, New York, 1905.

"The Plantation as a Civilizing Factor," in *Sewanee Review*, XII, 257–67.

"Black Belt Labor, Slave and Free," in *Lectures and Addresses on the Negro in the South*, 29–36. Charlottesville, Virginia, 1915. (In University of Virginia, *Publications, Phelps-Stokes Fellowship Papers*).

"Making Cotton Pay," in *World's Work*, VIII, 4783–92.

Memorial Day Address delivered in Battell Chapel, Yale University, May 30, 1931, in *Yale Alumni Weekly*, XL, 968 (June 5, 1931).

Excerpts from an Address, "The Professional Touch," delivered March

23, 1931, before the Yale Chapter of Phi Beta Kappa, in New York *Times*, March 29, 1931, Sec. III, p. 7.

3. CONTRIBUTIONS TO ENCYCLOPAEDIC WORKS

(a) In the *Dictionary of American Biography*

"John Caldwell Calhoun," III, 411–19.

"William Harris Crawford," IV, 527–30.

"Robert Y. Hayne," VIII, 456–59.

"Alexander Hamilton Stephens," XVII, 569–75.

"Robert Toombs," XVIII, 590–92.

(b) In the *Encyclopaedia of the Social Sciences*

"Jefferson Davis," V, 11–12.

"Stephen Arnold Douglas," V, 227–28.

"Popular Sovereignty," XII, 239–40.

"Slavery in Modern Times," XIV, 84–92.

"Robert Toombs," XIV, 651.

4. BOOK REVIEWS

(a) In *American Historical Review*

Alexander Letters, 1787–1900, Printed at Savannah for George J. Baldwin, XVI, 830–32.

Bassett, John Spencer, *The Southern Plantation Overseer As Revealed in his Letters*, XXXI, 589–90.

Catterall, Helen T., *Judicial Cases Concerning American Slavery and the Negro* (Vol. I), XXXII, 330–32.

Catalogue of the Wymberly Jones De Renne Georgia Library at Wormsloe, Isle of Hope, Near Savannah, Georgia (3 vols.), XXXVIII, 174.

Donnan, Elizabeth, *Documents Illustrative of the History of the Slave Trade to America* (Vol. I, 1441–1700), XXXVI, 407–408.

Dozier, Howard D., *History of the Atlantic Coast Line Railroad*, XXVI, 148–49.

Dyer, G. W., *Democracy in the South Before the Civil War*, XI, 715–16.

Jervey, Theodore D., *Robert Y. Hayne and his Times*, XV, 628–30.

Jervey, Theodore D., *The Slave Trade, Slavery, and Color*, XXXII, 169–70.

Harris, N. Dwight, *History of Negro Servitude in Illinois and of the Slavery Agitation in that State, 1719–1864*, X, 697–98.

Henry, H. M., *Police Control of the Slave in South Carolina*, XX, 672.

Lingley, Charles R., *Since the Civil War*, XXVII, 620–21.

Official History of the 82nd Division, American Expeditionary Forces, "All American" Division, 1917–1919. Written by Divisional Officers, XXVI, 151–52.

Sears, Louis Martin, *John Slidell*, XXXI, 590–91.

Shryock, Richard Harrison, *Georgia and the Union in 1850*, XXXII, 903–904.

Wade, John Donald, *Augustus Baldwin Longstreet: A Study of the Development of Culture in the South*, XXX, 181–82.

Wright, James M., *The Free Negro in Maryland, 1634–1860* XXVII, 365.

Wright, James M., *History of the Bahama Islands, with a Special Study of the Abolition of Slavery in the Colony*, XI, 444.

(b) In *Yale Review* (New Series)

"Under Letters of Marque" (review of William M. Robinson, Jr., *The Confederate Privateers*), XVIII, 379–80.

"Fifteen Vocal Southerners" (review of Twelve Southerners, *I'll Take My Stand*; Broadus and George S. Mitchell, *The Industrial Revolution in the South*; Howard W. Odum, *An American Epoch*), XX, 611–13.

"The Perennial Negro" (review of Charles S. Johnson, *The Negro in American Civilization*; Sterling Spero and Abraham Harris, *The Black Worker*; T. J. Woofter, *Black Yeomanry*; Rossa Cooley, *School Acres*; Samuel G. Stoney and Gertrude M. Shelby, *Black Genesis*; R. S. Rattray, *Akan-Ashanti Folk Tales*), XXI, 202–204.

"A Quest of the Common Man" (review of James Truslow Adams, *The Epic of America*), XXI, 402–403.

"Protagonists of Southern Independence" (review of Laura A. White, *Robert Barnwell Rhett*, and Avery Craven, *Edmund Ruffin, Southerner*), XXII, 642–44.

(c) In *Mississippi Valley Historical Review*

Johnson, Guion Griffis, A *Social History of the Sea Islands, with Special Reference to St. Helena Island, South Carolina*, XVII, 623–24.

McGregor, James C., *The Disruption of Virginia*, X, 331–32.

McLendon, S. G., *History of the Public Domain in Georgia*, XI, 442–43.

Paxson, Frederick Logan, *History of the American Frontier*, XI, 583–84.

Vance, Rupert B., *Human Geography of the South: a study in regional resources and human adequacy*, XX, 132–33.

(d) In Southern History Association *Publications*

Reed, John C., *The Brothers' War*, X, 116–17.

Stevens, Henry, *Thomas Hariot and His Associates*, and Hariot, Thomas, A *Briefe and True Report of the New Found Land of Virginia*, VI, 347–49.

Wooley, Edwin C., *The Reconstruction of Georgia*, VI, 175–76.

(e) In *Annals of the American Academy of Political and Social Science*

Lee, Guy Carlton, A *True History of the Civil War*, XXIII, 536–37.

Reynolds, John S., *Reconstruction in South Carolina*, XXIX, 434–35.

Smith, William Henry, *The Political History of Slavery*, XXIII, 154.

(f) In Other Periodicals

"Early Railroads in Alabama" (review of William E. Martin, *Internal Improvements in Alabama*), in *Gulf States Historical Magazine*, I, 345–47.

Malone, Dumas, *The Public Life of Thomas Cooper, 1783–1839*, in *North Carolina Historical Review*, IV, 328–29.

"A History of Texas" (review of George P. Garrison, *Texas: a Contest of Civilizations*), in *Sewanee Review*, XI, 497–98.

"The Black Belt" (review of Carl Kelsey, *The Negro Farmer*), in *Sewanee Review*, XII, 73–77.

5. LETTERS

Letters to the *Michigan Alumnus,* concerning war work, in the *Michigan Alumnus,* December, 1917 and February, 1918.

INDEX

Abolition: Northern political control, 279

Agriculture, Southern: along Gulf Coast, 15; problems of, 65–66; and production of staples, 65, 74–76, 97, 122, 153–54; in Reconstruction period, 67; share-cropping, 67, 77, 263; new plantation system in, 68–70, 78–79, 82. *See also* Cotton culture, Farm, Indigo culture, Plantation, Rice culture, Sugar cane culture.

Antiqua plantation: management of, 220–22; revenues and expenses on, 220–23; runaways from, 223

Barbados, 11–12

Biddle, Nicholas: and cotton speculation, 148

Black belts: produced by plantation system, 95–98; in Georgia, 98–100; as staple-producing areas, 119; in South Carolina, 191

Blue Ridge, 10

Bourbonism, 73, 75, 77–80

Brown, John, 60

Calvert, Charles, 41

Canals. *See* Transportation

Capers, William (overseer), 30

Charleston, S.C.: growth of, 19, 191–92, 199–200

Chesapeake lowlands, 14

Chronicle (Augusta), 30

Chronicle (New Orleans), 46–47

Colleton, John, 12

Cotton: sea-island, 15–16; upland, 15–16

Cotton belt: development of, 16–18, 19–20, 86; and Bourbonism, 73, 75, 77–80, 83; rigidity of slaveholding system in, 132–34

Cotton culture: origins, 16, 193; and War of 1812, p. 17; and development of cotton belt, 16–18, 19–20; over-production

Cotton culture—*cont'd*
in, 77–79, 133; in Georgia-Carolina lowlands, 201

Credit buying: of slaves and land, 131–32, 143, 145–46, 147

Daily Delta (New Orleans), 52–53, 55–56

Daily Tropic (New Orleans), 56

Economic provinces: Southern, 153–54

Evening Gazette (Charleston), 40

Faneuil, Peter, 39

Farm: as an agricultural unit, 6; in Virginia, 8. *See also* Agriculture

Farming population: increase in Virginia, 9

Finance: in South tied to cotton, 145–46; prosperity and depression, 147–48; crises in, 149–50

Frontier: as American industrial system, 4–5, 6; in South, 5; extension of, 10; first form of Southern society, 100

Helper, Hinton Rowan, 277–78

Hemp culture, 19

Indentured labor: on early American plantations, 6, 9–10, 14, 85, 118

Indians: relations with early whites, 23–25; as slaveholders, 24; confederacies of, 23–25

Indigo culture, 12, 13, 15, 21, 193

Industrial society; defined, 3; in America, 3; systems of, 4–5; types of Southern, 6–7

Industry: state regulation in South, 188–89; local regulation of, 189–90; in Carolina lowlands, 212–13. *See also* Frontier, Labor, Negroes, Plantation

301